Barriers and Bridges: Media Technology in Language Learning
Proceedings of the 1993 CETaLL Symposium on the Occasion of the 10th
AILA World Congress in Amsterdam

BAYREUTH CONTRIBUTIONS TO GLOTTODIDACTICS

BAYREUTHER BEITRÄGE ZUR GLOTTODIDAKTIK

Ed. Udo O. H. Jung

Vol. 4

PETER LANG
Frankfurt am Main · Berlin · Bern · New York · Paris · Wien

Heidrun Jung
Robert Vanderplank (eds.)

BARRIERS AND BRIDGES: MEDIA TECHNOLOGY IN LANGUAGE LEARNING

Proceedings of the 1993 CETaLL Symposiumon the Occasion of the 10th AILA World Congress in Amsterdam

PETER LANG
Europäischer Verlag der Wissenschaften

Die Deutsche Bibliothek - CIP-Einheitsaufnahme

Barriers and bridges : media technology in language learning : proceedings of the 1993 CETaLL symposium on the occasion of the 10th AILA world congress in Amsterdam / Heidrun Jung and Robert Vanderplank (eds.). - Frankfurt am Main ; Berlin ; Bern ; New York ; Paris ; Wien : Lang, 1994
(Bayreuth contributions to glottodidactics ; Vol. 4)
ISBN 3-631-46863-6

NE: Jung, Heidrun [Hrsg.]; Commission on Educational Technology and Language Learning; GT

ISSN 0721-409X
ISBN 3-631-46863-6

TABLE OF CONTENTS

III. Back to Basics

IV. Appendix

INTRODUCTION

The papers that make up this collection were either presented at the CETaLL (Commission on Educational Technology and Language Learning) Colloquium "The Autonomous Learner and the Media" held as part of the 10th AILA World Congress in Amsterdam, August 8-15, 1993, or were presented in other sections at the same Congress. Not only do they all share the common theme of exploring how media technology can be used to enhance language learning and teaching, but more than that, they all relate the excitement of breaking down barriers and building bridges with the help of both new and old technology.

Editing this collection proved to be a rich and rewarding experience. The spread of papers from Austria, Finland, Germany, Japan, Thailand, Britain and the United States is narrower than we would have liked but this is an inevitable fact of life when editing proceedings and we are grateful to the contributors for their hard work in trying to meet our deadlines. Nevertheless, we were pleased with the wide range of topics covered, from the latest hi-tech European Union funded multi-media project to the humble radio with its potential for interactivity in addition to its enormous richness and variety.

The contributors also offer a wide range of perspectives on the value of technology. While we may share a common interest in exploiting available technology, our answers to the perennial question "Why bother?" posed by many sceptical colleagues are diverse. The pragmatists among us hold that we bother because it is there and we should therefore seek ways to exploit it; those who are commercially minded are understandably seeking to define a product that will make a return on the investment; the pedagogues among us look for better ways of teaching and learning, raising motivation, overcoming classroom limitations, and so on, the idealists hope to overcome problems of cultural conflict and prejudice, while applied linguists appear to take two positions: using technology to produce better materials and well-designed courses as well as trying to gain insights into the very nature of language learning and acquisition.

All of the contributors mention bridges or barriers in their papers. While a substantial number are clearly trying to break down barriers created by time and space, whether through e-mail, video conferencing, and/or computer conferencing, others are trying to break down barriers with the outside world created by the classroom. Other contributors seek to build bridges between cultures, sometimes with rather dismaying results, and one contributor provides an excellent example of how we may build bridges between disciplines with the aid of technology. There are also contributions which focus on the potential and limitations of the technology itself and on how we can involve learners in the use and exploitations of the technology thereby changing the very roles of teachers and learners. Inevitably, many of us find that we have barriers in the way we perceive the value and uses of media technology which may limit our ability to exploit its full potential. Those contributions which seek to provide us with frameworks for thinking through the technology at our disposal and with methods for integrating what is available to best advantage are therefore particularly welcome.

Above all, what is heartening in this collection is the essentially learner-centred and learner-driven nature of much of the enquiry undertaken. All of us are only too aware of the dangers of letting the technology call the shots. A couple of decades ago much of CETaLL's work was concerned with "humanizing" the language laboratory, which, in its audio-active form, had more to do with the military parade ground than the classroom. The fact that the world of language learning has moved on in all respects is shown in the papers presented here. Time and again we find references to the learners as the prime motivating force, as the centre of activity, as task-definers and objective-setters. In turn the question arises, what of the teacher? What role is the teacher to have in the multi-media classroom or the language centre without walls? Is the teacher to become the software writer, the materials developer, the administrator, archivist, button pusher, or what? Just as the AA language laboratory could, if badly used, reduce the teacher to being a drill master, so the role of the teacher in the present-day situation needs careful re-assessment and re-definition.

The experience of the writers here suggests that a rich, varied and enhanced role as educators awaits teachers who use the tools offered. By providing our learners with access to the technology, training them in its use and guiding them, we not only give learners choice, control and responsibility, but give ourselves a more expert role, a role in which we can spend more time on evaluating, on revising and providing feedback, or stimulating and stretching our learners. Paper after paper emphasises how willingly learners take control, defining needs and objectives, setting and fulfilling tasks, exceeding teachers' hopes or revealing genuine problems that call for cooperative resolution.

All is not perfect in the garden, however. The explorations described here also bring out the limitations of the technology and new barriers to learning calling for yet more bridge building. We are reminded that learner isolation is a great problem in distance learning calling for such local initiatives as support groups and learner networks, that close cultural contact may lead initially to the reinforcement of cultural stereotypes and prejudice. Using radio phone-in programmes to bridge the gap between the classroom and the outside world may show how the slightest and silliest technical hitch can cause lengthy disruption. The technological solution of teletext subtitles to help learners gain access to TV documentaries may throw up the altogether more intractable problem that the structure and discourse of such programmes is not necessarily orientated towards educational exploitation, and the aims of the programme may in fact be in conflict with educational aims. The better a programme is in televisual terms, the more difficult it may be to learn much from it. E-mail messages sent out hopefully all over the world in search of willing communicators may prove to be as fruitful as messages in bottles.

And then there is the cost. All this technology does not come cheap. In the end there needs to be some cost-benefit analysis. Who will carry it out? Will it be accountants, managers, researchers, teachers or learners? Teachers are notoriously resistant to technology and for good reason: it goes wrong just when you need it most. Most of us are very careful to have back-up material just in case, and try not to become too dependent on technical wizardry. Perhaps this is why so many papers focus on the learner-centred, self-access element, why breaking down barriers of time and place and creating new networks of learner communication is accorded such importance. No one these days seems to be claiming that language learning is faster using media technology, but rather that it produces better results and is superior because it has the potential to involve the learner in key decisions and in the learning process. We all want to be involved in our own education and personal development and the large sums of money invested in both public and private sectors speak of the general acceptance of this position at the present time.

The papers in this collection have been divided into three notional groups: those that are concerned primarily with a wide range of media technology (Big Bucks and Grand Plans), those that focus on computer and video conferencing (Small World), and lastly those dealing with radio, TV, and video (Back to Basics).

In the first group, both Udo Jung and Robert Davis show how far the Language Centre has come in the past 25 years. They are now sophisticated multi-media foreign language resource centres, usually student-centred, student-driven, often integrating audio, video and computer courseware.

Udo Jung's paper provides us with a very valuable framework for considering media technology in terms of process and product media, and he argues that we should not neglect process media such as live radio, just because we are able to record and playback everything these days. Process media require careful preparation and planning, but have many advantages in being set in real-life and in real-time, thereby creating a "virtual reality" for learners.

Robert Davis stresses that multi-media offers wonderful opportunities for interdisciplinary study and research, citing the example of how students of literature, art and music at Smith College were brought together in a study of "Erlkönig". This study reminds us that not only has modern language teaching gained much from media technology but that teaching and research in Latin, Greek, Old and Middle English have all benefited greatly from technology. The limitations to exploitation are only those of the budget and the imagination.

Gabriele Fesl's description of the Berlitz "multi-media teleschool" describes the cutting edge of language learning at a distance, linking teachers and learners across Europe via computer and satellite. While her paper lacks a theoretical and critical framework, we can provide it for ourselves with the help of Kurt Kohn's paper which follows. Kurt Kohn argues that we now have so much technology at our disposal that we need a framework for thinking through coherent strategies for using technology and for integrating different media with one another and with our work and life. In a short space, he reminds us of what is available, what we can do with it, what the advantages and disadvantages of different technologies are, and the type of conceptual framework we need if we are to think through the potential of multi-media in humanistic terms. Kurt Kohn also highlights the paradox of distance learning: that while it is the nature of distance learning to create, accept and creatively exploit distance, the learner is at the same time distanced from the learning community. Emancipation may be in conflict with guidance, support and communicative authenticity.

The four papers in the second group all focus on using computer and/or video conferencing to overcome real or artificial barriers of time and space. Andreas Eck, Lienhard Legenhausen and Dieter Wolff describe an e-mail project involving schools in Germany, the United States and Canada. The paper provides useful insights for anyone contemplating an e-mail link-up between schools or colleges. Clearly there are enormous problems of planning and coordination to be overcome, in addition to mastering the technical know-how required. Even when an e-mail project is set up the messages take time to flow between the participants, five weeks in the case of the project described. Eck, Legenhausen and Wolff stress the value of such e-mail projects in terms of their student-centredness and their authenticity. Not only are the students in North America and Germany exchanging information and getting to know one another, but the messages that the German students receive are "recycled" to form a corpus of learner-produced texts, with many surprises for students and teachers alike.

Similar surprises were experienced in a three-year project involving contact between middle and high school students in Massachusetts and "Realschule" students in Karlsruhe described by Virginia Teichmann. The project used e-mail throughout with video conferencing at the end of the first year. Again the formidable amount of planning necessary is clear, but as Virginia Teichmann stresses, such contact is a lot cheaper than sending all the pupils abroad. This project was very much multi-media in the sense that all media, traditional as well as modern, were used. Students exchanged slides, art work, photographs, and audio-tapes, as well as corresponding by e-mail. At Christmas, even cookies were sent to convey smells and tastes. The important objectives of breaking down intercultural barriers and increasing understanding were not fully achieved in the short term, however. The project provides us with a useful reminder that previously held prejudices may be reinforced in the short-term rather than overcome by contact and exchanges of artefacts. As Virginia Teichmann concludes, we may need to wait a long time to reap the harvest that has been sown.

The two other papers in this group are both concerned with trying out media technology in order to overcome barriers of time and space in language teaching. In the study by Hiraga and Fujii, students at the University of the Air in Japan are given classes which are supplementary to broadcast lectures by teachers in Australia via two video conferencing systems. The findings are positive on the whole and we may be permitted to think that as video conferencing becomes cheaper, it may have a valuable role to play not only in the corporate training described by Gabriele Fesl in the first group of papers but also in encouraging public sector educational communities without borders.

Sirpa Leppänen and Paula Kalaja describe a less ambitious but nonetheless insightful project in which a guided discussion takes place between students using a campus-based computer conferencing network over a period of about a week. The ground rules are set by the teacher with each student agreeing in advance to make two contributions. The teacher fades into the background as the students take over responsibility for guiding the discussion, encouraging one another and occasionally chastising those who have not contributed. The teacher appears to have lost his role as students exchange not only messages but also comments on the structure of the discussion and on the language being used. It is quite clear that the teacher ought to have re-defined his position as the students took on the roles usually held by the teacher. This re-defining of student and teacher roles given the democracy of the computer technology is clearly crucial. Teachers need to become more expert, need to stretch students without dominating them. This study shows quite vividly the pitfalls that face us if we let slip our role and responsibility as teachers in the face of student-computer interaction. The technology is there to help us to achieve altogether better results in more satisfying ways, not to help us opt out of our responsibilities to learners.

The last group, Back to Basics, contains papers on radio, TV, and video. It is called Back to Basics because what we have are attempts to identify problems and weaknesses in using technology that may be considered basic these days in much of the world.

Eileen Vick and Gerlinde Hardt-Mautner focus on radio programmes. Eileen Vick's paper describes the positive effects of using radio phone-ins once a semester, real, live radio phone-ins. As she shows, careful modelling of the genre is essential in extensive practice sessions beforehand if full benefit is to be made. We need to know both what we want to say and how to say it appropriately before we speak on the radio. Eileen Vick also stresses the great boost to students' confidence that organising and seeing through such a "real-life" experience brings. Once again, we see an example of classroom walls coming down and barriers being broken as students take responsibility for producing something of value in real world terms.

Gerlinde Hardt-Mautner "revisits" radio in her paper. As she says, radio today is not the same radio in semiotic and cultural terms as it was in the 1920's. For a start, its status and social impact are quite different. Language teachers need to be aware of both cultural studies and studies of media language in using news programmes for comprehension practice. News programmes, she stresses, are carefully integrated into different networks and are adapted to the profile of the listener of a network. The BBC Radio 1 News listener is quite a different person from the BBC Radio 4 listener, and news stories are carefully edited and presented to reflect this fact. The implications for selecting news materials for particular sets of learners and increasing comprehensibility follow naturally.

Hubert Eichheim reminds us that learning a foreign language by radio is still a transglobal mass media phenomenon undimmed by the bright lights of satellite TV. "Deutsch - warum nicht?" is a highly popular language course with materials translated into 35 languages. The question, as always for broadcasters, was "who was listening and following the course?" If profiles of listeners could be established, then support could be provided to help overcome the well-known problems of learner isolation and at the same time bring a sense of a local learning community or learner network to listeners. Again, it is clear that the advantages of distance learning need to be balanced by local measures to overcome the problems that the barrier breaking and bridge building of distance learning brings with it. At some point learners must be encouraged to feel part of an interactive learning community, not mere passive recipients of programmes. It is the social aspect of language learning that must be retained as far as possible.

Robert Vanderplank in his paper on using broadcast documentary programmes for language learning develops a theme that will be familiar to all those who know the work of the Open University and other distance learning agencies. He argues that the very purpose, structure, and messages of television programmes may be a bigger barrier to their use as language learning resources than the difficulty caused by the speed and complexity of the language used. We can now make the language of television programmes accessible to language learners through teletext subtitles/closed captions, but the real challenge lies beyond the technology. Producers seek to engage viewers in interesting programmes which blend discourses, shifting from the expository to the narrative and the argumentative in minutes or even seconds. We attend, we respond, we value or reject. In analysing producers' intentions and viewers' responses, he calls upon taxonomies of cognitive and affective domains of learning developed in the early 1960's but since forgotten or neglected. There is a paradox here: the difficulty for learners in learning from television programmes when language is made accessible through teletext subtitles/closed captions arises from the very fact that they are so interesting and engaging. What makes a good television programme

may make a poor language learning resource unless learners are given a strong educational orientation to viewing and unless viewing is combined with other media such as print and radio.
The last paper, by William Savage, focuses on the interactive use and production of video programmes by students on a pre-sessional EAP course in Bangkok. William Savage's position like that of many video practitioners these days is that video has now reached that point in its pedagogical usefulness and technological simplicity that it needs to become a tool to accomplish some genuine purpose rather than being the focus of activity. The eight-week Talkbase course that he describes is not only learner-centred, it is also learner-directed. In the answers to questions such as "Who controls the camera?" and "Who sets the tasks and objectives?" we see how effective Talkbase is in breaking down traditional barriers not only in language learning, but in education as a whole. The teachers in Talkbase do not fade into the background. Not only do they train students intensively in the use of video production but they also work intensively with students in feedback sessions and in the final preparations for their presentations. Both teachers and students are clearly liberated by the technology, with, as William Savage puts it, learners "realizing opportunities for improvement, both of language ability itself and of educational potential, through the language being learned".
With William Savage, we are in a sense, back where we started. Media technology, whether it is video, computer, audio, interactive video, or all combined in multi-media, offers opportunities for task-based, experiential, learner-centred, and learner-directed work which may not only facilitate language learning but which may engage the learner in work of real educational value to the learners themselves. This is what humanizing media technology is all about. We are not simply interested in technology as language learning tools, we realize that there are goals of education that can be realized with the aid of technology, goals of better and more efficient learning, yes, but also goals of cross-cultural understanding, of understanding how the media work both for and at times against us, of enhancing the learner's own personal experiences, of understanding the language learning process, and even perhaps, of establishing our own value as teachers.
The last chapter of the collection is an updating of Udo Jung's *International CALL bibliography*. We have tacked this bibliography on to the present collection as this is, after all, a collection of CETaLL papers and CETaLL's role is to promote the intelligent application of technology to language education and encourage the dissemination of up to date information to AILA affiliates. In adding this bibliography, we feel that we are fulfilling exactly this role.

Heidrun Jung and Robert Vanderplank May, 1994

EXPERIENTIAL LEARNING: WHAT EDUCATIONAL TECHNOLOGY CAN CONTRIBUTE

Udo O.H. Jung
University of Bayreuth

Experiential learning is defined as a student-centered and student-driven learning mode which displays the characteristics of authentic communication. The process media are shown to be a much neglected aspect of educational technology and phone-in radio shows are described as a case in point. They create a virtual reality of foreign-language use and vitalize the alien community. Another example of educational technology in the service of the foreign-language learner is Datavision, a combination of radio and teletext. The latter is available both as a process and a product medium. Any model of media use in language teaching, it is maintained, must aim at a mix of product and process media, of lo-tech and hi-tech instruments to obtain optimal results.

1. Introduction

For many a foreign-language teacher educational technology translates into computers and language laboratories, into mechanical drills and written communication as opposed to spoken exchanges with target language speakers in meaningful situations. In the eyes of many, a concomittant feature of educational technology is the dehumanizing effect it is said to exercise on the learning process. That this must not necessarily be so I want to explain by adducing examples from the Language Centre at Bayreuth University. I want to look at language acquisition and learning through the eyes of a student who comes to the centre to either continue studying one or more foreign languages carried over from school or, maybe, to start completely from scratch. The latter do not have many linguistic vices. We can plan a successful career for the little Eliza Dolittles, teach them how to speak proper English or help the unhappy Cinderellas who lack both ballroom costumes and dancing shoes with their first steps to success. Some, even after they have learnt to go through the motions, remain in the heat of the kitchen. For them the kitchen must be transformed into a ballroom. The stunt can be done with the help of technology.

2. Parameter Definition

Let us proceed, however, in an orderly fashion. Whoever wants to talk about the contribution educational technology can be expected to make to the experiential learning of foreign languages owes his readers a definition of what is meant by experiential learning.

2.1 Experiential Learning

There is a whole gamut of catch-phrases associated with the concept of experiential learning. They are best understood if they are contrasted with their opposite number. David Stern's posthumously published book on Issues and Options in Language Teaching contains a table which enumerates constituent terms in opposition to each other.

Analytic	Experiential
objective	subjective
deliberate/systematic/structured	realistic/authentic/genuine
focus on code	focus on communication
predictability of response	information gap
controlled/restricted language forms	unrestricted/natural language forms
formal	informal
abstract	concrete/realistic
decontextualized	contextualized
emphasis on accuracy	emphasis on fluency
reaction to code	reaction to message
isolated utterances	incorporation of preceding utterances
medium centered	message centered
non-communicative	communicative
focus on language	focus on topic/purpose
language practice	language use
linguistic interaction	interpersonal interaction
skill-getting	skill-using
usage	use
observation	participation

Table 1 (adapted from Stern 1992)

Who has not heard the complaint that the increasing digitization of our lives results in an overemphasis on the objective, deliberate, systematic and the structured? CALL software production, for example, is dependent on a focus on code, the predictability of response, on controlled and/or restricted language forms. Not a few of the exercises students are exposed to can be demonstrated to be formal, abstract and decontextualized in their emphasis on accuracy. Students are observed to bark at code or heard to produce isolated utterances. Most of their language learning, in other words, is medium-centered and non-communicative.

Experiential learning is characterized by a different set of items, between seven and ten - depending on how you group them. There must be focus on the topic and, ideally, "the students should play a part in the choice and treatment of topics" (Stern 1992: 315). A related criterion is "purposeful activities": This translates into "projects, enquiries, games, or problem solving, in which the focus of attention is planning the task, carrying the plan into effect through different stages, and finally completing it satisfactorily" (Stern 1992: 315). Stern then enumerates the following additional characteristics:

(1) Use of the target language.

(2) Information gap exercises where only one of a pair or group of students has the necessary information to bridge a gap with, so that only if the information provider is activated the task in hand can be completed.

(3) Next, there is the sustained speech-requirement. One-word or one-sentence utterances are considered insufficient evidence of language proficiency.

(4) Student reaction must be to message, not code.

(5) Implicit in the previous requirement is the demand that preceding utterances be registered by the students and incorporated in their responses.

(6) A further point concerns student initiative in discourse. Classroom talk is normally dominated by the teacher. This trend should be reversed.

(7) Finally, control of linguistic form should be largely abandoned.

To reassure the seasoned teacher, who has experienced the clash between theory and classroom reality, Stern is quick to add that "it seems right to assume that the attempt to encourage meaning and fluency is justified provided it is matched by an equivalent attempt to develop accuracy" (Stern 1992: 319). The pendulum, it seems, has swung back. Methodologists now agree that the motto of the nineties must be fluency and accuracy (see also Hammerly 1991).

2.2 Student-centered Learning

Whatever the differences may be, all methodologists agree that the student should be placed in the centre (Figure 1). Our imaginary student finds himself opposite a native speaker/teacher whose job it is to inculcate the elements that the target language system - the langue - is made up of. The teacher also represents the authority who from time to time assesses the student's progress or lack thereof. In testing terms, at least two varieties of language proficiency can be distinguished: BICS and CALP. The distinction was brought up by Jim Cummins (Stern & Cummins 1981). Basic Interpersonal and Communicative Skills (BICS) are primarily acquired in natural language acquisition situations, whereas CALP (Cognitive/Academic Language Proficiency) is mostly the result of schoolroom learning. There may be a third element, CUP (Common Underlying Proficiency) which has to do with what first and second languages have in common. There is no easy or direct way for the teacher to impart one of the two proficiencies to the learner, who is surrounded by a number of elements which may hinder or promote learning. The outer ring is made up of acronyms and abbreviations pointing to societal institutions and influences: BSRI stands for Bem Sex Role Inventory; SCT represents Syllabus and Curriculum Theory; R&D is Research and Development. The inner circle is closer to the learner's personality: BALLI refers to the Beliefs about Language Learning Inventory; FLASR stands for Foreign Language Anxiety Scale of Reactions; LA is Language Aptitude; AMI represents the Attitude and Motivation Index; IQ stands for Intelligent Quotient and CA for Chronological Age. And of course, the learner is "encapsulated" in the languages learnt so far.

Tasks/Situations conducive to LEARNING

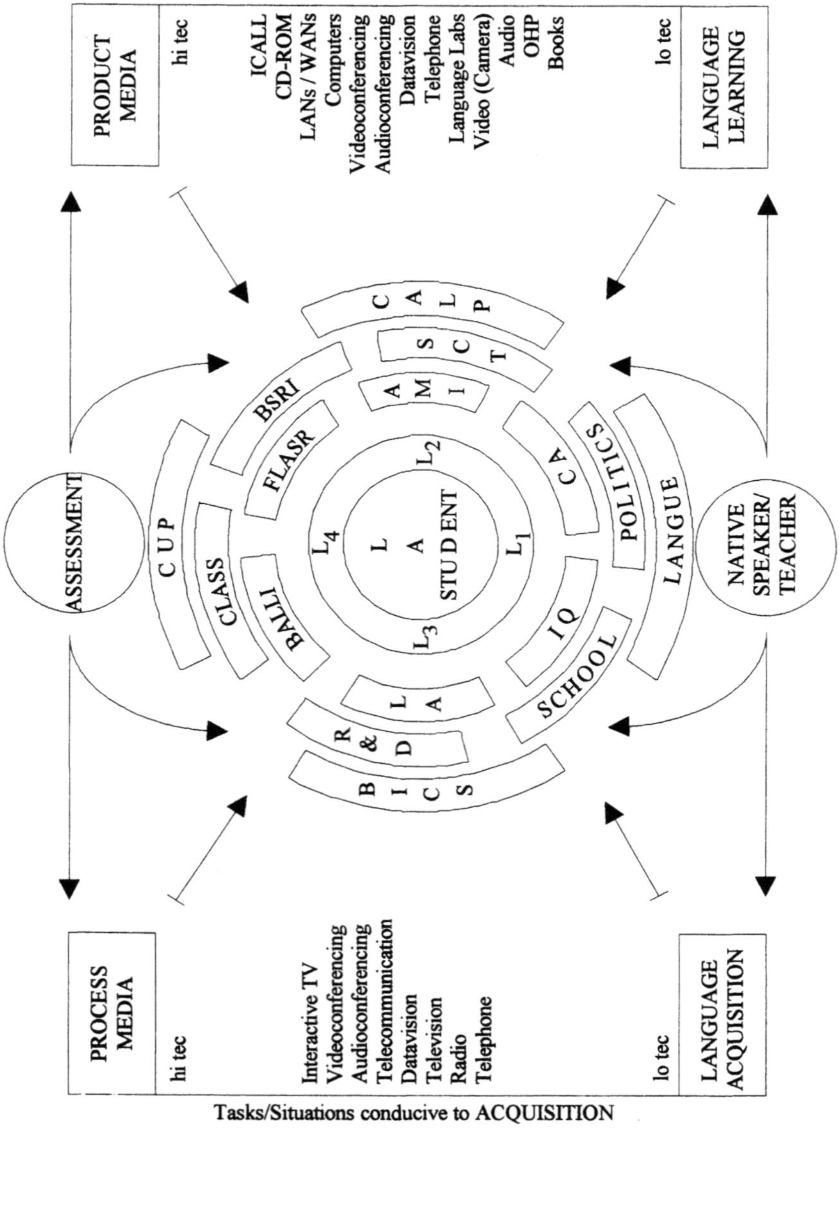

Tasks/Situations conducive to ACQUISITION

At the deepest level of abstraction, that is, if the student is stripped of all the characteristics that make up individual personalities, what remains is a language acquisition device, a LAD. In an ideal teaching situation the input data are maximally and optimally ordered and the acquisition device is not impeded in any way. In reality, to get to the heart of the matter the input data bump into or must slalom around a number of obstacles: age, sex, attitude, anxiety, beliefs etc. The workings of the LAD are thus obscured from view. But it is responsible for building up grammars - somehow. Its job consists in making a copy of the Langue and to place it firmly in the learner's head.

First (and second) language acquisition is concerned with this phenomenon (Ellis 1992; Felix 1987; Krashen 1982; Wode 1981). After four monographs and countless articles on the subject Rod Ellis's answer to the question of what the contribution of SLA to language learning is reads as follows: "SLA is of some value in deciding on *approach* but of very little value in clarifying which techniques ... to use" (Ellis 1992: 246). And he adds: "It is easy ... to view the contribution of SLA to language pedagogy as nugatory" (Ellis 1992: 245). At the same time, researchers like Rod Ellis are convinced that "classroom learners, like naturalistic learners, have the capacity to acquire a new language "naturally" as a result of participating in classroom communication" (Ellis 1992: 245; see also Kempen 1992).

2.3 Educational Technology

Let us take his word for it and step back a bit to ask how Stern's dual requirement of fluency *and* accuracy can be achieved with the help of educational technology.

As in the case of experiential learning it may be useful to start with a definition of what we mean by educational technology. There is the well-known distinction between technology *of* education and technology *in* education. The latter is machinery employed in the teaching process, the former an articulated sequence of educational measures aimed at achieving a goal, or to put it in the words of the US Commission on Instructional Technology "a systematic way of designing, implementing and evaluating the total process of learning and teaching in terms of specific objectives, based on research in human learning and communication and employing a combination of human and non-human resources to bring about more effective instruction" (Ellington & Harris 1986: 56).

This means we shall have to take into consideration questions of language acquisition and curriculum design as well as teaching techniques and evaluation processes. But we shall begin with the traditional, more narrow notion of technology which is understood to mean computers and language labs, radio and television, overhead projectors and laser disks, CD-ROMs and recording machines, video cameras and tapes. It is customary to distinguish between the media according to the senses they appeal to. If you are a native speaker of the language it makes sense to say that a tape recording of a dialogue is an auditory representation of the event or that an accompanying slide is a visual means which helps you to better understand the constellation of speakers. This is how the traditional distinction between auditory, visual and audiovisual means came about.

2.4 Process vs. Product Media

However, as soon as one starts looking at the media through the learner's eyes, it becomes clear that there are qualitative differences between a radio broadcast and an audio recording thereof or between an AC- and an AAC-language laboratory. Let us call radio, television and AC-laboratories *process media*, because their messages are fleeting phenomena which must be grasped on the spur of the moment, whereas audio, video and AAC-laboratories can be manipulated - rewound and replayed - at will by both teachers and students: they are *product media*. This distinction between process and product media is an important one. It has frequently been overlooked in the past even to the extent of renaming a video cassette *cassette TV* - a contradiction in terms.

In the past, the negative aspects of the process media have been overemphasized, their positive aspects ignored. After the invention of audio- and videorecorders only very few teachers have attempted to harness the process media to the language teaching cart. It is my contention, however, that foreign-language teachers should and can avail themselves of *all* the opportunities available to them. At Bayreuth we have already begun a fruitful co-operation with both the local commercial radio station and the state-wide Bavarian broadcasting authorities.

3. Phone-in Radio Shows

At the time of writing, the most spectacular event is only 3 months away: a radio link-up between Munich and Washington, DC. American and German students will discuss matters of common interest for as long as one hour, with the two target languages - German and English - spread about evenly across the available time schedule. This has been attempted before (Wicke 1991), and it has been attempted in the US on a much bigger scale. American teachers of German were fortunate enough to have one TV satellite and one audio (back) channel available to them on several occasions (Eddy 1986; Eddy 1989). Their students spoke to scholars at the Maritime Museum in Bremerhaven and learnt about German emigration to America in the 19th century or they conversed with rock star Klaus Lage. A third exchange was between American college and German university students. The model proposed and discussed by Eddy was criticized mainly on financial grounds (Herbst & Wiesner 1988): thirty thousand US dollars was deemed too high a price for a one-hour tele-conference. Thirty thousand US dollars is an exorbitant sum of money to spend on a one-hour teaching experiment if only 30 students are likely to profit from it. But if thirty thousand students profited from it? The trick to bring about an acceptable cost-effect relationship is as simple as it is practicable: the number of listeners and participants is stepped up by

(a) broadcasting the event and

(b) allowing listeners to voice their opinions by calling into the programme.

This is what will happen on 20 November 1993, and it has happened before. Phone-in radio shows bring about highly valued qualitative changes (see also Eileen Vick's paper in this volume).

First and foremost: Classroom walls are dismantled, broadcasting is to the real world beyond the confines of the studio. In the extreme case, the whole world will be listening and responding, an invisible and temporary college including many a native speaker of the language to be taught is set up. Communication within this college depends on all the participants accepting the rules of the game. Students cannot fall back on their native language, because the language of communication of some of the callers from outside may be the only vehicle available to transmit messages. Foreign-language phone-ins do no longer simulate reality, they create a foreign-language reality of their own. The actual verbal exchanges between student broadcasters and target-language callers constitute an important phase of the learning process. To put it in David Stern's words: "If an experiential strategy is applied, the classroom language will have the characteristics of authentic communication as it occurs in ordinary conversation" (Stern 1992: 315). In many parts of Europe we nowadays find large pockets of alien residents. Phone-ins might well turn into rallying points of a movement to preserve the emerging community languages in order to begin and maintain a continual intercultural dialogue. At the same time, they could be part and parcel of the movement for peace education (Raasch 1993), a necessary addition to language curricula in view of the atrocities committed almost daily in Central Europe and elsewhere.

In preparing such a spectacular event the teacher brings about a change of atmosphere which is palpably present in the participating classrooms. A phone-in is a most effective teaching instrument at all stages of its "life cycle" - the planning and training phase, as well as the execution and aftercare period, when students and teacher return to the classroom to discuss the pros and cons. There are a number of reasons why phone-ins are worth the foreign-language teacher's while:

(1) The broadcasting studio is still a very prestigious theatre of operation (*Prestige Value*).

(2) A radio station is a very powerful instrument to foist your views on other peoples' minds (*Power Aspect*).

(3) It is also a tremendous challenge to the language learners, who, by exposing them-

selves, get an opportunity to test their mettle in public (*Educational Value*).

(4) Once they have decided to participate in the production of a radio broadcast, students start anticipating language needs. They must take stock and make predictions as to the structural and content elements that are likely to crop up and therefore need revision. After they have discovered seeming or real language deficits there is a great willingness to accept advice from their teachers as to how the situation can be remedied. Syllabus building (see also Savage & Storer 1992) is set afoot (*Student Involvement*). Questions like the following are heard:

(a) Could we listen to a recording of an original English-language call-in broadcast from AFN, BBC or VOA?

(b) How do you start a conversation on the phone and how do you keep it going? Both telephone-beginnings and endings are language and/or culture-specific (Godard 1977; Clark & French 1981).

(c) Is there a specialized vocabulary that we are supposed to know?

(d) Are there any tricks to ward off unwelcome callers?

(e) Can the art of saying nothing in so many words be learnt quickly?

(f) What are our most salient language deficits? How does our grammar, pronunciation/intonation compare with the norm? Should we go to the language laboratory and work in pairs?

(g) What are the foreseeable controversial aspects of the topics to be dealt with?

(h) Do we need canned materials (interviews, reports, birthday greetings etc., music items) to spark off a lively discussion or to fill gaps?

(i) Should we have a rehearsal and invite a few native speakers, who could be asked to participate in a test-run?

(5) On the day of the broadcast there are thousands of listeners in the circumference of the radio station. A schoolhouse as big as this has yet to be built (*Multiplication Effect*).

(6) Some of the listeners may turn into callers and voice their opinion over the phone (*Activation Effect*). A class of 10 to 15 students may thus actively involve a huge number of people for the duration of the broadcast. If the event has been publicized well in advance, other classes may be enticed to participate in the experiment.

(7) The actual verbal exchanges between student broadcasters and target-language callers constitute an important phase of the acquisition process (*Acquisitional Aspect*).

(8) The value of such broadcasts does not, however, stop here. They can be recorded and made the subject of enquiry in an aftercare phase where questions like the following are asked and answered: What went wrong and why? How could conversational breakdown have been avoided? Recorded broadcasts are not the sole property of the

students actively involved. Multiple copies can be used even in those classes who were prevented from listening to the broadcast itself. (How would *we* have solved such a problem?). A process medium turned into a product medium may not be as attractive as the original, but it can nonetheless be put to good use (*Spin-off Effect*).

4. Datavision

It could be argued that ab initio students are barred from participating in foreign-language phone-ins* and that it has yet to be shown that and how a deschooling process can be initiated with the help of process or other media. Here is an example. Let us call it *Datavision.* It is an extension of Radiovision, which is a French invention popularized by the BBC in the 1960s (Lefranc 1967). In radiovision participating schools are sent visual materials (film strips, OHP-transparencies) in advance of the broadcast so that teachers can preview and integrate them into their lesson plans. The characteristic feature of radiovision is the simultaneous presence of both visual and auditory materials. Datavision is a combination of broadcast videotex, also called teletext (Jung 1990), and radio. Broadcast videotex is signals encapsulated in ordinary TV programmes; they ride piggy-back on the TV waves. A decoder built into the receiver reads the information and then blows up a few spare lines of the TV picture to screen size. Teletext pages can be called up anytime in conjunction with the TV programme currently being transmitted: this results in intralingual (Vanderplank 1990) or interlingual (Battarbee 1986; Titford 1982) subtitles. Teletext pages can also be called up independently of the TV programme currently showing. Hundreds of pages of information (weather forecasts, exchange rates, lottery results, news flashes, small ads, train and/or plane departures and arrivals etc., etc.) become available that way throughout the day. The advantages of this message system are many:

(1) It does not collide or interfere with regular TV programmes, because it can be used as a separate and independent programme source.
(2) It can easily be updated at short notice.
(3) It has colour pages.
(4) It is interactive to a certain extent: users can turn the pages by pressing a key on their remote control device or they can browse through the data and scan for information.

Teletext also has a number of disadvantages. One of them is that it does not have a sound source of its own. To produce a full-fledged audiovisual aid teletext must be combined with radio signals which represent the auditory part. For datavision the learner needs both a TV

*There are no a-priori reasons why beginners should be barred from phone-ins. On the contrary, a Dear Abby- or Professor Grammar-Corner for learners of foreign languages as part of a radio show would be an ideal way, a valve, so to speak, for learners to let off steam: "I can't for the life of me see when anybody and when everybody should be used. Can you explain the difference?" Students are taught nowadays from a very early date to ask questions in class. These same questions can equally well be asked in public with the additional advantage that a lively discussion between a number of participants - acting vicariously for thousands of listeners - may ensue.

and a radio receiver, which must be switched on simultaneously. If the audio component is broadcast, users cannot manipulate the speed of delivery or the sequence of the items. They are at the mercy of the broadcasting station, so to speak, the broadcaster's rate of speech, the course planner's decision concerning the flow of information. If, however, the marketing department attached to the station sends out pre-recorded audio-cassettes to registered course participants, the latter can freely manipulate both the audio and the visual information during time-removed individual sessions. The same effect is obtained if course participants record broadcasts on their own initiative. There are thus two modes of using Datavision in language training, which could be named *learning* mode (product) and *testing* mode (process). They can be combined to obtain optimal results. It may thus be useful to occasionally broadcast lessons which are not available otherwise. A certain measure of interactivity can also be introduced on such occasions. Course participants are instructed to select, say, table 236, to next read the contents and to finally address another table mentioned. Pandemonium may, of course result from such a measure, because learners can get lost in the jungle of video tables. The flock must be herded together again after a while to continue lock-step.

The amount of written or graphic information which the TV screen can accommodate at one time may also cause problems: a single page cannot take in more than 24 lines of 40 characters each. Pages must be "turned" quite often if longer texts are to be transmitted. Datavision is thus best described as a partly interactive, audiovisual starter medium, which changes and enhances the quality of educational broadcasts. It can present tests, text reconstruction exercises, for example, and divulge the results immediately after. In doing so, Datavision contributes to an initiation to computer literacy, or if this quality of Datavision is disputed, it, at least, helps to dispel technophobia or the fear of technologically mediated language learning.

The example of Datavision also shows that process media need not only contribute to basic interpersonal communicative skills. Process media - especially if they are transformed into product media - have been and can be used to promote cognitive academic language proficiency.

Let us, therefore, cast a final look at a possible language learning scenario with Datavision as the principal means of message transport. Our target group consists of German and Italian housewives, although other learners of these two languages could also participate. The women live next door to each other, but do not normally speak to each other, because their foreign-language deficits do not allow them to. A bilingual Italian/German and German/Italian language course via Datavision could address and redress this problem. For their camping holiday at the Ligurian coast the German family must be able to buy the ingredients necessary to cook their meals, preferably following instructions in an Italian cookery book. The problem which the Italian woman faces is almost a mirror image of the one the German housewife must tackle. A Datavision course solves both these problems. It also resolves the conflict that has been raging between adherents of the monolingual and the bilingual method. The course addresses problems faced by both groups simultaneously. In doing so the two source languages which are target languages at the same time, are accorded equal rights. If the course begins with a recipe and if the women can be persuaded to wear badges identifying them as course participants, they might meet at the grocer's from the very start of the programme and henceforth tutor each other during the programme intervals. The language-learning situation initiated by Datavision can thus be complemented by acquisition-rich encounters between language twins.

5. Digital Equipment

Not much has been said about the machine which has hit the headlines more often during the last ten years than the language laboratory in its long career as a teaching aid. The computer, elected man of the year in the early 1980's, or its carrier-medium variants, the LANs and the WANs, had to cede pride of place for reasons of space to technology-in-education instruments which have been unduly neglected lately. Computers (more than 3000 entries in the two volumes of the international CALL bibliography published in 1988 and 1993) are the talk of the town, and eventually this piece of hardware will have acquired enough human characteristics to justify its election as man of the year. In the meantime, its unintelligence, to use John Higgins's term (Higgins 1988), is powerful enough to mediate between written and spoken forms of communication. Written communication between humans who are five thousand miles apart or maybe only a few blocks away tends to display many of the qualities of spoken dialogue if the exchange is via computers. Colette Daiute (1985) was the first to notice this qualitative difference, which was confirmed independently by Dam et al. (1990: 333; see also Eck et al. in this volume), who attest to the fact that computer-written texts are "reminiscent of spontaneously produced informal spoken language". Two researchers from the USA reported last year on experiments with synchronous computer networks (Beauvois 1992; Kelm 1992), where students exchanged messages in the foreign language in a manner which was also reminiscent of spoken dialogues. One of the authors, therefore, subtitled her piece "conversation in slow motion", and the other stated that "the discourse flows like an oral conversation" (Kelm 1992: 446). Indeed, it looks as if the missing link between speaking and writing had been discovered to the advantage of both learners and teachers.

On the whole, it can be said of computers and computer-driven configurations that, quoting Stephen Hagen, "the technology is impressive", but can it be used in schools in such a way "that it adds value to the sum of existing language learning technologies?" Stephen Hagen goes on to say that "until models have been developed for integrating these systems and their courseware into the curriculum, a flexible learning approach, mixing and matching technologies to achieve the best results would be the only way forward" (Hagen 1993: 8). It is true, the 21st century is just around the corner, but it is also true that the future begins today, and in order not to antagonize present and future generations of language teachers an integrative model of technologically supported language learning and teaching must include both low-tec and hi-tec elements. In the model described here computers are stepping stones on the students' way to communicative competence. Stepping stones, by definition, are temporary not permanent footholds for students to tread on.

6. Conclusion

So, what is the contribution educational technology can be expected to make to experiential learning? It is twofold, if the distinction between product and process media is accepted as relevant.

The classical function of the media consists in simulating reality. They bridge the gap between the classroom and the reality of the target culture. Drawings, photos, audio and video are praised, because with their help reality (the semblance thereof) can be brought into the classroom. A closer look reveals that it is the product media which mainly fulfill this function. If the process media are not removed from the foreign-language teacher's tool-box, as they have been since the invention of audio- and videorecording machines, and exploited to the utmost instead, a new dimension is added to language teaching in non-target surroundings. In conjunction with the telephone, radio and TV can *vitalize* the alien community within the indigenous community they are servicing. These media, then, create a virtual reality of language users. The whole thing can stop here, the moment the power is shut off. But it can also go one step further. Off-line meetings can be arranged both between the foreign residents of a town and between native speakers and language learners.

The media thus prepare and anticipate what Europe and other parts of the world will look like in a few years. The place will be teeming with multilingual and multiethnic communities, little Englands and little Italys will be found everywhere so that learners can make a long-distance call for the price of a local call and school children can be taken abroad for the price of a bus ticket. It is this experiential learning ticket that deserves the support of language teachers.

REFERENCES

Battarbee, K. (1986). Subtitles and soundtrack. In: Gambier, Y. (ed.). *Trans*. Turku, University of Turku: School of Translation Studies, pp. 144-165.

Carlisle, C. (1993). English talk show in Poland: the lighter side of being "on the air". *English Teaching Forum* 31 (2), p. 54.

Clark, H. & French, J. (1981). Telephone goodbyes. *Language in Society* 10, 1-9.

Daiute, C. (1985). *Writing and computers*. Reading, MA, Addison-Wesley.

Dam, L. et al. (1990). Text production in the foreign language classroom and the word processor. *System* 18 (3), 325-334.

Eddy, B.D. (1986). Live from Germany: a look at satellite instruction. *Die Unterrichtspraxis for the Teaching of German* 19, 213-219.

Eddy, B.D. (1989). Interactive tele-classes from Germany. In: Smith, W.F. (ed.). *Modern technology in foreign language education*. Lincolnwood, IL, National Textbook Co., pp. 211-217.

Ellis, R. (1985a). *Classroom second language development*. Oxford, Pergamon Press.

Ellis, R. (1985b). *Understanding second language acquisition*. Oxford, Oxford University Press.

Ellis, R. (1990). *Instructed second language acquisition*. Oxford, Blackwell.

Ellis, R. (1991). *Second language acquisition and language pedagogy*. Avon, Multilingual Matters.

Ellington, H. & Harris, D. (comps.) (1986). *Dictionary of instructional technology*. London/New York, Kogan Page/Nichols Publishing Company.

Felix, S.W. (1987). *Cognition and language growth*. Dordrecht/Providence, RI, Foris.

Godard, D. (1977). Same setting, different norms: phone call beginnings in France and the United States. *Language in Society* 6, 209-219.

Hagen, S. (ed.) (1993). *Using technology in language learning*. London, City Technology Colleges Trust in association with CILT.

Hammerly, H. (1991). *Fluency and accuracy: toward balance in language teaching and learning*. Clevedon, Multilingual Matters.

Herbst, H. & Wiesner, P. (1988). Nicht alle Satellitenträume reifen: Bilanz nach der dritten Teleklasse. *Die Unterrichtspraxis/Teaching German* 21 (1), 119-122.

Higgins, J. (1988). *Language, learners and computers*. Human intelligence and artificial unintelligence. Harlow, Longman Group.

Horwitz, E.K. (1986). Preliminary evidence for the reliability and validity of a foreign language anxiety scale. *TESOL Quarterly* 20, 559-562.

Horwitz, E. & Young, D.J. (1991). *Language anxiety: from theory and research to classroom implications*. Englewood Cliffs, NJ, Prentice Hall.

Jung, U.O.H. (1988). *An international bibliography of computer assisted language learning*. Frankfurt a.M., Peter Lang Verlag.

Jung, U.O.H. (1990). The challenge of broadcast videotex to applied linguistics. *International Review of Applied Linguistics in Language Teaching* 28 (3), 201-220.

Jung, U.O.H. & Lieber, G. (1993). *An international bibliography of computer assisted language learning*. Volume 2. Frankfurt a.M., Peter Lang Verlag.

Kempen, G. (1992). Second language acquisition as a hybrid learning process. In: Engel, F.L. et al. (eds.). *Cognitive modelling and interactive environments in language learning*. Berlin, Springer, pp. 139-144.

Krashen, S.D. (1982). *Principles and practice in second language acquisition*. Oxford, Pergamon.

Lefranc, R. (1967). Radiovision as an aid to literacy teaching in Niger. In: Unesco International Institute for Educational Planning (ed.). *New educational media in action: case studies for planners - III*. Paris, Unesco, pp. 43-57.

Raasch, A. (ed.) (1993). *Language teaching in a world without peace / L'enseignement des langues dans un monde sans paix / Der Fremdsprachenunterricht in einer Welt ohne Frieden*. Saarbrücken, Universität des Saarlandes.

Savage, W. & Storer, G. (1992). An emergent language program framework: actively involving learners in needs analysis. *System* 20 (2), 187-199.
Scovel, T. (1978). The effect of affect on foreign language learning: a review of the anxiety research. *Language Learning* 28, 129-142.
Stern, H.H. (1983). *Fundamental concepts of language teaching*. Oxford, Oxford University Press.
Stern, H.H. (1992) [edited by Patrick Allen and Birgit Harley]. *Issues and options in language teaching*. Oxford, Oxford University Press.
Stern, H.H. & Cummins, J. (1981). Language teaching/learning research: a Canadian perspective on status and directions. In: Phillips, J.K. (ed.). *Action for the '80s*. Skokie, IL, National Textbook Company, pp. 195-248.
Titford, C. (1982). Subtitling - constrained translation. *Lebende Sprachen* 27 (3), 113-116.
Vanderplank, R. (1990). Paying attention to the words: practical and theoretical problems in watching television programmes with uni-lingual (Ceefax) sub-titles. *System* 18 (2), 221-234.
Wicke, R.E. (1991). Conference Call. Interkulturelles Lernen durch Rundfunkkontakte. *Der fremdsprachliche Unterricht (Englisch)* 25 (4), 38-41.
Wode, H. (1981). *Learning a second language*. Tübingen, Narr.

MULTIMEDIA AND THE FOREIGN LANGUAGE RESOURCE CENTER: ITS PROMISE FOR THE LEARNER

Robert C. Davis

Smith College, Northampton

This paper will document the planning, organization, and implementation of the Center for Foreign Languages and Cultures (CFLAC), describing many of its technological features including, among others, networked digital audio, interactive video, digital video slides, and our latest project, interactive digital video interactive. It will furthermore address staffing questions including the participation of students in the operation of the center as well as their key role in the development and evaluation of curricular materials.
The report will also illustrate how the implementation of integrated audio, video, and computer courseware components has fostered the integration of linguistic, cultural, and literary aspects of the learning process in foreign language and culture courses at Smith College. The relationship between the open learning and instructor-directed uses of the center as well as the use of multimedia as a presentation tool in the media classroom will be considered. We will likewise investigate the role technology and media can play in bridging the gap that many perceive between language teaching and literary critical scholarship. Finally, a case will be made for the revaluation of multimedia projects as a legitimate area of coursework for students (as an alternative to the traditional "term paper") and of research for faculty (equivalent to a publication in a scholarly journal).

1. Objectives

One of the primary concerns for instructors and researchers in the field of foreign language, literature, and culture studies is developing strategies to assist learners in achieving proficiency in a language other than their own together with an understanding of the new cultural context which insures true communication. This has led to an increased demand for culturally authentic materials and to their introduction earlier in the learner's foreign language studies. The "new technologies" offer a variety of multimedia assistance in the presentation and processing of culturally authentic materials. A well-conceived and managed foreign language resource center can play an integral part in helping both instructors and learners achieve these curricular goals. At Smith College, linguistic proficiency and cultural proficiency represent indivisible components of the pedagogy of our foreign language media center, a fact we sought to accentuate, beginning with the name of the center, the Center for Foreign Languages and Cultures (CFLAC).

2. Electronic Classroom

Our plans called for a center which would support individual and small group learning but, for logistical reasons, would not be used for entire classes. Since faculty, however, wanted the opportunity to use the same technology as in the Center for their classes, we began our project in 1988 with the Electronic Classroom (EC). We renovated a small seminar room in the same building as CFLAC and equipped it with 15 student stations and one presentation station connected to the center by a 10 Mbit Ethernet network. Each student station features an IBM PS 2 Model 30 with M-Audio Capture/Playback card and Tandberg TLH 82 headset for digital audio, while the presentation station includes a Model 57slc with 486 processor, M-Audio Capture/Playback and M-Motion video overlay cards as well as an internal CD-ROM drive. An IBM PS 2 Model 80 located in the Center was designated as server. A Barco RCVD 400 Quad projector coupled to a Panasonic AG-W1 multi-standard VCR and a Pioneer LD-V8000 laser disc player capable of playing both CAV and CLV discs provides large-screen video and VGA projection. In addition to the video players, the media cabinet includes an Onkyo TA-2120 Stereo Cassette Tape Deck, NAD Stereo Amplifier 3220PE, and a TOA MX-401 powered audio mixer.

Voice and sound from video sources, conventional audio cassette tape, and computer digital audio are available over speakers, while students record through the digital audio system with headsets at their individual stations. Since video in the Electronic Classroom is designed for group rather than individual work, it is projected through the Barco and can be controlled interactively from the presentation station where the videodisc player is attached to the RS 232 port of the PS/2 Model 57. Plans are currently underway to upgrade the EC into a fully interactive multimedia classroom. The student stations will be replaced with PS/2 Model 77s equipped with digital audio and digital video cards (IBM Action Media II) to allow for digital interactive audio and video at each station.

The room is laid out with a perimeter horseshoe of 15 student stations and a central seminar table which also houses the equipment cabinet and faculty station. Students can now work privately or in pairs at the work stations and then swivel around to the seminar table for class interaction. Until the Center was completed, the EC also served as a test lab for the network, hardware, and software. Its prime use has been as a demonstration site and instruction facility for both videotape and disc use in all languages as well as for intensive phonetics drill (primarily in East Asian languages). Furthermore, translation and composition classes are conducted regularly in the EC with the assistance of the network and VGA projection as an electronic blackboard, where the process of writing and translation can be explored and analyzed "live."

3. Resource Center

Work on renovation for the Center proper began during the summer of 1989. CFLAC was designed with space for 61 workstations, four of which are all-access stations to accommodate wheelchairs. We sought to create a varied arrangement of stations, including both islands and perimeter placement, which offer privacy, yet a sense of community, with a view of others working nearby. Roughly one half of the stations are individual units while the other half are doubles which can be changed into singles by extending a retractable divider. These dual stations have proved especially popular with students for video assignments, and their spontaneous interpersonal interaction constitutes an essential component of their interactive learning experience in the Center. In this respect, the technology serves to enhance rather than inhibit person-to-person communication.

3.1 Student workstations

The workstations were designed to support multimedia applications on a networked PC. The desktop provides enough room for the keyboard, mouse, and a notebook while a shelf above the monitor can house either videotape, videodisc, or CD-players. Except for applications which require the players mentioned above, all applications can be accessed at any of the workstations. CFLAC currently supports 30 networked IBM PS 2 Model 55sx all with M-Audio Capture/Playback cards and 20 with M-Motion cards as well as 10 IBM PS 2 Model 57 slc with M-Audio Capture/Playback cards and Action Media II digital video cards. The Model 55s are connected via a 16 Mbit Token Ring network to an IBM PS 2 Model 80 with 4 external hard drives for 3 gigabytes of storage. The Model 57s are linked to a PS/2 Model 95 with a 486 50 MHZ processor which is dedicated as our digital video server and connected to external drives with 7.2 gigabytes of storage. The M-Motion and Action Media cards allow us to use a single standard computer monitor at each workstation for all our applications, including linear and interactive video. Nine of our stations also include Pioneer LD-V4200 videodisc players and five feature Selectra AG-1960 computer controllable VCRs for interactive videotape use.

As is evident from our hardware selection, a guiding principle in equipping the Center was to choose components which could be modified or extended in order to keep pace with the rapid changes in multimedia technology. Thus far, this philosophy has served us well. For example, we were able to upgrade our earlier alternate-screen approach to interactive video to single-screen video overlay including windowing of moving images and digital still-capture capability by adding IBM's M-Motion adaptor. A pilot project in interactive digital video using Microsoft's *Video for Windows* and Action Media II digital video cards is well underway. With the addition of the new server, storage and computers with digital video cards, we are able to digitize and store motion video as well as send video images from this single source over the network much in the same way we now provide digital speech.

Likewise, software development at CFLAC has followed the same component principle which allows us to combine, for example, our digital audio programs with M-Motion digital stills to create listening comprehension exercises with visual cues or to attach our dictionary program to a word processor, a reading program, or in support of transcripts with our interactive video controller.

3.2 Permanent and Student Staff

CFLAC operates with a full-time staff of three including the Director, Multimedia Programmer, and Secretary as well as 16 part-time Student Consultants. The Consultants are trained in *DOS, Windows*, and the various applications run in the Center. In addition to assisting students and faculty in using the equipment and materials in CFLAC, the Consultants also participate actively in the design and testing of applications and perform much of the data entry, scanning, and command input for exercises in the Center. This work/study approach not only benefits the Center in terms of the amount of work the staff can accomplish, but also affords the Consultants the opportunity to expand their computer literacy. Initial concerns during the planning stages that a "high tech" multimedia center would need the constant attention of specialized technicians, programmers, and a highly trained staff quickly proved unfounded. Evening and weekend hours are routinely staffed solely by our Student Consultants, and in over eight semesters of operation we have experienced no major disruptions.

4. Courseware Menu

Since our students' primary concern in visiting CFLAC is learning about foreign language and culture, we attempt to keep the operation of the computer simple and the delivery system as invisible as possible. With the exception of applications which require a video or CD-player, students can access any program at any station through the menu system from *Novell Netware 3.11*. The student may choose from a menu related to coursework which begins by listing the languages taught at Smith followed by a submenu listing those courses for which CFLAC provides materials. A further submenu lists those computer, audio, and video materials available to students specifically for that course. Students may also select the "Browse" option which allows access to language offerings regardless of course. From the submenu, the student selects either "Audio," "Data Bases," "Laser Discs," "Linear Video, "Word Processors," or "Workbook Exercises" and is presented with a listing of the materials available in each language.

4.1 Digital Audio

Within the "Audio" option, students access one of the unique features of CFLAC: the exclusive use of digital audio for recorded speech and speech recording. Although students may check out audio cassette tapes for their listening comprehension exercises at the Audio Tape Library window connected to CFLAC, in the Center itself, all recording by faculty and students is conducted using digital speech. With the Audio Capture/Playback adapter we can digitize analog audio, capturing the natural sound and storing it as a digital file. Once on computer disk, this file can be combined with other computer files such as text, graphics, or digital video and sent over the network to individual workstations. At the student stations, the audio adapters convert the digital audio back to analog sound which is played over a headset attached to the adapter. Conversely, when students record, their responses are converted to digital format and stored on server's hard drives. With the central storage of all digital audio materials which the network allows, only a single copy of any audio material needs to be produced and stored on the file server. This material can then be selected at any time for independent use by any number of students. In contrast to the old audio tape system, students have access to the same audio materials simultaneously and can proceed at their own pace, without having to leave their workstation or wait for another student to finish. Students currently have access to a self-correcting digital audio dictation program, which replays the word or words missed as the corrected text is displayed, a "question and answer" program which can provide closely coordinated text as well, and a "tape recorder" program. These digital audio programs and applications were created in-house by the Academic Computing and CFLAC staff.

While these audio / text programs represent a distinct improvement over audio only exercises where students had to refer to a book or lab manual, the addition of a visual cue has stimulated interest among students and faculty alike. M-Motion technology has made digital still-frame capture a convenient alternative to slides and adds flexibility to the type of exercises which can be developed. Instructors can capture stills from any video source and save them on the computer as digital files. These files can then be combined with other programs to create stimulating and challenging applications. For example, in intermediate Chinese, students view digital stills and listen to a passage and questions about what they have seen. The digital audio "Question and Answer" program which plays the speech also allows the student to record her responses to computer disk. A sample recorded answer is then offered as feedback.

4.2 Word Processing

Under "Word Processors," both *DOS*-based and *Windows* programs are available. In *DOS*, students choose commercial word processing packages such as *système D* and *Salsa* for French and Spanish, *XyWrite* with a specifically mapped keyboard for foreign diacritics for many modern European languages, or a Russian version of *Xywrite* with a Cyrillic font created by Academic Computing. Chinese students have access to the *TianMa* word processor to produce text with Chinese characters. Under *Windows, Word for Windows 2.0* is available with *Exceller Keyboard Mappers* for modern European languages and Cyrillic, while Japanese characters can be generated using *TwinBridge*.

4.3 CALL Exercises

From the "Workbook Exercises" menu students can select CALL (computer-assisted language learning) exercises. Students currently use "electronic workbooks" in beginning German and intensive French developed using the *CALIS* authoring system, while exercises for intermediate German are available using the *Written Language Lab*, with similar "workbooks" currently in preparation for beginning Spanish and Italian as well. Other drill and practice exercises which accompany foreign language texts are also available. Many students and instructors prefer these CALL exercises to traditional workbooks because they offer students immediate feedback as to the nature of their mistakes, which helps guide them to the correct answer. While the need for such independent programs will continue, it is their integration into multimedia lessons with video and audio components which makes the CALL learning experience truly interactive and exciting.

4.4 Linear Video

The "Linear Video" menu option allows the student access to video controlled in traditional fashion by the VCR or videodisc player. In the past several years, video has come to play an ever-increasing role in the foreign language and culture curriculum. Smith courses currently feature *French in Action*, the Yale University series by Pierre Capretz; *Destinos*, the "Telenovelle" series for beginning Spanish; *Alles Gute!*, the successor to *Guten Tag!* by Inter Nationes and Langenscheidt; the Portuguese video series, *Travessia*, by Tollman, Paiva, Jensen, and Parsons; Eleanor Jordan's *Japanese: The Spoken Language*; as well as a variety of culturally authentic discs and tapes including ads, news, soaps, cartoons, weather, and feature films. Our interactive controller program now runs computer-controllable VCRs so that video tape lessons can quickly become more interactive.

4.5 Interactive Videodisc

Under "Videodisc," students choose a language from the submenu and receive a list of the discs available for that language. The learner accesses and manipulates the videodisc and support materials through an interactive controller developed in the Center. Currently, students can call up transcripts which accompany the video materials and, in German, access an on-line dictionary. With the on-going addition of CALL exercises for judging comprehension, the videodisc program is becoming increasingly interactive.

Under *Windows*, faculty and students at CFLAC have been using two multimedia authoring system, *WinCalis* developed at Duke University and Assymetric's *ToolBook*. In the *WinCalis* interactive videodisc project, designed for intermediate German, students view video clips, are presented with text questions and true multimedia feedback which includes motion video, video stills, and audio as well as text clues. This feedback is tailored to the student's level of proficiency and to the pedagogical goal of the exercise. Instructors often plan interactive assignments for their students in the Center as linguistic and cultural preparation for class where they can then concentrate more on in-depth discussions and analysis or practice in the target language.

5. Language and Culture Studies

CFLAC has offered two summer workshops in *ToolBook*, and in that short time some 1/5 of the entire foreign language faculty at Smith have received basic training in interactive multimedia. During fall semester 1992-93 the first of these *ToolBook* applications was introduced as an integral part of an intermediate Spanish course. Instead of simply watching a video about the topic, students were actively engaged in learning customs and cultural attitudes, communicative strategies, as well as vocabulary and useful expressions. In using the program, they responded to questions either by recording their impressions and analyses digitally or in writing with the aid of an on-line Spanish word processor and glossaries. At times, their responses were registered by identifying and "clicking" on persons on the video screen. At the end of the semester, they were also tested using a similar multimedia program. These programs which allow for student recording and composition (as well as the traditional self-correcting text exercises) have effectively brought instructors back into the loop and engaged them actively in the projects undertaken in the learning center. Furthermore, with the expansion of our campus networks, materials from the learning center are also available in the classroom and will soon be accessible from faculty offices and student residences.

In contrast to the audio-only language lab, then, CFLAC is able to offer support in all four "skill" areas of foreign language learning: listening, speaking, reading, and writing. The integration of video and interactive video allows the student to work towards becoming culturally as well as linguistically proficient. Yet this is only a small portion of the potential which a modern media center offers to foreign language students and faculty. We need to look to the areas of literary study and research and see where technology and media can bridge the gap that many perceive between language teaching and literary critical scholarship. I would offer just a few examples in the following sections.

6. Literary Studies

Faculty often complain that many of their students lack training in basic poetic diction, rhetoric, and literary analytical terminology. Moreover, there remains the added difficulty of determining rhyme and meter in a foreign language. While several CALL programs offering tutorials on poetics already exist, they could be made much more effective if combined with the addition of sound. Digital speech allows for a close coordination of segments of sound with text from complete works to individual words or syllables. In a similar manner, by using a reading and repeat program with digital speech, students could practice the almost lost art of poetic recitation or dramatic reading. Furthermore, we have been experimenting with a word cruncher and the data bases in *Pfeffer's Basic Vocabulary for German* to study especially the use of non-translatable flavoring particles like "doch." As literary and cultural documents become more readily available on disk, similar techniques can be employed to make the search for "beauty and truth" or "truth and beauty" that much simpler and more effective. The researcher's efforts can be devoted to the analysis of the text rather than to the previously laborious search for appropriate passages.

6.1 A Multimedia and Literature Project

In order to demonstrate the effective potential of multimedia in literary studies, I have been developing a *ToolBook* application based on the "Erlkönig" or "Erl-king" motif as depicted in the well-known 18th-century German ballad written by Johann Wolfgang von Goethe. This dramatic piece lends itself particularly well, since its theme has often been adapted and interpreted by graphic artists and musicians alike. The program invites the learner to compare works of graphic art expressing the theme through a series of video and scanned images of artwork from Pl^{n}dermann in the 18th century to Barlach in the 20th. Digital sound allows the learner to investigate three individual performances of the Schubert rendition, by simply first clicking on a name of the singer and then on a line from the text. Similarly, a further "page" in the toolbook offers the opportunity to compare a single performer singing the three contemporaneous compositions of Erl-King, by Schubert, Reichert, and Loewe with a video window for viewing the performances. Biographies with accompanying slides, source information, cultural background materials, translations, and a parody round out the project at this stage.

The *Erlkönig* Project aims at fulfilling several objectives. Pedagogically, it is designed to promote trans- or interdisciplinary studies by bringing students of literature, art, and music together and affording them the opportunity to discover links between their fields as well as some of the methods of interpretation which vary between the fields. In addition, the *Erlkönig* study seeks to involve students actively in the creation of their own multimedia research projects. Using this application and the various templates which were produced in creating it, students can then begin any number of multimedia investigations comparing elements of style in the three singers' individual interpretations of Schubert's Romantic composition, documenting each point of their analysis with the audio or video evidence they have discovered. A further investigation might entail the non-traditional use of light and darkness in the paintings and woodcut depicting the character of the Erl-King. The true value of multimedia in such projects lies in the opportunities it affords users to create links and understand connections across disciplines, opportunities simply not available or manageable without this technology.

7. Film Studies

Interactive video permits the precise manipulation of the medium including single-frame access and frame-by-frame progression so essential for in-depth sequence analysis. Video overlay and digital video technology allows for the windowing of the screen where video stills can be captured and compared with each other or with a window running motion video. Professor Gabriele A. Wittig Davis of Mount Holyoke College has been working in cooperation with CFLAC developing a project which focuses on comparative film analysis, that is, the comparison of similar motifs and techniques within one film, and of two or more filmings of the same literary text, Theodor Fontane's *Mathilde Möhring* (composed 1891-96, first published 1906). Using *ToolBook* and the windowing capabilities of M-Motion video overlay, the project illustrates possibilities for detailed sequence analysis and a close comparison of three different *Mathilde Möhring* films produced around the end of WWII, during the late sixties, and in contemporary Germany. Templates based on the toolbook are being developed which will enable students to document similar analyses. Included are, furthermore, components which allow for the comparison of the film with the original print text as well as manuscript drafts and different editions of the Fontane novel and transcripts of the films' dialogues. Finally, the project includes through various media (scanned images, digital slides, digital audio, etc.) supplemental materials for exploring the era and culture under discussion. A film terminology dictionary with video, computer graphics, and animated graphics to exemplify key terms assists the learner in "translating" the filmic language and understanding the process of metamorphosis from the linguistic to the filmic code.

As the above applications illustrate, access to this technology should not be limited to the instructor. Students should be encouraged and assisted in using multimedia as an expression of their creative and analytical ideas. Most multimedia authoring programs like *ToolBook* are designed to create templates, that is, routines in which the scripting or programming of functions can be copied and linked to new content material. As a media center develops more materials and hence templates for different multimedia functions and combinations, the time and effort necessary to create new applications can be drastically reduced. Both faculty and student users can then concentrate more on the *what* they wish to express rather than *how* they might make it work.

8. Learning "Networks"

At CFLAC, we remain convinced of the revolutionary potential that educational technology holds for the learner, especially in light of the many ways in which it has already influenced pedagogy. Just as the word processor has illustrated and then formalized the concept of writing as process and not product, so too have non-linear media like interactive video forced us to rethink the way we teach and the way students learn. Some of the last vestiges of linear word-for-word comprehension and translation have been challenged by the need to work from global comprehension to more detailed understanding, which the use of culturally authentic media brings. Furthermore, as technology makes access to and management of huge amounts of information more transparent, it enables the learner to participate more directly and fully in original research. Shared technology allows learners and instructors to become closer partners in scholarship.

The freedom of students to choose how best to use the Center to serve their individual learning needs reflects the basic CFLAC philosophy which considers that the Center is not only a place where assignments are completed as an integral part of the foreign language curriculum, but is also an environment which students feel free to visit on their own to explore a foreign culture. Similarly, faculty should consider CFLAC both a service facility in support of their coursework and a research resource for curricular development and investigations into second-language acquisition.

In our planning and implementation of the Center for Foreign Languages and Cultures at Smith, then, we have attempted to create networks: physical networks between the classroom and the learning center; intellectual networks between disciplines; and interpersonal networks between instructors, learners, and researchers. In the end, however, the learners are proving to be the prime motivating force. As they have become more and more convinced of the extent to which technology and the use of media benefits their learning, it is their enthusiasm and their persistence which is convincing greater numbers of our colleagues that technology and media should comprise integral parts of their teaching and scholarship and of their students' learning experience.*

---

*It occurred to us that readers of this article might also profit from a number of articles on the same subject contained in a book recently put on the market. A British view of present-day and future developments is found in Stephen Hagen's 1993 publication *Using Technology in Language Learning*. London: CILT. [Editors' note].

EUROPEAN FOREIGN LANGUAGE LEARNING IN THE MULTIMEDIA TELESCHOOL

Gabriele Fesl

Berlitz European Projects, Frankfurt

The "Multimedia Teleschool for European Personnel Development" is the major application project of the research and development programme DELTA of the European Commission. The project focuses on foreign language distance learning with cross-border learner groups based on European computer conferencing systems and interactive programmes. It started in January 1992 and will run for 3 years. Advanced learning technologies based on electronic networks and interactive satellite broadcasting are integrated in corporate personnel development systems and tested in a "real life approach". Satellite and terrestrial networks are linked to provide broadcast communications with interactive real and delayed time feedback. "Computer supported cooperative" learning systems with interactive satellite broadcasting will offer feedback links from students and student groups to tutors.

1. On the verge of a market breakthrough

'Multimedia' is a catchword which promises the user not only technical sophistication but also a communicative experience which is both varied and integrated. ISDN, HDTV, Windows-based software for computer conferencing, networks and storage media such as CD-I form the basic framework for virtual environments for which the potential user is often unable to find useful applications. Now the Multimedia Teleschool provides an application which usefully combines technical developments with the need for advanced company training in the countries of Europe.

The need for advanced training within companies is growing, a trend which is dictated not only by ever stiffer internal requirements for qualifications but also external changes in the economy. Even now, the European market for staff development and advanced training within companies is estimated to be worth some 27 billion marks (Fahle 1992). It is in this context that "Multimedia Teleschool" (MTS) is providing a distance-learning concept which involves the use of up-to-date teaching aids. MTS uses telecommunications technologies in an attempt to create virtual study centres for students from European companies, and in this way, to meet the need for real and effective advanced training. The main aim behind this approach is to overcome two problems associated with conventional distance learning, namely interactivity and integration. Inter-activity allows for the use of various feedback technologies at the workplace, such as telephones, faxes, computer conferencing and even video conferencing. Students and tutors have the option of communicating synchronously or asynchronously. An interactive approach of this type, coupled with the assignments which are given to students on the courses, is designed to ensure integration of students within study groups at both national and international corporate level, and also integration of students drawn from various companies in a particular sector.

2. Courses and Scenarios

From the teaching point of view, MTS attempts to bring about four different educational scenarios:

(1) individual learning (with a tutor),

(2) team tuition (students A, B and C - tutor),

(3) supracorporate tuition (branch A: study group - tutor - branch B: study group), and

(4) supranational tuition (country X: study group - tutor - country Y: study group).

The last of these four scenarios merits the European Commission's particular attention, despite all the problems surrounding it, as it is committed to the idea of European integration. The courses "English for Telecommunications" and "English for Business" which are currently being run bring together students from Germany (Telekom), Spain (Telefónica, GATE/Universidad Politécnica de Madrid), France (France Télécom), Sweden (Ovemi), Finland (Technet), Russia (Baumann Institute), Italy (University of Catania), Czech Republic (Telekom) and Belgium (European Commission).

Six courses are currently offered by MTS for around 1,600 students in eight European countries. Companies also have the opportunity now of sending students off on these courses. In the case of Western Europe, there are no technical barriers and in principle, Datex-P (packet switching) and satellite technology open up the possibility of reaching students in eastern Europe, even in places as far away as the Baltic States and Russia. Initial attempts at meeting language training needs in Eastern Europe are being made using the EC's Tempus and Comett programs.

3. Interactive television for distance learning

The first interactive television service for staff development in European companies was launched on 27 October 1992.

Between October 1992 and June 1993, 12 one-hour programmes on core topics of "English for Banking" and "English for Telecommunications" courses were broadcast live throughout Europe from Strasbourg by Arte, the new European cultural channel, and also by Eurostep. Two other courses of MTS, "Environmental Awareness" and "Camélia" have broadcast another 4 programmes each up to the time of writing.

On 26 October 1993 the new series "Business on Line" was launched, which gathers all members of the "English for Business" and "English for Telecommunications" courses. At three-week intervals, all learners are now following 90-minute live programmes, and many of them are linked *directly* with the studio via videoconference using ISDN technology.

Course members in the European branches are of course also linked up with experts in the television studio via the Teleschool's computer conferencing system. It is via this system that all students receive their correspondence lessons from the Berlitz correspondence course centre in Eschborn, and they also use it for returning homework to their tutors. In addition, the conferencing system is used by students for studying in groups with other course participants across Europe, for putting questions to the experts during live broadcasts and for making their own contributions.

The broadcast lesson comprises a presentation by the experts lasting about 20 minutes, 15 minutes of film on the topic being studied and a discussion lasting about 20 minutes which deals with students' queries and contributions. And of course, a large amount of time is dedicated to the live interaction with the learner groups by video conference, including debates, negotiations and role plays. In addition to the experts and the moderator, tutors are present in the studio, and the latter receive incoming contributions via their monitors and pass them on to the experts. The contributions made by the students or study groups will have been prepared with the tutors in the accompanying correspondence course.

4. The Teleschool Technology

Fairly recent developments in the field of computer conferencing and satellite technology are being used in the initial phase in order to provide the Teleschool with technical support. Teletutor, developed by the Berlin company Condat, will be used during the second stage and this will even enable ISDN synchronous multimedia communication between students and tutors to take place.

The computer conferencing system is installed on a host computer in Berlin and is ideally suited to the needs of the Teleschool. In particular, this is where all interactive processes are carried out, i.e. distribution and return of course material, group work and direct access to the television programme. Individual participants work locally on PCs which are networked with the host computer via Datex-P. All basic functions required for communication are controlled via a top Windows level.

The computer system is also configured as a distributed system with several host computers in different countries. This means that conferences can also be transmitted to other host computers, opening up the way for supranational conferences in which students do course work together. Such "cross-border" learning is an important element of the Teleschool's approach.

Television broadcasts from the Arte studio in Strasbourg are being broadcast by TDF 1 and EUTELSAT. The computer conferencing system and video conferencing via ISDN provide communications facilities for live interaction by participants in the TV studio.

5. Participating Companies

The following companies currently arrange for their staff to receive advanced training from the Teleschool on the courses mentioned above: France Télécom and SNVB in France, GATE and Telefónica in Spain, British Airways, Exxon Chemicals, Carneaud Metalbox, Earthwatch, IPC and Orfeus in England, Deutsche Bundespost Telekom and Detemobil in Germany, Technet in Finland, the Baumann Institute in Russia, The University of Catania in Italy, SPT Telekom in the Czech Republic, the Agricultural Bank of Greece and Macedonia Thrace Bank in Greece, and Ovemi in Sweden. In 1993 and 1994, more than 1,600 working people in Europe will be following courses organised by the Teleschool.

6. The MTS Project Consortium

Management and coordination activities associated with the Teleschool are carried out at Berlitz. Courses are currently offered by Cleo (F), Southampton University (GB), and Berlitz. The communications software for the computer conferencing facility is supplied by Cecomm (GB) and Condat; responsibility for interactive television and satellite transmission is borne by the European culture channel Arte, Eurostep, La Sept, France Télécom, University College Dublin and Berlitz. Evaluation activities are carried out by the Scientific Institute for Communication Services in Bad Honnef and the Polytechnic University of Madrid.

REFERENCE

Fahle, R. (1992). Mit Elektronik Zeit gewinnen — leichter lernen. *CAPITAL* 2, p. 53.

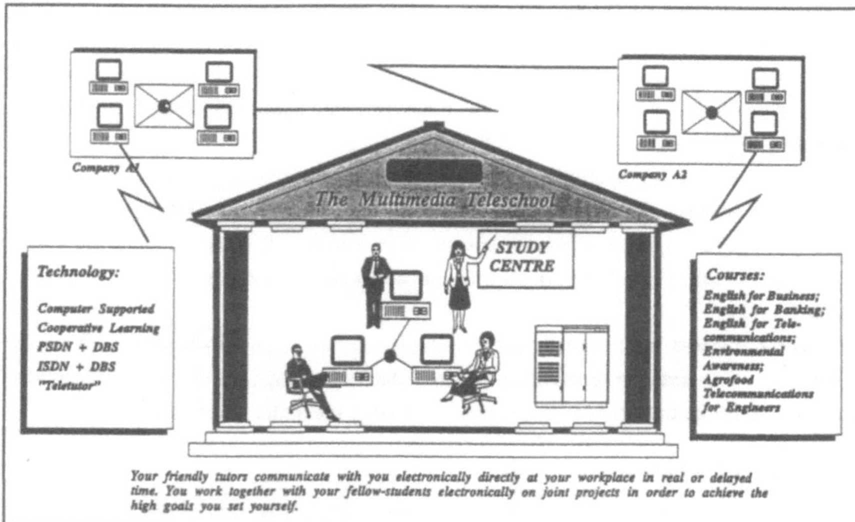

Your friendly tutors communicate with you electronically directly at your workplace in real or delayed time. You work together with your fellow-students electronically on joint projects in order to achieve the high goals you set yourself.

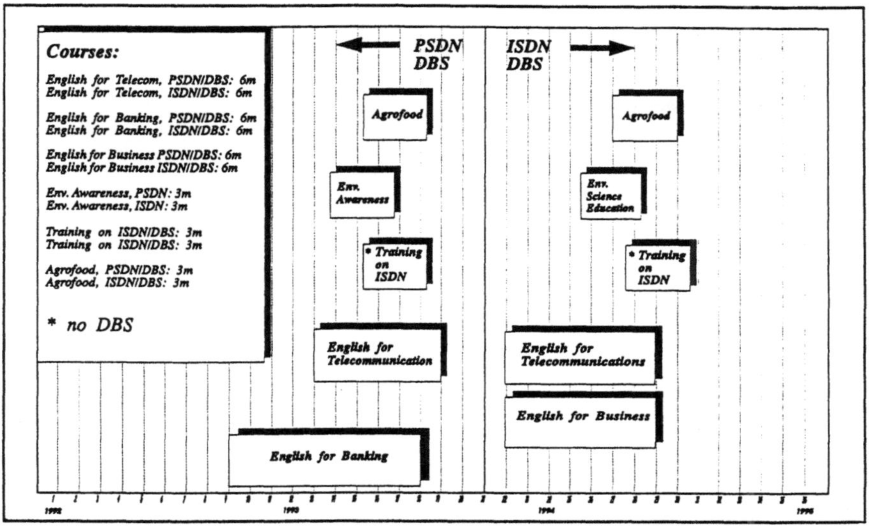
Courses:
English for Telecom, PSDN/DBS: 6m
English for Telecom, ISDN/DBS: 6m
English for Banking, PSDN/DBS: 6m
English for Banking, ISDN/DBS: 6m
English for Business PSDN/DBS: 6m
English for Business ISDN/DBS: 6m
Env. Awareness, PSDN: 3m
Env. Awareness, ISDN: 3m
Training on ISDN/DBS: 3m
Training on ISDN/DBS: 3m
Agrofood, PSDN/DBS: 3m
Agrofood, ISDN/DBS: 3m
* no DBS
PSDN
DBS
ISDN
DBS
Agrofood
Env. Awareness
* Training on ISDN
English for Telecommunication
English for Banking
Agrofood
Env. Science Education
* Training on ISDN
English for Telecommunications
English for Business
1992
1994

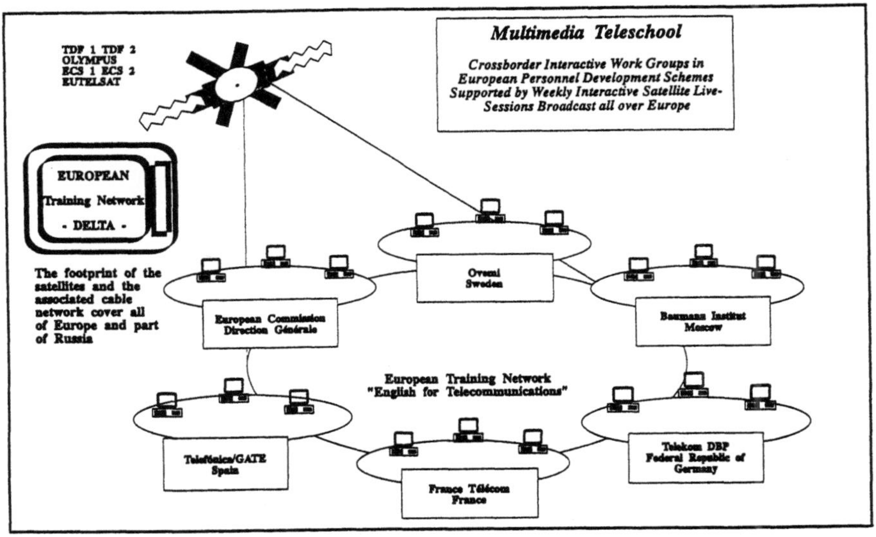
Multimedia Teleschool
Crossborder Interactive Work Groups in European Personnel Development Schemes Supported by Weekly Interactive Satellite Live-Sessions Broadcast all over Europe
TDF 1 TDF 2
OLYMPUS
ECS 1 ECS 2
EUTELSAT
EUROPEAN
Training Network
- DELTA -
The footprint of the satellites and the associated cable network cover all of Europe and part of Russia
Ovemi
Sweden
European Commission
Direction Générale
Baumann Institut
Moscow
European Training Network
"English for Telecommunications"
Telefónica/GATE
Spain
France Télécom
France
Telekom DBP
Federal Republic of
Germany

DISTRIBUTIVE LANGUAGE LEARNING IN A COMPUTER-BASED MULTILINGUAL COMMUNICATION ENVIRONMENT*

Kurt Kohn

University of Tübingen

The future of technology-based language learning and teaching is seen in an open communication and learning environment, which integrates generalised multi-purpose tools and is powerful and flexible enough to be used by different users, i.e. learners and tutors, for different purposes on different levels of sophistication. Two concepts will be of particular importance - *distributive integration* and *life/work-embedded language learning*. According to these concepts, learners should be enabled through technology to combine and integrate various learning and teaching modes - from direct to distance to self-access - depending on their purposes, needs and learning styles. Technology should also provide a basis for the integration of a diversified range of second-language activities - from communicative processing to communicative interaction, from communication support to learning support - in a real-life context of (work-related) multilingual communication. The technological potential is available; what is still missing, however, is a 'humanistic' approach providing imaginative guidance on the basis of user needs and a research-informed understanding of technology-based multilingual communication and second-language learning.

1. CALL Perspectives

During the past decade, technology-based approaches have become an increasingly relevant factor in the overall discussion on language learning and teaching (Hagen 1993). A variety of trends can be observed ranging from 'traditional' to 'interactive' to 'intelligent' computer-assisted language learning (CALL) (Kenning 1990; Fox et al. 1992).

In its traditional version, CALL may support activities ranging from vocabulary practice to cloze tests/exercises and text reconstruction, from problem solving and simulation to branching stories and adventure games - but the main emphasis is always on those lexical, grammatical and textual aspects of language performance which lend themselves to formal practice.

Among the more recent developments in the field of CALL, 'interactive video' (IV) has raised considerable interest in the language learning world, combining computers and video /audio technology. The advantage is obvious. While the video/audio component provides authentic aural and visual data, the computer itself serves as a control centre for restricted human-machine interaction. As the processing power of a computer can be fully exploited only with digitised data, the availability of digitised speech and video will be of crucial importance for future development of IV towards a full-blown interactive communication and learning environment.

---

*I have benefited from many discussions of these issues with colleagues in the Lingua project Eloquent and the Delta Concerted Action on Technologies in Language Learning and Teaching. In particular, I would like to thank Joe Farrell, Petra Hoffstaedter, Peter Isackson, Nigel Reeves and Peter Roe for their comments on earlier versions of this paper.

Learning a language for the purpose of real-life communication is a demanding task, and any attempt to develop congenial computer-based learning-support tools is soon confronted with major limitations. Certainly, there is a particular challenge in the fact that the natural 'intelligence' of a computer, fast algorithm-based processing, is hardly the kind of intelligence required for the strategic processing of discourse in natural communication.

There have been attempts in CALL development to bypass such restrictions, in particular, by putting some of the burden of the human-machine interaction on learners and tutors. But in the long run, the need for 'intelligent' CALL will increase, that is, applications will be needed which simulate relevant aspects of the typically human competence underlying the comprehension and production of meaningful discourse. Grammatical parsing, semantic interpretation, context-based inferencing, interactive text processing, advanced text categorisation - these are only some of the research topics that will be relevant in this context. Even modest success in these areas will have a great impact on the future development of technologies in language learning and teaching (Engel et al. 1992; Swartz & Yazdani 1992).

Although the overall development seems to be rather promising, it is nevertheless true that current CALL applications still tend to fall short of hopeful expectations. This is mainly due to the following:

(a) unimaginative traditional learning approaches combined with poor linguistic modelling and little attention to recent advances in psycholinguistics, cognitive linguistics and second-language acquisition research;

(b) insufficient deployment of Natural Language Processing technologies;

(c) emphasis on specialised ('dedicated') language learning (and teaching) tools;

(d) a corresponding neglect of the kind of multi-purpose 'common ground' technology that would be required for a flexible and diversified approach;

(e) last but not least, a neglect of the 'human' dimension in technology-based language learning.

2. Distributive Integration

With learners becoming increasingly dependent on being able, for various professional or private reasons, to choose their own time and location of learning, direct teaching has lost much of its natural appeal. In addition, the need for specialised work-embedded language learning requires a type of integrated learning/working environment which, on the basis of direct teaching alone, could not be optimally supported.

As a result of changing needs and the promise of technological advances, the traditional unity of learning and teaching with regard to 'time and place' is no longer valid. In the recent past, it has come under attack along two interdependent battle lines:

(1) the *separation* of learning from teaching in terms of time and place resulting in various types of distance learning;
(2) the *emancipation* of learning from teaching in terms of learner autonomy resulting in various types of self-access learning.

Due to these trends the language learning world is witnessing an ongoing evolutionary process of *diversification* producing a wide range of mutually overlapping and interacting learning and teaching modes, in particular:

(a) technology-based classroom teaching;
(b) tutored self-study;
(c) 'pre-fabricated' teaching 'packages';
(d) interactive distance tutoring;
(e) autonomous self-access learning.

Given the cognitive, linguistic and social complexity and sophistication of human language learning in the context of multilingual communication within real-life discourse communities, it is difficult to see how any of the various learning/teaching approaches currently emerging could be successfully used in isolation. An obvious answer to this problem is the concept of *distributive integration*. This concept encapsulates a flexible and comprehensive learning approach which supports the selective combination and integration of different language learning modes in such a way that any restrictions and negative effects present in each single mode are neutralised and the learner is given maximum customised support (Hoffstaedter & Kohn 1992; Kohn & Roe 1993). A distributive integration approach may combine direct teaching with distance tutoring and autonomous self-access learning and is thus responsive to individual needs, aptitude, preferences and situational conditions.

The idea is to adopt a more global perspective in order to be able to integrate the best that is available in language learning and teaching to the benefit of the individual learner.

The kingpin of all this would be an innovative learnware platform allowing for the dynamic representation and flexible (learner) navigation of integrated multimedia learning materials *across different (technological) modes of flexible and distance language learning and teaching* - from direct to distance, from tutored to autonomous. What is needed is a type of generalised learnware technology that is powerful and flexible enough to adapt to varying conditions and modes of language learning and teaching, thereby providing a necessary pre-requisite for flexible and customised integration.

3. From Communication to Learning

The fundamental role and relevance of the *discourse community*, the communicative social environment within which language learning takes place (for example the workplace), can hardly be overemphasised.* Learners acquire a considerable and vital part of their communicative (linguistic) competence through communicative social interaction. It is the discourse community (and/or community of practice) which determines the learning needs and at the same time offers a potential for co-operative 'group-learning' (cf. Brown & Duguid 1991).

This emphasis on the role of discourse communities is paralleled by the view that second-language learning is embedded in *multilingual communication*. People communicate across language boundaries, and they learn languages in order to extend their range of communication. Second-language learners are, primarily, language users who need (and want) to deploy their second-language knowledge in order to communicate in their work environment, their everyday life, or their leisure time. Second-language learning stems from multilingual communication, in particular, from second-language-based communication problems.

The natural situation in which learners are confronted with deficits in their second-language knowledge and related second-language learning challenges is the communicative situation encountered in daily working life, not in the 'classroom'. Natural communication in a discourse community and/or a community of practice thus not only defines the target of language learning, it also provides the setting in which the need arises to learn specific things in order to overcome specific problems of communication.

Looking at multilingual communication not only as the *goal* but as the *necessary condition, cause* and *natural environment* of second-language learning has the advantage of integrating a wide range of second-language activities in life/work-embedded multilingual communication beyond the traditional language-course approach (Jung in this volume). The following four dimensions, in particular, need to be distinguished (see Figure 1):

(1) *Communicative Processing* - comprehension, production, translation of computer-based multimedia communication materials from text to sound to video;

(2) *Communicative Interaction* - technology-based distance communication with others within a discourse and/or learning community as well as distance delivery of multi-media communication materials;

(3) *Communication Support* - including lexical/terminological and encyclopaedic look-up facilities, grammatical and phraseological production help, as well as computer-based

*The notion of discourse community in second-language learning calls to mind a number of topics in second-language acquisition research that were dominant, and gave rise to much heated discussion, in the seventies and eighties (Kohn 1990), in particular, the distinctions between language *learning* and *acquisition* (Krashen 1982), and between *use* and *usage* (Widdowson 1979), the relevance of comprehensible input and output (Krashen 1982; Swain 1985), and the consequences of socio-psychological distance (Schumann 1978).

mediation (translation, interpreting);

(4) *Language Learning Support* - access to technology-based 'local' or 'global' language learning modules.

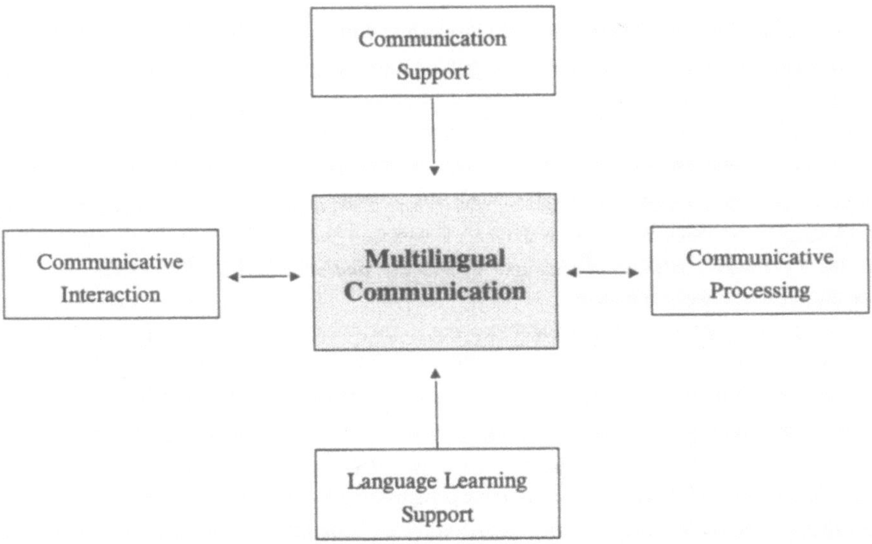

Figure 1: Dimensions of Multilingual Communication

It should be noted that language learning takes place on each of these four dimensions of multilingual communication. While in communicative processing and communicative interaction language learning is a welcome by-product of the type of 'learning by doing', it is more targeted in communication support and more systematic in language learning support.

This approach, which sees language learning as integrated within multilingual communication, opens up new perspectives into a hitherto neglected area of demand. There is considerable potential for product-orientated research into technology-based support facilities for language learning. The multilingual communication approach has the advantage of, in particular,

(a) taking into account the most comprehensive framework for language learning, which is language learning in a natural and relevant life/work environment;

(b) integrating language learning with other activities in multilingual communication, such as dictionary look-up, style and grammar checking, or translational mediation;

(c) providing a unifying basis for the development of multi-purpose common ground tools.

4. Flexible and Distance Language Learning

Distance education, and distance language learning in particular, seem to be bedevilled by a fundamental conflict. On the one hand, it is in the very nature of distance learning to create, accept and creatively exploit distance, distance in the sense of a *temporal/spacial separation of learning from teaching*, and distance in the sense of the *learner's emancipation from teaching* (see above). The advantage is obvious as the learner is liberated from time, place and teacher constraints which are characteristic of traditional classroom learning. On the other hand a third type of distance, that is, distance in the sense of the *learner's separation from a discourse community and/or community of practice* clearly operates against these advantages.

In distance language learning this negative force seems to have an even stronger impact than in other types of distance education. The distance of the learner from the target discourse community, in particular from native speakers and real-life socio-cultural interactions, reduces the potential for relevant language learning. While this detrimental effect is present already in the traditional classroom, it is even stronger under conditions of distance learning, where the learner is separated from a supporting learning/tutoring community.

Distance language learning is thus faced with the fundamental challenge of exploiting distance and overcoming it at the same time. Emancipation seems to be in conflict with guidance, separation with communicative authenticity.

This seemingly paradoxical situation requires a substantial reorientation of the traditional concept of distance (language) learning. What is needed is an approach which goes beyond the rigidity and restrictions of the earlier approaches characterised by 'industrialised' pre-fabrication and introduces a substantial degree of flexibility and individualisation (Keegan 1990; van den Brande 1993).

In a truly 'flexible and distance' approach toward language learning the following aspects will be of crucial importance:

(1) *Distributive Integration* - integrating distance language learning with a wide range of relevant learning modes (including 'direct' ones) with appropriate links and 'gateways' for flexible navigation;

(2) *Life/Work-Embedded Language Learning* - integrating (distance) language learning into the (professional) world of multilingual communication in order to provide access to relevant communities of practice and/or discourse communities;

(3) *Learner Autonomy* - supporting and strengthening the individual dimension of

language learning in terms of user needs and purposes, learning goals and self-instruction, as well as self-evaluation;

(4) *Communicative Interaction* - supporting and strengthening distance communication and delivery of materials in order to create an efficient platform for dispersed learning /tutoring communities.

This conceptual reorientation needs to be backed up by an ensemble of tools which draws, in particular, on technologies in distance communication, multimedia and Natural Language Processing. At the same time, it provides a framework for humane and relevant technology development.

5. General Principles of Technology Development

One of the main challenges of technology development for language learning purposes is to devise new learning techniques that treat technology as an integral part of an activity which, in spite of considerable modifications brought about by technological factors, will and must always remain essentially human.

To begin with, a general caveat concerning the interpretation of 'virtual classroom/teacher' might be in place. While these terms may capture the creative potential of computer-mediated simulation, they also carry the danger of trivialising this potential by merely transferring traditional ways of learning onto a computer platform. The future of computer-mediated language learning should certainly not be restricted to substituting the 'real' class-room and the 'real' teacher by 'virtual' replicas.

It needs to be emphasised that the 'new' world of computer-mediated language learning will (have to) be dramatically different from what we have been used to in the 'old' world. Computer-based technologies clearly have the power to change the world of language learning - provided, however, that the process of technology development is creatively informed, shaped and controlled by a thorough understanding of, in particular:

(a) language-based communication;
(b) the principles, conditions and processes of 'good' language learning;
(c) learner needs in the wider context of real-life multilingual communication;
(d) the pedagogic potential of current technology and future technological trends.

With recent developments in distance communication systems, computer power and multi-media processing, the vision of flexible and distance language learning in a distributively integrated life/work-embedded approach is now fast becoming a tangible possibility with a promising commercial perspective. Success, however, will depend largely on our ability to integrate the relevant *technologies*, from video conferencing to computer simulation to

distance delivery systems, in such a way that the learner can move flexibly between functionally different yet compatible learning modes according to private and professional needs in the context of multilingual communication.
The two general principles that should be observed in the course of technology development for language learning purposes are *humanistic orientation* and use of *generalised multi-purpose tools*.

- Humanistic Orientation

Technology-based language learning has an intrinsic humanistic orientation. It is first and foremost about human beings: about their cognitive power to creatively acquire and learn a second language for communication purposes, and about the socio-psychological forces shaping the intent, direction and manifestation of the individual learner's learning activities.
The development of advanced technological applications in the area of language learning and teaching (and in any other area, for that matter) is not at all a purely technological task; nor is the relationship between application design and the processes and conditions of language learning a trivial matter. There is a growing awareness that exclusive attention to technological aspects is not generally conducive to success in language learning.
It should be noted that the cohesive force underlying flexible and distance language learning is not technology as such. Cohesion derives from conceptual design. What is needed are integrative approaches linking, from the very beginning, the development of technological applications to the field of application itself, in our case, to what is known about the cognitive, the linguistic, and the socio-psychological dimensions of language learning and teaching.
We are on the brink of a new era of technology-based language learning. With the advent of advanced standards in distance communication, 'intelligent' Natural Language Processing-based techniques and powerful hypermedia tools, a great technological potential becomes available. But technology development needs guidance, it needs to be made dependent on two things: user purposes and needs, and a research-informed understanding of the human processes and conditions of language learning.

- Generalised Multi-Purpose Tools

Flexible learning styles and increasingly diversified user profiles require generalised multi-purpose tools. The innovative potential of technology-based language learning is not in the area of dedicated single-purpose tools. What is required instead are tools that are flexible and diversified enough so that they can be used by different users (learners, tutors) for different purposes, on different levels of sophistication, and with the potential of serving the needs of a wide range of approaches, from direct to distance, from tutored to self-access, from simple to complex, from general to specific. The representation and navigation of multimedia communication and learning materials across different modes of language learning and teaching will thus be of vital importance. Generalised solutions accounting for underlying functional similarities are required to provide the technological 'common ground' necessary for free and easy navigation across a full range of support modules within a flexible and distance learning environment.

6. Action Themes for Research and Development

Language learning is one of the most complex and most diversified human learning activities involving any type of human knowledge from intuitive to analytic, from encyclopædic to social, from declarative to procedural to functional. Language learning imposes the highest demands on flexible and distance learning; and it provides a challenging framework for the development of innovative and relevant advanced systems.
Research and development of technologies in language learning should have a clear focus on communication- and language-specific technologies within a comprehensive approach integrating second-language activities and multilingual communication. The integration of these two domains will make it possible to provide language learning with a much-needed dimension of real-life relevance; at the same time, it will help to make multilingual communication more efficient.
Some of the main action themes in the area of computer-based flexible and distance language learning will be briefly characterised below.

6.1 Distance Communication Infrastructure

Technological support of learner-tutor communication is especially in demand in distance language learning, where much of the success depends on the linguistic power and flexibility of the delivery system used. The tools should allow for a bi-directional and interactive learner-tutor communication, including the exchange of a wide range of linguistic learnware materials comprising text, speech, discourse, and video. Other areas relevant to distance language learning include video conferencing and telecommunications. Again, it is essential to avoid reducing the question of how to support distance learner-tutor communication to a purely technological one. Innovative concepts are needed that pay sufficient attention to the wide range of learner-tutor and learner-learner relationships relevant in this context as well as to the specialised communication activities involved. Specific provisions should be made for supporting the establishment of communities of practice and/or discourse communities.

6.2 Multilingual Communication Support Systems

A wide range of communication support facilities need to be integrated into a computer-based multilingual communication environment which helps learners working in their second language to cope with communication problems caused by knowledge gaps and performance deficits. These may include techniques for reducing the learner's processing load through, for example, subtitling, dubbing, visual display and the ability to create or access on-line synchronised commentaries supplied by the learning or teaching communities or individual tutors. It is also of central importance that learners have access to linguistic and encyclopædic/cultural information resources. Traditional support tools, dictionaries and grammars, are basically of this type. Research and development in this area should creatively exploit the potential of hypermedia technology and advanced Natural Language Processing in order to produce (semi-)automatic look-up facilities fully geared to a learner's information and processing needs with regard to comprehension and production problems in a multilingual communication and learning environment.

6.3 Language Learning Support Systems

As part of their multilingual communication and learning environment learners should be provided with learning support facilities in the form of:

(1) language exercises related to specific lexical, grammatical, etc. problems and specific performance skills relevant in a particular stretch of discourse (= 'local' learning);
(2) free-standing language learning units including broader lexical and grammatical areas as well as the full range of relevant performance skills (= 'global' learning);
(3) learner access to a multimedia learnware base, serviced and tailored to the learner's specific needs by an external tutor.

In this connection it will be of special importance to explore innovative and 'intelligent' ways of computer-based language learning and practice.

6.4 Analysis and Diagnosis Systems

Three interrelated dimensions of analysis and diagnosis can be distinguished:

(1) needs analysis and specification of learner profiles
(2) language proficiency diagnosis
(3) progress assessment

Tools supporting the diagnostic analysis of learner output are of central importance for monitoring the learning progress. They should be made available to the tutor for external monitoring as well as to the learner for feed-back and internal monitoring. In this connection, it is important to note that in the area of language-related analysis and diagnosis there is a great demand for 'intelligent' tools involving the type of higher-level processing currently under focus in Natural Language Processing, such as grammatical parsing, semantic interpretation or context-dependent inferencing.

6.5 Computer-Simulation Systems

Following on from role-play techniques, much of the effort in the development of advanced computer applications in language learning goes into the simulation of communicative situations designed to promote language acquisition. The driving force behind all this is the assumption that communication is not only the goal but also the means of communicative language learning and teaching. The facilities available for distance communication call for the exploitation of the potential of computer simulations for creating 'virtual' discourse communities.

6.6 Multimedia Learnware Representation and Processing Systems

Technology-based flexible and distance language learning (and tutoring) requires as its centrepiece rich learnware corpora of multimedia (text/audio/video) materials, analysed and categorised for learning purposes (that is, according to domain, topic, communicative function, linguistic structure, complexity, difficulty), represented in a robust hypermedia structure, and accessible through powerful user-oriented navigation procedures. They should support a sufficiently wide range of communicative situations and functions, represent the relevant linguistic means of expression on various levels of complexity, difficulty and style, and be integrated with various kinds of learning-related language activities, from communication to practice, from exploration to diagnosis/testing.

6.7 Language Learning Management Systems

The more diversified and complex the learning and tutoring process, as in a distributive integration approach, the more important it is for tutors and learners to have the backup of efficient management tools. It would be a great mistake to see the development of such tools as something separate from the 'real' language learning and teaching tools. The management dimension should be addressed right from the start as an integral part of the overall process of tool development.

These action themes need to be integrated into the broader framework of a computer-based *multilingual communication and learning environment* featuring:

(1) a diversified and interconnected distance communication system for communicative interaction and delivery, including broadcasting, video conferencing, e-mail, fax;

(2) a learnware platform featuring the dynamic representation of integrated multimedia learning materials coupled with a flexible (learner) navigation system *across (technologically) different modes of flexible and distance language learning*.

Such an environment (see Figure 1) should enable learners in particular to

(a) access and process communicative multimedia materials (video, animation, pictures, audio, text) in different modes or with varied aims (comprehension, production, translation . . .), the utility of the documents not necessarily being restricted to language learning purposes (= Communicative Processing);
(b) communicate with others (learners, tutors) across a distance and to exchange learnware/testware materials (= Communicative Interaction);
(c) access various kinds of support facilities in connection with language-specific processing and communication problems (= Communication/Learning Support).

Empirically sound and innovative *user modelling* and real-life *formative evaluation* should be an essential part of this undertaking (Dillon & Gunawardena 1992; Eisner 1993; Reeves 1992). Of particular importance in this connection are user-friendliness and assessment support.

User-friendliness includes the following things:

(1) the ergonomic adaptation of a tool to a learner's predispositions in order to make it non-obstructive, natural and efficient to handle;
(2) the integration of flexible help information;
(3) the training of learners to use specific tools and, more importantly, to adapt to new ways of technology-based learning.

With regard to the *Assessment of user profiles*, emphasis should be put on:

(a) the *integration* of software solutions for the elicitation and analysis of data concerning the various linguistic and non-linguistic dimensions of the user profile;
(b) the promotion of 'intelligent' and interactive tools for the assessment of communicative/linguistic needs in the context of diagnostic tools in general.

Through the imaginative exploration of the user dimension it will be possible to gain valuable insights for a humanistic orientation of technology-based language learning in a flexible and distance approach.

REFERENCES

Brown, J.S. & Duguid, P. (1991). Organisational learning and communities of practice: toward a unifying view of working, learning and innovation. *Organisation Science* 2 (1), 40-57.

Dillon, C.L. & Gunawardena, C. (1992). Evaluation research in distance education. *British Journal of Educational Technology* 23 (3), 181-194.

Eisner, E.W. (1993). Reshaping assessment in education: some criteria in search of practice. *Journal of Curriculum Studies* 25 (3), 219-233.

Engel, F.L. et al. (eds.) (1992). *Cognitive modelling and interactive environments in language learning*. Heidelberg, Springer.

Fox, J. et al. (1992). *New perspectives in modern language learning*. Sheffield, Dept. of Employment in association with the University of East Anglia, Norwich.

Hagen, S. (ed.) (1993). *Using technology in language learning*. London, City Technology Colleges Trust in association with CILT.

Hoffstaedter P. & Kohn, K. (1992). Learning and teaching business communication. A linguistic perspective. Proceedings of the XVII Annual Symposium: Language Needs in Business, Nijmegen 15 - 16 October 1992.

Jung, U.O.H. (1994). Experiential learning: what educational technology can contribute. In this volume, pp. 1-14.

Keegan, D. (1990^2). Foundations of distance education. London / New York, Routledge.

Kenning, M.-M. (1990). Computer-assisted language learning. *Language Teaching* 23 (2), 67-76.

Kohn, K. (1990). *Dimensionen lernersprachlicher Performanz*. Theoretische und empirische Untersuchungen zum Zweitsprachenerwerb. Tübingen, Narr.

Kohn, K. & Roe, P. (1993). Computer-assisted language learning in a holistic approach. In: Commission of the European Communities (ed.). *LINGUA - DELTA: Foreign language learning and the use of new technologies*. Conference proceedings London 1993. Brussels, Bureau Lingua, pp. 67-78.

Krashen, S. (1982). *Principles and practice in second language acquisition*. Oxford, Pergamon Press.

Reeves, N. (1992). Our European future and the challenge of language learning. Inaugural Lecture; Monday, 3 February 1992, Aston University.

Schumann, J.H. (1978). *The pidginization process*. A model for second language acquisition. Rowley, MA, Newbury House.

Swain, M. (1985). Communicative competence: some roles of comprehensible input and comprehensible output in its development. In: Gass, S.M. & Madden, C.G. (eds.). *Input in second language acquisition*. Rowley, MA, Newbury House.

Swartz, M.L. & Yazdani, M. (eds.) (1992). *Intelligent tutoring systems for foreign language learning*. Heidelberg, Springer.

van den Brande, L. (1993). *Flexible and distance learning*. Chichester, John Wiley & Sons.

Widdowson, H.G. (1979). *Explorations in applied linguistics*. Oxford, Oxford University Press.

ASSESSING TELECOMMUNICATIONS PROJECTS: PROJECT TYPES AND THEIR EDUCATIONAL POTENTIAL

Andreas Eck, Lienhard Legenhausen, Dieter Wolff
Universities of Münster and Wuppertal

This article is concerned with the educational potential of telecommunications and explores the question of how e-mail projects can be systematically analyzed and evaluated. It focuses on the experiences with an AT&T Learning Circle project involving 6 schools in the USA and Canada and 2 schools in Germany. In a follow-up activity the texts produced by learners and native speaker peers within this project were analyzed by the German students. It is shown that e-mail texts can serve as valuable learning materials and research data for the learners themselves.

1. Underlying principles of language learning and teaching

Research into second language acquisition and classroom experience have made it increasingly clear that it is first of all meaningful authentic communication which promotes language learning. Only if the interactions derive from a need to communicate and if they serve a real communicative purpose do the utterances reach a processing depth which can affect the learning system. These assumptions lead to a social organization of the foreign language classroom in which work in peer groups figures prominently. Group work favours multi-faceted negotiating processes and allows a high degree of independent and self-determined learning. However, in order for the group dynamic processes, to set in and develop effectively, group work should preferably be based on long-term projects and entail a communicative purpose that reaches beyond the group. The ideal classroom should therefore provide opportunities for learners to explore the sociocultural dimension of language and prepare or even engage them in intercultural communication.
It is within this setting that the technology of e-mail telecommunications suggests itself as a possible partner. There are many reasons why e-mail appears to be especially suitable for creating authentic and purpose-oriented interaction situations, for stimulating group and project work, and for providing intercultural learning opportunities. Some of the more important aspects will be dealt with in the following section.

2. The educational potential of telecommunications

2.1 Telecommunications transcend the confines of the classroom

It has always been a traditional teaching goal to prepare students for 'real' communication outside the classroom. And there has always been a feeling that there is little the school can do systematically in this respect, apart from organizing exchange programmes and promoting pen-friendships.
All this has changed with the advent of telecommunications, which bring the world into the

classroom or links the classroom with thousands of other classrooms all over the world. McLuhan's global village metaphor has become concrete and tangible for learners working with e-mail. Getting into contact with peers outside their own learner group, peers who live in different countries and cultures, quite naturally leads to a host of talking points and starts intercultural communication and, by implication, intercultural learning. In other words, learners now produce texts not just for the teacher and within the narrow educational context but for real addressees outside their learning groups, and they act as real addressees for incoming messages. As a consequence, students view their own texts as much more purposeful. They are generally quite aware that these texts are no longer non-committal, and that they themselves are accountable for what they are writing. This higher degree of commitment produces texts of obviously better quality.

2.2 Telecommunications enforce a division of labour and thus promote group work

Compared to standard classroom procedures, running e-mail projects is a highly demanding task, which requires extensive planning phases, long-term coordination, and a certain amount of technical know-how. The multitude of tasks cannot be carried out by either one individual student alone or by the whole class together. These tasks are therefore best managed by small groups. Telecommunications thus create a learning environment in which a division of labour becomes not only important but a prerequisite for successful work.

2.3 Telecommunications enforce the integration of additional tool functions of the computer

Many teachers and learners have already come to appreciate word-processing and data bases as important tools in the EFL classroom. In connection with telecommunications, however, their use becomes an integral part of the project routine. Transmitting messages, for example, presupposes word processing; it is our experience that once students are working within this technological environment, they also want to exploit the speed of electronic dictionaries. Telecommunications thus lead to an authentic and purpose-oriented environment which exploits and draws on various computer functions.

2.4 Telecommunications contribute to the authenticity of (learning) materials

It stands to reason that telecommunications also contributes to the authenticity of materials in the foreign language classroom. In traditional classrooms course materials are to a large extent especially designed for learning and teaching purposes, and since the students immediately and automatically associate these materials with the learning purpose, they very often cannot help dealing with them and processing them with pedagogical motivations only. Pedagogical motivations, however, are likely to be very unstable and to vary considerably from student to student.

Incoming e-mail messages are authentic texts in the sense that they have not been primarily produced with a didactic purpose in mind. The focus is solely on the meaning of the message which has to be reacted to in real-life terms. These texts are therefore processed with a different attitude of mind, with effects on processing depth which again seem to correlate with learning effect (see Craik & Lockart 1972).

2.5 Telecommunications make electronic processing and the analysis of texts possible

One factor which distinguishes e-mail from other communication technologies such as telefax is of particular interest in this context. The e-mail user has access to texts in electronic form, i.e. texts which can, on the one hand, be easily edited and reformated in various ways, and which can, on the other hand, be analyzed linguistically and statistically by computer programs. This feature can and should be exploited for language-awareness activities in the foreign language classroom since text-processing programs such as concordancers are available and also suitable for use by learners (see section 4).

3. Projects and project topics

There are quite a few applications where telecommunications can even play a role in short-term learning tasks, for example, looking up search words in an online encyclopedia or retrieving information from a newspaper database. But if electronic communication goes beyond mere information retrieval, that is, as soon as there are "real" persons at both ends of the communication channel, telecommunications are best applied in long-term projects, lasting from at least 3-4 weeks to about half a year. During our research project we tested the effectiveness of various kinds of e-mail projects in the foreign language classroom. So far we have identified and explored three different types of project: bilateral, open, and closed.

3.1 Project types

- Bilateral projects

Here the two groups involved in a joint project already work closely together in the planning phase of the project, often making use of already existing contacts. Projects of this kind have the big advantage that topics and procedures are the result of a joint negotiation process where the foreign language is already functional and authentic in preparatory stages.

- Open projects

In this case there is an initiating learner group which typically plans the project independently: contents, duration, forms of organization, and presentation of results are designed to suit the needs and wants of this particular learner group. Classes in other parts of the world are invited to join the project. As a result, an asymmetrical working relationship very often develops, in that the partners are (at least in the first project phase) often confined to a mere contributory or information-supplying role. They provide data on the project topic from their particular point of interest and experience. If they are speakers of the target language and members of the target culture they can make their special linguistic and socio-cultural expertise available.

When organizing open projects the number of responses might be unexpectedly small. In general, the return rate ranges around 10% to 15% of all the parties contacted. In a pilot project we tried to get a clearer picture of response rates and patterns (see Figure 1). The addressees - about 100 mailboxes all over the world - were asked to write back a short note stating who they are and where they are from. Days 3, 4, 10 and 11 were Saturdays and Sundays.

The human and institutional factors are often underestimated, especially the problems involved in getting many partners to work on one specific project within a specific time span. Institutional and curricular constraints make it difficult for participants to agree on a project plan. From the response rates in open projects it follows that about ten times the number of schools should be contacted or that the project should be announced well in advance via existing and globally distributed newsletters. With the help of telecommunications technology this is not difficult at all.

- Closed projects

The defining feature of closed projects is their fixed organizational structure. Only a predetermined number of participants is admitted. Typically, these projects are not organized by schools or learners, but are more likely to be offered by universities or private companies. They are centrally organized, which means that students are neither involved in finding partners nor in the internal structuring of the project. Even though the students do not have any influence on who they are going to work with, how long the project is going to last or what form of presentation will be chosen, closed projects make up for some of the problems one typically faces in the case of open projects, as mentioned above.

In the course of our research project we cooperated with seven classes from three German schools (Bad Essen, Jena, Kettwig). They took part in e-mail projects of all three types. For lack of space we cannot report on all of these, we will instead focus on one particular project type and illustrate techniques of project evaluation.

3.2 The AT&T Learning Network

Two of the schools took part in a closed e-mail project offered biannually in the AT&T Learning Network (LN) scheme. The AT&T LN is run by the US-American communications company AT&T and offers pre-planned projects in the educational sector.

Normally, there are eight to ten schools from regionally and culturally diverse locations working together in what is called a Learning Circle. The participating students work over a time span of 11 weeks (autumn) or 15 weeks (spring) on a joint project focussing on a topic chosen from various areas (curriculum). Several Learning Circles can work independently within one curricular area. Usually there is a choice of six curricular areas that cover a wide range of interdisciplinary topics:

(1) Society's Problems
(2) Global Issues
(3) Places and Perspectives
(4) Mind Works
(5) Computer Chronicles
(6) Energy Works

Once placed in one of the Learning Circles the participants communicate through a joint mailbox, i.e. messages are not sent to the individual group members (although this possibility exists), but rather to the Learning Circle as a whole. This mailbox is called a *shared folder* and can be accessed by all the participants of a certain Learning Circle.
In autumn 1992 two classes of the schools we were working with (students aged between 16 and 18) took part in the same Computer Chronicles project. This is a curriculum in 'language arts' and journalism. Students adopt the roles of reporters and editors and the eight schools work together to produce a newspaper (the "Computer Chronicles") featuring the news, opinions, sports, and lifestyles at each of the Learning Circle sites. Schools from the following cities were participating in the project: Jena (Germany), Bad Essen (Germany), Watford, Ontario (Canada), Basking Ridge, New Jersey, Edmond, Oklahoma, Cherokee, North Carolina, Keene, New Hampshire, Mililani, Hawaii.
This regional spread ensured that there was a certain amount of cultural diversification even among the five US-American schools. The following time scheme was suggested by the project organizers:

(a) Opening the Circle (1 week)
(b) Planning Circle projects (2 weeks)
(c) Exchanging students' work (5 weeks)
(d) Organizing publication (2 weeks)
(e) Closing the Circle (1 week)

The topics chosen by the students were typical of a newspaper edited by school-students: education (graduation, school-systems etc.), current events (U.S. elections etc.), social problems (racism, discrimination etc.), travel, entertainment, sports. The newspaper produced within our project was based on more than 300 pages of students' messages.

In the following section we are going to illustrate how certain features of e-mail projects, in particular the intensity of interactions, can be analyzed and assessed.

3.3 Describing e-mail interactions

Our analysis of e-mail interactions is based on Levin et al. (1990) who introduced a procedure for analyzing message flow and intermessage reference.
Message Flow Analysis (see Figures 2-4) is a simple way of displaying graphically the number or density of messages (y-axis) across the time of the project (x-axis). There are several conclusions that can be derived from these graphs:

(1) It takes quite a long time for the interactions to get going and develop. In our example the first peak of message flow is reached as late as five weeks after the start of the project (see Figure 2). This means that the intensity of the interactions within short-term projects might suffer.

(2) In Figure 3 the messages written by adults (teachers at the various Learning Circle sites and organizing network staff) and by students are displayed separately. It clearly demonstrates that the majority of the texts were written by students. E-mail projects seem to be well-suited to a student-centred approach.

(3) There are peaks and troughs showing the number of messages sent throughout the project. Peaks indicate a high level of activity at all participating schools. Troughs usually occur during holiday periods at one or several schools. Figure 4 shows that peaks and troughs at the participating schools do not coincide. This lack of overlap is very often a first indicator of a less than smooth communication flow. The obvious fact that schools in different parts of the world have different school schedules often tends to be neglected when planning e-mail projects. It is, for example, not very likely that many Australian schools will become involved in an e-mail project in January or February, the summer holiday period in the Southern hemisphere.

In *Intermessage Reference Analysis* (see Figures 5-6) messages are grouped in clusters according to the topics discussed. Intermessage Reference Analysis helps to structure an unordered set of e-mail texts. It makes it possible to follow the various thematic threads and to answer questions such as: Which group initiated a topic? Who referenced whose messages? At first sight, an Intermessage Reference Analysis looks very confusing, even when it covers only a one month time span (see Figure 5). Therefore it is advisable to isolate clusters to get a better overview (see Figure 6).
These methods of analyzing texts sent and received by students make it easier to compare the efficiency of different e-mail projects. At the same time, they can be used as a starting point for more in-depth text studies.

4. E-mail texts as research data and learning material

In a communicative language classroom as we envisage it, learners should not just be supplied with suitable materials but ought to be actively involved in contributing to their own learning material. In other words, learner-produced texts could be recycled, as it were, into the classroom and made use of by the whole group. This means that learner texts should not just be publicly shared, but that learners should also be asked to approach them from a researcher's point of view, i.e. their own texts could be made the object of analysis and thus be used for awareness-raising activities.

If this is a generally agreed approach, it is especially e-mail texts which lend themselves to a closer analysis by learners. There are two reasons for this, the first of which has already been mentioned: E-mail texts are electronically stored and can thus be processed by text analysis programs, i.e. by research tools like concordancers and style checkers. Secondly, in e-mail projects native speaker peers produce texts which belong to exactly the same text type and which can thus be used as a point of comparison for evaluating one's own learner texts.

It is in this way that we used the texts from the AT&T Learning Circle for awareness activities in the classroom, and as material for 'data-driven learning'. We produced two different corpora from these texts. One native speaker corpus comprising about 51,000 words and a non-native speaker corpus which consisted of approximately 28,000 words. This statistical imbalance has to be kept in mind when the tables below are interpreted.

These two text corpora were used in the classroom for text analysis purposes. One of the German classes taking part in the AT&T Learning Circle was shown how to use Longman's MiniConcordancer. We had the students work in small groups and discuss possible differences between German learner texts and native speaker peer texts. They then tried to verify their hypotheses by means of the MiniConcordancer. The students compared and analysed problems such as:

(a) type/token ratios, i.e. number of different words used by L1 and L2 speakers,
(b) frequency lists, and especially content words,
(c) forms of address or greetings,
(d) sentence beginnings,
(e) discourse structuring devices, especially *conjuncts* such as *well, also, furthermore, moreover* etc.
(f) contracted vs uncontracted forms as indicators of degree of (in)formality

These were the more promising and fruitful research questions, some of which originated in teacher-led plenary discussions. The students came up with several findings which were highly interesting, some of them even took students - as well as teacher and observers - by surprise. The type/token ratio is a point in case.

▪ Type/token ratio:

American and Canadian high school students used 5,771 different words, which means the type/token ratio was 1:8.77. By contrast, L2 students used 4,266 different words in a corpus which is about half the size of the L1 corpus. This yields a type/token ratio of 1:6.47. In other words, the number of different words used in the L2 texts seemed to have been greater. Although the L2 corpus was too small to allow for statistically significant conclusions, this did not actually matter in the pedagogic context. Students entered into heated discussions as to the possible reasons for the difference in type/token ratio. One interpretation read like this:

> "L2-Texte [sind] z.T. ausgeschmückter als L1-Texte. Grund dafür: Wir sind darum bemüht, so schöne grammatische Formen wie möglich einzustreuen, für Amerikaner würde das vermutlich eher künstlich und hochgestochen klingen."
> [L2 texts are to a certain extent more elaborate. The reason for this: We are trying hard to put in as many nice grammatical forms as possible; to Americans this would probably sound rather artificial and over-formal.]
>
> Questionnaire Bad Essen

Although there was no time left to elaborate on this interpretation in the classroom, it could easily have been linked to the learners' interest in certain conjuncts and their distribution in L1 and L2 texts (see Additives in Table 1).

	L1	L2
and	1403	748
also	106	63
besides	-	4
furthermore	-	4
moreover	-	4
in addition	-	2

Table 1: Additives (sentence-initial and internal)

If the different corpus sizes are taken into account, then it becomes obvious that the overall frequencies of the conjunct *and* and the adverbial *also* are about the same in the two corpora. More formal conjuncts, however, are not found in the L1 texts.

▪ Sentence beginnings

The assumption that sentence beginnings might differ in the two corpora also turned out to be quite justified. Table 2 shows that informal discourse-initiating items like *well* and anyway occur much less frequently in L2 texts, whereas resultative or summative *so*, *therefore* and adversative *but* are overrepresented in L2 texts.

	L1	L2
Well	56	5
So	25	20
And	22	13
But	20	45
However	16	4
Also	15	3
Anyway	9	-
Therefore	5	10
Actually	4	-
In fact	1	-

Table 2: Sentence-initial conjuncts

To our students' surprise, though, L1 sentences started much more often with the personal pronoun *I* than L2 sentences (L1 - 623 times vs. L2 - 137 times).

- Stylistic variability

Some of the figures mentioned above might easily have been interpreted in terms of an overall greater stylistic variability of L2 texts. This slightly misleading conclusion could have been counterbalanced if further data relating to lexical differentiation had been adduced. The corpora include, for example, welcoming messages in which the students describe themselves and their hobbies. If the frequencies of *I like/love/enjoy*-structures are compared it becomes obvious that the L2 distribution pattern shows little variation (see Table 3).

	L1	L2
I like	72	46
I love	38	1
I enjoy	36	2

Table 3: Frequencies of *like/love/enjoy*

Data such as these could be used for analyses contrasting the two languages. The under-representation of *I love*-structures has probably also got something to do with the semantics and usage of the German translational equivalent *lieben*.

■ Contracted and uncontracted forms

The students quickly realized that their L2 texts tended to be more formal, and they wanted to verify the higher degree of formality of learner texts. They therefore compared contracted and uncontracted forms of the copula *be*. And again the results were quite unexpected. There is a pronounced tendency for L2 learners to use contracted forms more often than their L1 peers. Table 4 contains only high frequency forms arranged in a descending order of frequency.

	L1		L2	
	contracted	uncontracted	contracted	uncontracted
sum total	475	451	250	99
I'm - I am	219	137	84	5
ratio	1.6	1	16.8	1
don't - do not	119	27	58	2
ratio	4.4	1	29.0	1
it's - it is	49	110	58	26
ratio	1	2.2	2.2	1
isn't - is not	24	35	9	13
ratio	1	4.6	1	4.4
that's - that is	31	29	30	2
ratio	1.1	1	15	1
there's - there is	18	61	2	20
ratio	1	3.4	1	10
we're - we are	15	62	9	31
ratio	1	4.1	1	4.3

Table 4: Contracted vs uncontracted forms

The L1 ratio between contracted and uncontracted forms is about 1:1, whereas L2 students used contracted forms two and half times more often than uncontracted forms. These tendencies might be interpreted along the following lines: When the German learner group received the first e-mail messages from native speaker peers, they were struck by the number of informalisms and slangy terms. Although they were quick at picking up the odd colloquialism, they had to resort to markers of informality that they were familiar with. Since textbooks of English used in German schools tend to introduce contracted forms from the very beginning, the preference for the more informal forms might also be considered the result of transfer of training.

This means that Table 4 contains data that are also of interest to textbook authors and second language acquisition researchers. It reveals, for example, that the ratio between contracted and uncontracted forms varies considerably, and at first glance the preferred forms seem to be randomly distributed. However, with one exception (*it's* vs. *it is*), the general trends are identical in the two corpora. This seems to be a first indication that there are underlying regularities which can be explained from a phonological and/or syntactic point of view.

- Forms of address / greetings:

The German students were very quick at picking up different forms of address and good-bye formulas. And again, when it comes to analyzing greetings such as *hello* and *hi* from a research perspective, slightly different usage patterns emerge. For German students there is a more pronounced tendency to mention the addressee after *hi* and *hello*, and they tend to use both forms in exactly the same way. In the L1 corpus, by contrast, isolated *hi* occurs more often than isolated *hello*.

	L1		L2	
	f	%	f	%
hi	49		39	
isolated *hi*	46	93.9	23	59.0
hi + NP/ *there etc*	3	6.1	16	41.0
hello	33		24	
isolated *hello*	25	75.8	14	58.3
hello+NP/*there etc*	8	24.2	10	41.7

Table 5: Comparison of hi and hello patterns

Different usage patterns of this kind, which are of special interest to contrastive pragmatics, might be the starting point for a unit on intercultural differences. In this context the students' self-descriptions could be looked into more closely.

- Self-descriptions

E-mail projects usually start with welcoming messages, in which the participants introduce themselves. These texts are, on the one hand, highly conventionalized with fixed language patterns (cf. *Hi. My name is x. I have ...*), on the other hand, there are some noteworthy differences in the self-descriptions.

Mentioning one's age seems to be obligatory in German L2 introductions, but not for L1 speakers. Almost one third of L1 students (80 out of 134) do not mention their exact age, although this is partly compensated for by specifying whether they are juniors or seniors. By contrast, height seems to be more important to American students. It is mentioned by 19.4% (N=26) American students, whereas only three out of 35 Germans (8.6%) find this of interest.

- Free-time activities / hobbies

Concordancers allow students a rough statistical analysis of spare-time activities by searching for collocations of *I like/love/enjoy* and by looking up search words such as *hobbies / spare time / free time*. It is amazing the extent to which these activities are similar across continents. The ranking scales of 16- to-18-year-olds are almost identical; only the categories 'sports/games' and 'music' show a reversed order. The category 'travelling' does not seem to exist for American/Canadian high school students.

	L1 (f=199)		L2 (f=74)	
sports / games	57	28.6 %	10	13.5 %
music	37	18.6%	24	32.4 %
parties	17	8.5 %	5	6.8 %
cars/motorcycle/bike etc.	14	7.0 %	3	4.1 %
school-subjects	7	3.5 %	3	4.1 %
reading	7	3.5 %	2	2.7 %
computers	5	2.5 %	5	6.8 %
movies / TV / videos	4	2.0 %	4	5.4 %
travelling	0	-	4	5.4 %
other preferences	51	25.6%	14	18.9 %

Table 6: Free-time activities

In conclusion we can say that the students' motivation to work with their own texts and compare them with native speaker texts was extremely high. In the final questionnaire, in which the learners were asked to evaluate the follow-up activity with the concordancer, they almost unanimously referred to the difference between their classroom English (*Schulenglisch*) and everyday English (*Gebrauchsenglisch*), which were clearly understood to form two different registers.

5. Brief summary

It has become quite obvious that e-mail projects, no matter whether of the bilateral, open, or closed type, are well-suited to implementing vital language learning and teaching principles such as

- student centredness
- authenticity of social interactions
- authenticity of learning materials etc.

Furthermore, they provide opportunities for gaining experience in using the new communication technologies through developing

- keyboard and word-processing skills
- network management skills
- information retrieval skills.

REFERENCES

Craik, F.I.M. & Lockart, R.S. (1972). Levels of processing: A framework for memory research. *Journal of Verbal Learning and Verbal Behavior*, 671-684.

Levin, J.A., Haesunk, K. & Riel, M.M. (1990). Analyzing instructional interactions on electronic message networks." In: Harasim, L. (ed.). *Online education: perspectives on a new environment*. Westport, CT, Praeger, pp. 185-213.

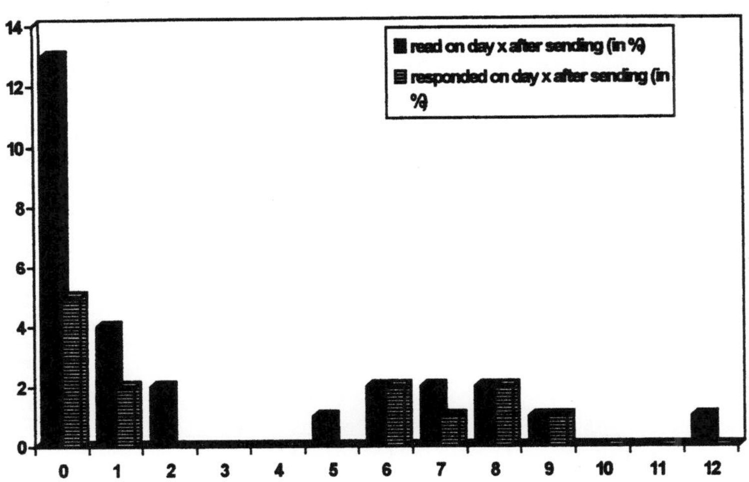

Figure 1

Message Flow Analysis

Project: *Computer Chronicles*

Network: *AT&T*

Time: *17/09 - 11/12/1992*

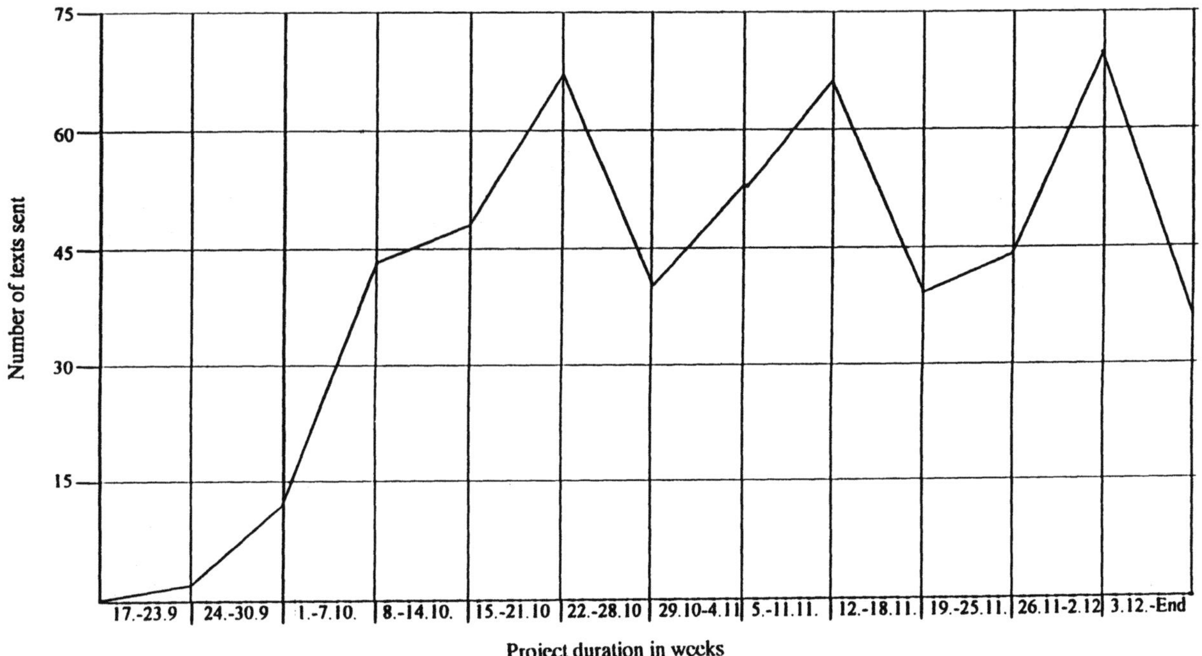

Figure 2

Message Flow Analysis

Project: *Computer Chronicles*

Network: *AT&T*

Time: *17/09 - 11/12/1992*

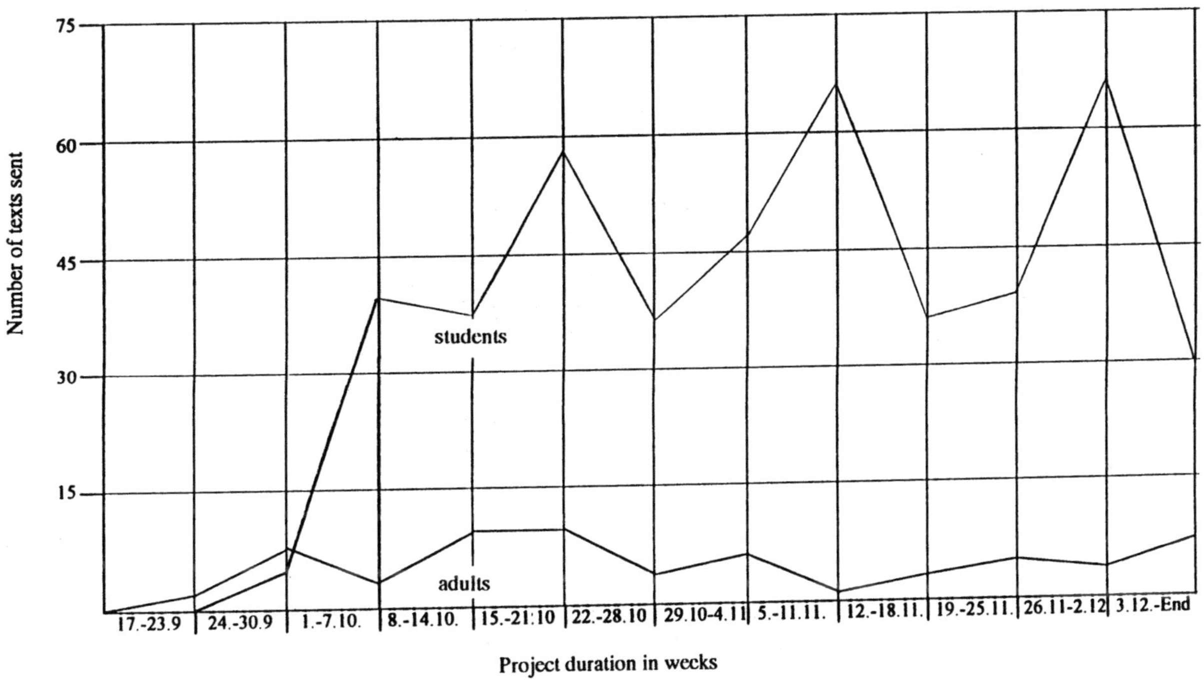

Figure 3

Message Flow Analysis
Project: *Computer Chronicles*
Network: *AT&T*
Time: *17/09 - 11/12/1992*

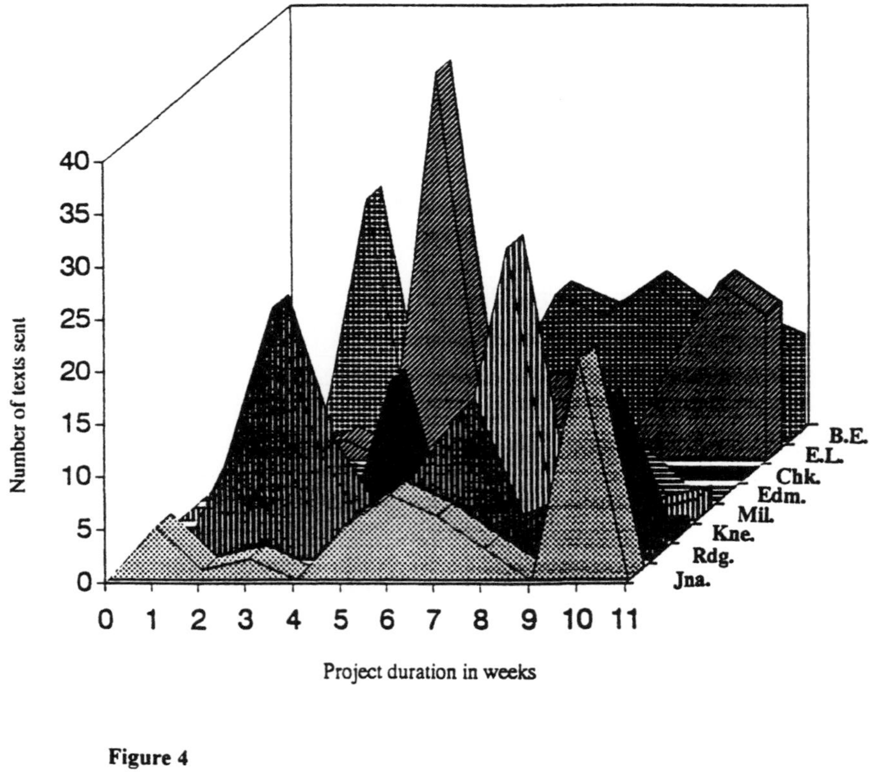

Figure 4

Intermessage Reference Analysis (Computer Chronicles / all texts / November)

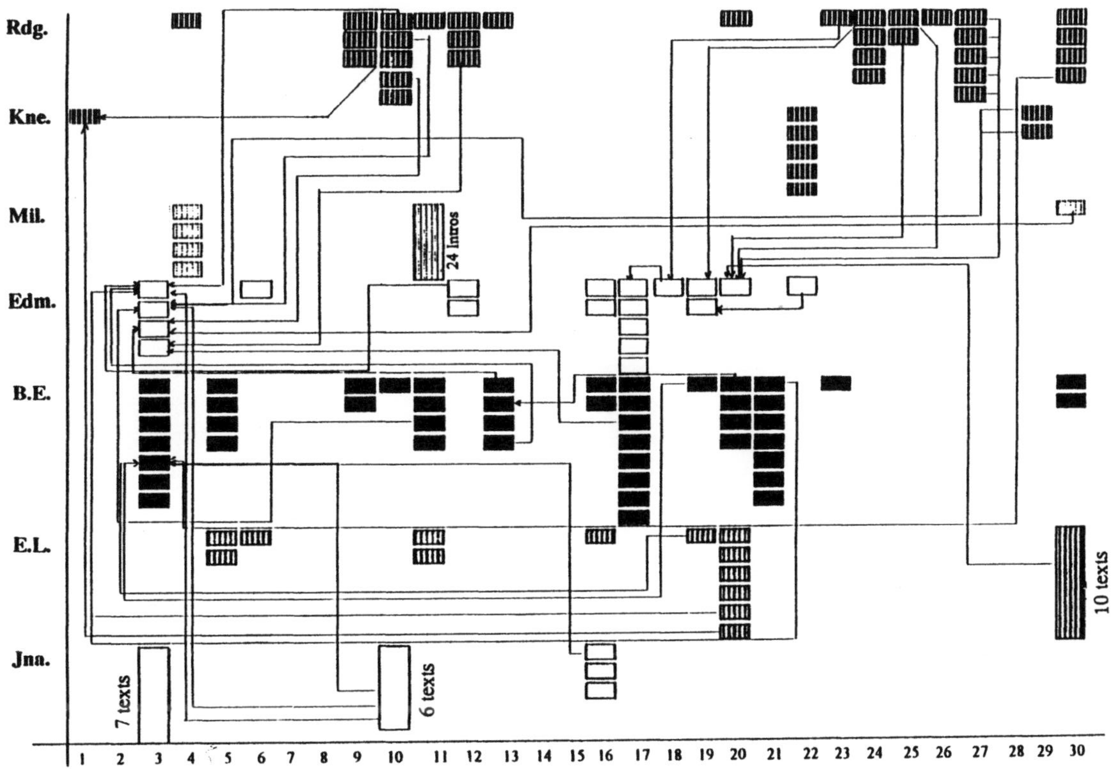

Figure 5

<u>Intermessage Reference Analysis</u>

Project: *Computer Chronicles*
Network: *AT&T*
Time: *17/09 - 11/12/1992*
Topic: **Abortion**

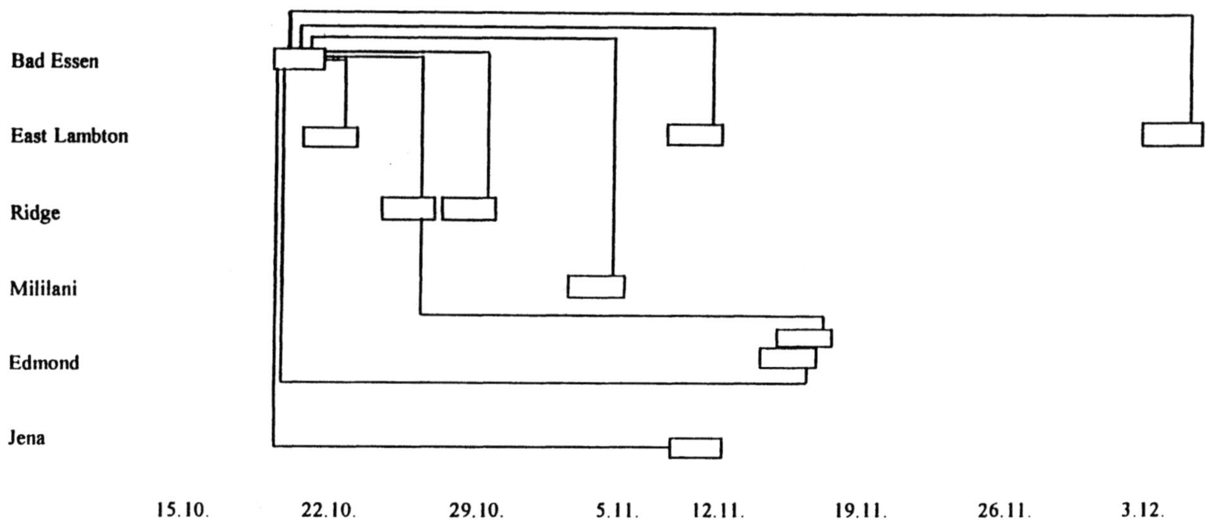

Figure 6

AN INTERDISCIPLINARY PROJECT ORIENTATION USING TELECOMMUNICATIONS MEDIA IN FOREIGN LANGUAGE TEACHING

Virginia Teichmann
Karlsruhe College of Education

This interdisciplinary project orientation combining traditional and telecommunications media was used in a three-year partnership between middle and high school pupils in Massachusetts (USA) and "Realschule" pupils in Karlsruhe, Germany. The goal of the project was to create an authentic communications framework within which the participating language learners would be motivated to use the foreign language to discuss a variety of topics of their choice with partners whom they would gradually get to know almost personally. Each medium was implemented in a way that used its particular strength.

1. Introduction

Foreign language teaching often suffers from the syndrome of "trying to learn to swim without water", that is, the application of what is learned takes place in a separate, later phase from the learning itself (if at all). In an attempt to establish whether telecommunications media can contribute to the solution of this problem by replicating the authentic communication experience to an extent that increases pupil motivation and foreign language performance (without the prohibitive cost of sending all foreign language learners abroad), German and American pupils were linked in the KITES project by means of electronic mail and video-conference. (KITES = Kids Interactive Television Experience by Satellite; German title = Internationale Schülerkontakte durch moderne Kommunikationsmittel.) The project ran from September 1988 to June 1991, first with middle school pupils without any knowledge of German in Lowell, MA and then with third to fifth year learners of German in Amherst, MA; the German participants were 8th and 9th grade pupils (fourth and fifth year learners of English) in a "Realschule" in Karlsruhe. The German pupils took part in the project in addition to their regular English instruction, while the project was integrated into the curriculum on the American side.

2. Media Employed

The telecommunications media employed in this project were electronic mail throughout the entire project and a video-conference at the end of the first year. This video-conference used full-motion two-way television technology and allowed the pupils to see and talk to each other in real time for ninety minutes. (Without any didactic changes, the much cheaper compressed video technology could be employed, available in Germany as "Videokonferenz" through Telekom.) The video-conference gave the pupils a chance to "make their own television" and to respond immediately to their partners "face-to-face".

All the communication necessary for preparing the video-conference, which involved very careful, minute-by-minute planning, was done by e-mail. E-mail was also used between the teachers and scholars working on the project as well as by the pupils themselves to set up the time plan for each school year and to agree on the themes to be treated within each segment of the plan. Since one of the main goals of the project was to increase pupil motivation to use the foreign language, the pupils were directly involved in selecting the themes and modifying them in cooperation with their partners. Some themes were of the usual partnership nature (i.e., introducing themselves, getting to know each other and their immediate environments), some were connected to topics treated in school subjects other than English (i.e., environmental protection issues, esp. atomic power plants), some were topics of particular youth interest (i.e., fashion, pop music) and some developed as the project progressed in direct response to issues of current interest (i.e., the Gulf War).

Once the framework for each year had been negotiated and agreed upon by e-mail, the project took an eclectic approach: each national group could interpret a given theme in whatever way it wished. The realization could include any medium desired, not only modern ones; (the form of interpretation itself was a culturally characteristic expression). Traditional airmail was used to send packages of conventional artefacts. This aspect of the project was not designed to limit the use of the more modern media, but was meant to create a framework in which the pupils would work out for themselves the strengths and weaknesses of each medium. Each medium suggested by the pupils for the interpretation of a theme was assessed critically and used in a way that realized its own potential. The pupils quickly came to recognize the computer, for example, as the only appropriate tool for some purposes (i.e., bar and pie graphs to represent the results of their own questionnaire), but as inadequate for conveying the smells and tastes of Christmas (communicated by boxes of cookies baked in home economics classes with instructions about the appropriate music, candles and pine branches necessary to create the whole experience). One class decided to format their curricula vitae on the computer to give them a more professional look (in connection with their school unit about the job world), but another class opted for a more personal touch and used hand-writing. Other media used included completely traditional ones like art work (done in art class), photographs (developed and enlarged in the school darkroom), slides and audio tapes. Semi-modern media included many videos the pupils conceived, scripted and made themselves.

Upon receipt of each set of artefacts, the responses and questions were transmitted to the partners by e-mail. The principle of the project is clearly visible here: e-mail is the best link available at a reasonable price for immediate, spontaneous questions and replies, for a casual written dialogue. Because the number of keyboard steps necessary to use the communications software is limited and transparent (connection to gateway, self-identification with log-in code, opening mailbox, checking and printing out new mail, entering address of recipient and messages, logging out, etc.), it is a very effective use of the computer for pupils not yet experienced in this field, does not require extensive use of the whole keyboard for long periods of time and produces the desired results (answer from partner) within a time frame comfortable for today's fast-living teenagers. (For many of these youngsters, the time lag between sending a conventional letter and receiving an answer from abroad pushes them to the limits of their abstraction ability and patience.) And, of course, for a development like the Gulf War, unforeseen at the time of planning the school year in advance, but of crucial interest to both American and German teenagers, e-mail provided an ideal means of communicating attitudes and questions quickly.

3. Project Orientation

The use of both the traditional and modern media described above had a crucial side effect that was at least as important for the improvement of the participants' foreign language skills as the final artefact and media products themselves: the working process that led up to the completed artefacts and the steps necessary to carry out the telecommunication linking require constant verbal communication that allows a close reproduction of the primary language acquisition situation in the classroom. All these activities - designing and making a collage, taking, sorting and choosing slides, following the correct series of steps on the computer to obtain the e-mail link, etc. - are very concrete, very action-oriented and are conducive to the constant questions, requests, reinforcement that are necessary for the success of the activity. In other words, project activities of this concrete type are the closest one can come to reproducing the continuous verbal give-and-take of the normal primary language acquisition phase. As the class is divided into groups to carry out different parts of the whole project (a division necessary for effective work of this type), many participants can be using the foreign language at once (more efficient use of time than in the traditional classroom, where only one person can speak at a time); the conversation is about objects visible and goals clear to everyone involved, so concepts not completely verbally understood can be readily inferred; and, most important psychologically, comprehension errors are immediately apparent and can be corrected within the discourse flow without the learner's having a sense of failure. These characteristics of project work make it ideal for foreign language learning, because the learner is really simultaneously a language user. It does not replace, but provides a crucial additional dimension to the structured course work of traditional language teaching.

4. The Intercultural Angle

This project had a wide variety of goals, some of which were directly connected to school subjects like foreign language (improvement in language skills, increase in knowledge about institutions and life in partner country), mother tongue (mastering particular genre forms like report or letter) or natural sciences (background necessary to understand environmental issues). Other goals were part of the general syllabus for this age group, like the entire field of media awareness and critical media analysis. While the improvement in language skills could be measured in comparison to a parallel control group not involved in the project and quantified (modified C-tests administered at commencement and end of project), other aspects of the project did not lend themselves as easily to quantification and were, in fact, the source of some irritation during the course of the project. Foremost among the unexpected irritants was the field of intercultural understanding, or, as it developed, occasional misunderstanding.

Beyond the factual knowledge about life in the partner country, it was anticipated that the pupils would recognize differences between the contents and presentation forms of the artefacts they created and those created by their partners. A discussion of these differences and their possible or probable sources would lead to an appreciation of cultural differences and the ways in which such differences develop and can be understood. It became clear very quickly however, that such an impartial recognition of differences and non-judgemental discussion of them were often beyond the immediate horizon of the pupils involved.

Examples of these misunderstandings occurred independently of the media used. The fact that one set of American cards of self-introduction was made on pieces of cardboard ripped by hand from old folders no longer needed, had very amateur photographs and were written in pencil in what would be classified in Germany as poor handwriting led to the incensed interpretation by the German recipients that the American partner pupils obviously were not really interested in the project and had not taken care to produce high quality results. In other words, they interpreted the appearance of the American artefacts by reference to their own cultural standards of the importance of neat external form and orderly appearance and the economic possibilites of their school to provide quality, new cardboard and photographic equipment and expertise. Similar negative interpretations on the German side arose from videos about school life in the American partner junior-senior high school ("When do they actually get down to real school work?") and about Christmastime in the partner town ("Don't they know the difference between Christmas and `mardi gras'?"). The same kind of inability to see the artefacts of the partner within the appropriate context was apparent when the American pupils had no favorable or even particularly emotional response of any kind to the German Christmas season cookies ("These taste funny.").

This kind of reaction fits neatly, of course, into the pattern described by prejudice researchers: confrontation with the reality of a different culture can lead at first to a reinforcement of all the prejudices previously cultivated, instead of contributing to overcoming them. It was conceived as a strength of a project such as this one that the pupils' reactions would be expressed within a situation guided by teachers with a more profound understanding of the cultures involved and with some insight into intercultural communication. The teachers viewed their role as one of guidance toward an appreciation of any cultural phenomenon, including the pupils' own, as something to be understood within the appropriate cultural context, not automatically judged negatively by the standards of another culture. The reality of everyday discourse during the project showed however, that whatever went beyond the apparently internationally bonding world of pop youth culture and material consumption (pop music and name brands were lowest common denominators) often aroused dismay and rejection on the part of the pupils, or, at best, disinterest. At the same time, the degree of confidence and friendship created by the various means of communication, including e-mail, was not great enough to allow for an open controversy about negative perceptions.

The reasons for this apparent failure to realize some of the intercultural goals of the project may be found in several factors, (beyond what may be a general human tendency to dislike anything that is different from one's own personal experience). The very fact that all the pupils involved in the project on both sides came from schools with a varied ethnic and social mix in pupil intake, while it might arouse an expectation of previous practice in tolerance, could mean that the pupils had already reached the limit of their ability to cope graciously with cultural differences. These limits are probably also determined by the type and age of the pupils participating in the project. In particular, the German pupils were not in the university-entrance stream of the German educational system. (This would be less so for American pupils in their third to fifth years of German instruction, for example, most of whom would be likely to go on to a college education.) German "Realschule" pupils have chosen this type of secondary school because a theoretical and abstract approach to learning is not their strength, and they respond better to a more practice-oriented and concrete learning style. The nature of the project would seem to cater precisely to this type of learner, and the more concrete phases of the project did arouse the most pupil enthusiasm, but the aspect of intercultural understanding seemed to require just that degree of abstraction, that leap of imagination to picture a world very different from one's own, that was extremely difficult and sometimes impossible for these pupils. The age group involved may have also been a negative factor in this field. It was determined by the age at which a certain basic level of foreign language mastery is available within the normal school systems of the countries involved. This automatically places the participants in the middle of puberty in most western industrial countries. This is, however, the very age group least able and least willing to accept anything beyond their own very particular view of the world. The reactions of eighth and ninth graders differ in this way from the more spontaneous, uninhibited approach of younger children as well as from the more mature and worldly style of eighteen or nineteen year-olds. (It must be kept in mind however, that participants of a younger age would be less able to work effectively on an independent basis.)

Thus it sometimes seemed, during the actual day-to-day work of the project, as if the teachers were fighting an uphill battle on the intercultural front. Not even the immediacy of modern telecommunications could completely compensate for this tendency to reject the foreign and different, although other aspects of the project were clearly successful. The first group of German project participants has now been out of school for three years, however, and although contact with them is too sporadic and unsystematic to allow any kind of generally valid scholarly interpretation, it is worth noting that occasional chance feedback from these original participants is now positive, glowing, and often stresses that side of the project that originally seemed so problematic, the exposure to another culture. This suggests that foreign language teaching including the use of telecommunications media, while in many significant ways more immediate and effective than traditional classroom instruction alone, must nevertheless reap some of its harvest long after sowing, no differently from all other forms of education.

REFERENCES

LeBaron, J. & Teichmann, V. (1989). KITES: A Middle School Environmental Science Telelink to West Germany. *Educational Technology* 29 (12), 51-53.

LeBaron, J. & Teichmann, V. (1992). Internationale Schülerkontakte - ein Telekommunikationsprojekt. *LOG IN* 12 (5/6), 43-49.

Teichmann, V. (1991a). Fremdsprachenunterricht und moderne Telekommunikationsmittel: die Fremdsprache sofort anwenden und dabei dem Partner in einer anderen Kultur begegnen. In: Raasch, A., Herold, D. & Kiupel, C. (eds.). *Fremdsprachen lehren und lernen: Perspektiven für ein Europa nach 1992*. Saarbrücken, Universität Saarbrücken, pp. 214-221.

Teichmann, V. (1991b). Interkulturelles Lernen im Englischunterricht. Projekt "Internationale Schülerkontakte durch moderne Kommunikationsmittel". *Englisch* 26 (4), 142-146.

Teichmann, V. (1992). Voraussetzungen für schulische Partnerschaftsprojekte mit Telekommunikationsmitteln. *Mitteilungsblatt des Fachverbands Moderne Fremdsprachen Landesverband Baden-Württemberg* 5, 24-33.

TEACHING ENGLISH FROM AUSTRALIA TO JAPAN VIA INTERACTIVE VIDEO CONFERENCE SYSTEMS*

Masako K. Hiraga and Yoko Fujii
The University of the Air, Japan

This is a report of a project on the use of an interactive video conference system for teaching English as a foreign language, jointly undertaken by the University of the Air (UA), Japan and the University of New England (UNE), Armidale, Australia. The findings of the project indicate that given appropriate settings, face-to-face instruction by the low-bit rate video conference system is a viable alternative to direct classroom teaching.

1. Introduction

The purpose of this paper is to report the results of a project on the use of an interactive video conference system for teaching English as a foreign language, jointly undertaken by the University of the Air (UA), Chiba City, Japan and the University of New England (UNE), Armidale, Australia.

The significance of our project of teaching English by the interactive video-conference system can be understood in the context of the expansion of the University of the Air and the increasing demand for face-to-face instruction. The University of the Air offers about 300 courses through the medium of broadcast (either TV or radio) lectures and more than 80 courses by classroom instruction at study centers. The major purpose of classroom instruction is to supplement broadcast lectures and to provide students with an opportunity to interact face-to-face with the instructors and other students. As the University of the Air plans to expand its instruction nationwide in the coming five years, we face increasing problems in ways of maintaining the quality and the quantity of face-to-face interaction with students who are scattered throughout Japan.

To address some of these problems, the University of the Air conducts on-going research with the National Institute of Multimedia Education and other institutions of higher education in Japan and overseas. This includes research on distance education via an interactive cable TV network, by a personal computer communications system, by a satellite link and by a low-bit rate video-conference system such as ours. A low-bit rate video-conference system looks most promising at the present time, as it uses ordinary telephone cables. Several experimental projects (Hiraga & Wilkinson 1988; Wakamatsu et al. 1989; Arger 1990) have indicated that given appropriate settings, face-to-face instruction via a video-conference system is a viable alternative to direct classroom teaching. Hiraga

*This research was supported by a 1991 Special Grant of the University of the Air and a 1993 Travel Grant of the International Communications Foundation, Tokyo, to which we want to express our gratitude. We also wish to thank Kumie Fujimori, Ruth Nicolls, and Graham Patterson for their assistance in the preparation and the actual sessions of the experiment, to Geoff Arger, Yoshihiko Kawakami, Sam Meredith, Stan Tonkins and Shigeru Wakamatsu for their technical assistance. We appreciate the generous financial support given by O.T.C., Australia, Australia TELECOM, and Sony Corporation, Tokyo.

and Wilkinson (1988), Wakamatsu et al. (1991), among others point out that interactive small-size classroom instruction, such as used for foreign language courses, is most handicapped by the introduction of video-conference systems. It is our urgent task to clarify the merits and demerits of this type of instructional medium, to develop optimal uses of its merits and to devise effective ways of compensating for its demerits. In this regard, our project is beneficial not only to foreign language education at a distance, but also to the development of teaching techniques that are applicable to any interactive small-size class of any subject.

2. Development of Teaching Materials and Presentation Techniques

The University of New England in cooperation with the University of the Air developed teaching materials and audio tapes for use in the experimental sessions using 64/128 kbps compressed video via ISDN. The materials were designed to cover various aspects of daily interactions in Australian life and culture for intermediate-level Japanese students. To facilitate preparation and review by the individual learners, a set of audio tapes and exercises were devised.

In accordance with the teaching materials, various presentation techniques were examined. They included traditional interactive techniques such as comprehension questions and answers, substitution drills, "show and tell" role play, and games as well as new presentation techniques such as the use of a display camera with photographs and the use of flash cards and answer cards to elicit simultaneous responses in multiple classrooms.

3. Technological Set-Up

The system set-up of each classroom at the University of the Air is shown below.

UNE site	UA site
Telecom's CLI Rembrandt II/06 codec Summit System 2000 multiplexer Jtec Macrospan AC 1200 echo cancellor Dataplex modem	Sony Compact Type 134VP S1-2B ISDN-2B; 1/room Hand Microphones AMX-26 (Shure); 3/room Display Camera Sony Vid-P10; 1/room

The video conference system was temporarily installed in the ordinary classrooms at the University of the Air, whereas the linked studio at the Distance Education Center of the University of New England is equipped with the facility permanently.

Figure 1 illustrates the link between UNE and UA:

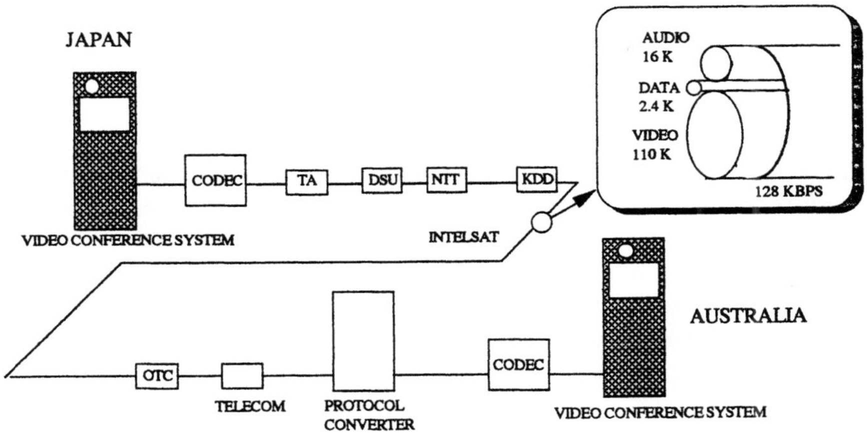

FIGURE 1: NETWORK LINK BETWEEN UNE AND UA

4. Experimental Sessions

Two sets of five one-hour experimental class sessions were conducted in February and March 1992 with a total of 32 students. The objectives tested were: (a) technological issues — the acceptability of transmission speeds (64 kbps and 128 kbps), layout of seats and microphones; (b) pedagogical issues — the number of sites, the instructors and the presentation techniques; (c) individual issues — the level of English ability and the age of students.

A one-site experiment was conducted with 12 students and one male Australian instructor with the speed of transmission changing from 64 kbps to 128 as shown in the table below. A two-site experiment was conducted with 10 students on each site and two Australian instructors of different sex, accent, and length of experience in interactive video teaching. The change in the speed of transmission in the two-site experiment was reversed from the one-site experiment so as to minimize the effect of the order affecting the results of the evaluation.

	students	1	2	3	4	5
one-site	12	64 (M)	64 (M)	64 (M)	128 (M)	128 (M)
two-site	10/room	64 (M/F)	128 (F)	128 (M)	64 (F)	64 (F)

The students were given the hearing test part of the TOEFL (Test of English as a Foreign Language) on the last day of the experiment. Their TOEFL scores varied from 12 to 80 (out of 100) with an average of 40. The age of the students varied from 31 to 69 with an average age of 51.

5. Results

Evaluation was carried out by questionnaires (see Appendix) answered by the students, the teachers and the observers of the experiment. The 54 items were divided into TECHNOLOGY and PEDAGOGY factors. TECHNOLOGY factors included sound, image, room, and camera, whereas PEDAGOGY factors included preparatory materials, learning situation, reactions, content, teacher, teaching techniques, and follow-up activities. After the last session, the students were asked to answer an overall evaluation questionnaire, where they were asked to compare the experience with a traditional class and to suggest which aspects of the project required most improvement. Open-ended comments were also obtained.

5.1 Technological Issues

All the items in the Technology category received very positive reactions, although the evaluation of technology generally attracted lower scores than the evaluation of pedagogical effects as indicated in Figure 2:

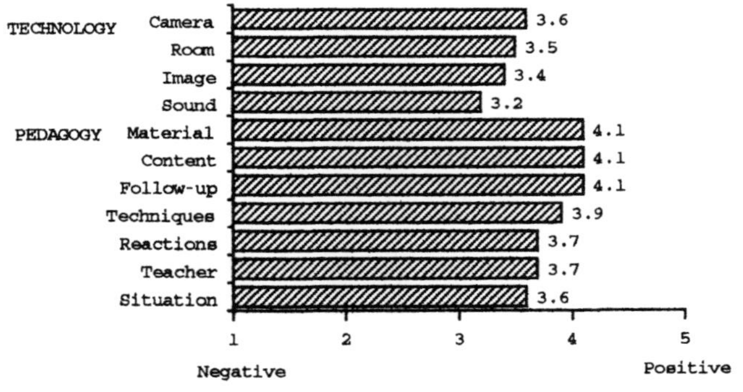

FIGURE 2: OVERALL EVALUATION

The overall evaluation ranking of the need for improvement indicates that technological problems such as the quality of sound and image were felt to need more improvement than other aspects. In both experiments, improvements in sound were felt to be of primary importance, while improvement of picture quality ranked second. The majority of the students, i.e., 87%, indicated that items in the Technology category (sound, picture, room, or camera) should be given highest priority for improvement as shown in Figure 3:

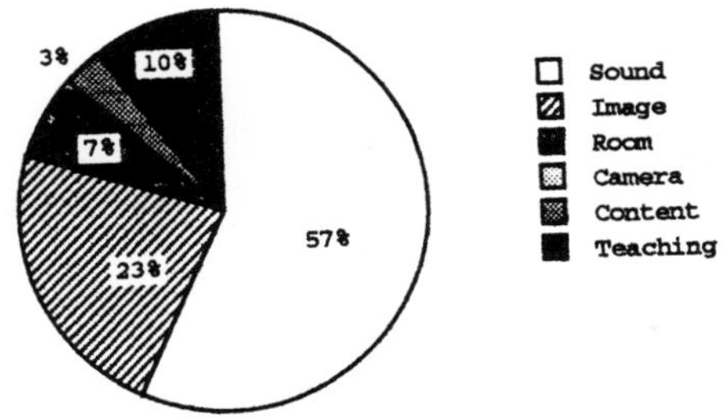

FIGURE 3: HIGHEST PRIORITY FOR IMPROVEMENT

The amount of exposure of the students to this technological environment was another important factor. The more they were exposed to interactive video, the higher they evaluated the technological items, as Figure 4 shows:

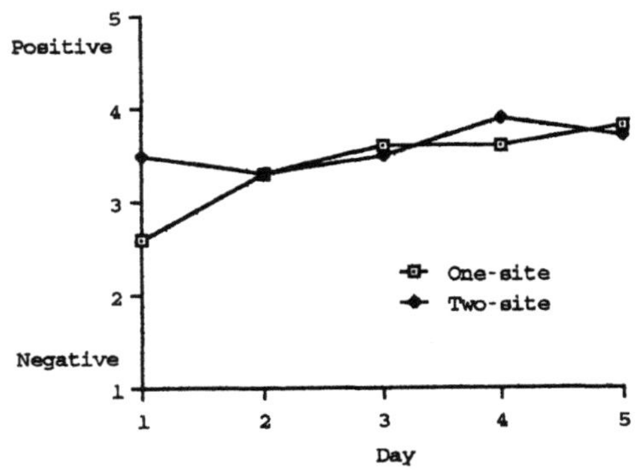

FIGURE 4: TECHNOLOGICAL EVALUATION DAY BY DAY

The sudden improvement in the assessment of the technology on the second day of the one-site experiment, as shown in Figure 4,was due to the change of microphones: the instructor's microphone in the ceiling and the students' boundary microphones were all replaced by hand microphones. This indicates the importance of the quality of microphones for sound effects.

However, there was no significant difference in the evaluation of technology between the one-site and the two-site experiments, nor was the sex of the instructor a significant factor.The different of transmission speeds, 64 kbps or 128 kbps, did not affect the students' evaluation of the sound or the picture quality either, as Figure 5 shows.

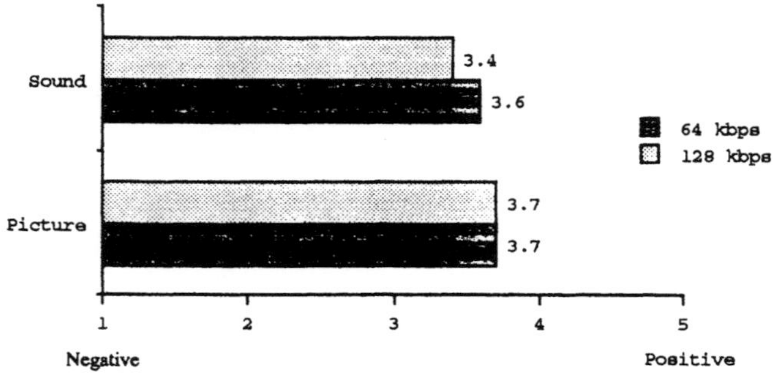

FIGURE 5: SPEED OF TRANSMISSION

There was a seemingly confusing result in the evaluation of sound, which seemed to suggest that 64 kbps was preferred to 128 kbps. However, this was due to the confusion of sound and picture transmission caused by the fact that the Multi-point Communication Unit (MCU) at 128 kbps was set to switch picture transmissions automatically when triggered by sound. Therefore, we strongly suggest that the instructor should have full control of the shift of picture transmission from one site to another.

5.2 Pedagogical Issues

With regard to the number of classroom sites, the two-site experiment obtained a more positive evaluation than the one-site experiment as indicated in Figure 6.

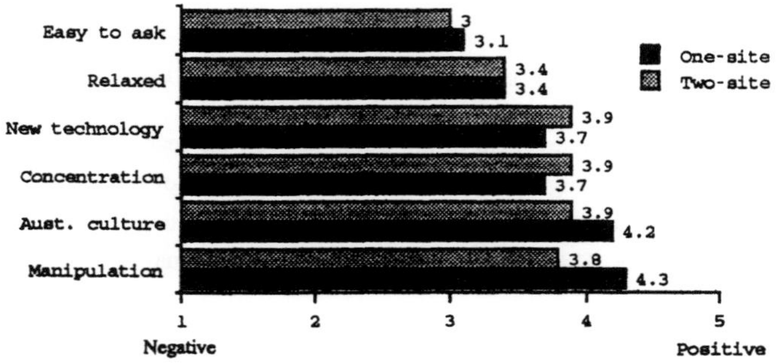

FIGURE 6: STUDENTS' REACTIONS

As for students' reactions, the subjects in the two-site experiment gave a higher score to such items as ease of concentration and motivation stimulated by the new technology, whereas the one-site subjects gave a more positive evaluation to other items such as easy manipulation of technological facilities and interest in Australian culture. Evaluation of the ease of asking questions obtained the lowest score among the items on students' reactions. Physical and psychological remoteness of the instructor from the students' point of view might explain this result. Nevertheless, the differences in evaluation scores between the two groups was fairly small, which indicates that connecting two sites did not affect the reactions of the students at large.

Students rated the instructors highly, regardless of their differences in voice pitch, speed of talking, and length of experience in video conference language teaching. We had two instructors: a male instructor with a low-pitched voice, a fast speaker with a heavy Australian accent, with longer experience of interactive video teaching; and a female instructor with a high-pitched voice, a slow speaker with a British accent, with shorter experience. As indicated in Figure 7, students gave very similar evaluations to the skills of both teachers.

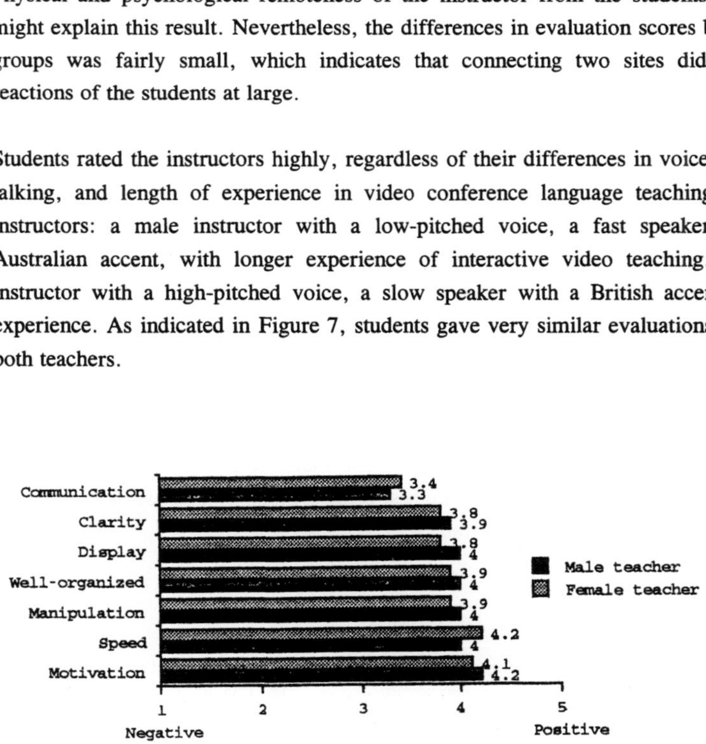

FIGURE 7: EVALUATION OF TEACHERS

A closer examination of the evaluation of teachers on a day-by-day basis indicates that the scores increased gradually as the course progressed. This was the case in the one-site experiment, in particular, as shown in Figure 8.

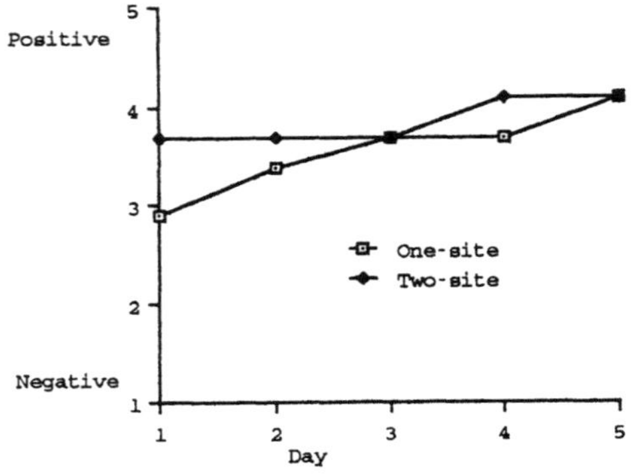

FIGURE 8: EVALUATION OF TEACHERS DAY BY DAY

Consequently, it can be assumed that the amount of experience shared with the instructors in the interactive video classroom contributed to the higher evaluation of the instructors by the students. Furthermore, there is a correlation between the evaluation of the instructor and almost all other items. Namely, students who rated the instructor highly also rated other items highly. This suggests that the teachers play the most crucial and influential role in conducting effective interactive video classes.

Evaluation of teaching techniques showed high scores as indicated in Figure 9. Show & tell and photo display/explanation obtained the highest scores, probably because they utilized both audio and visual dimensions in an optimal way.

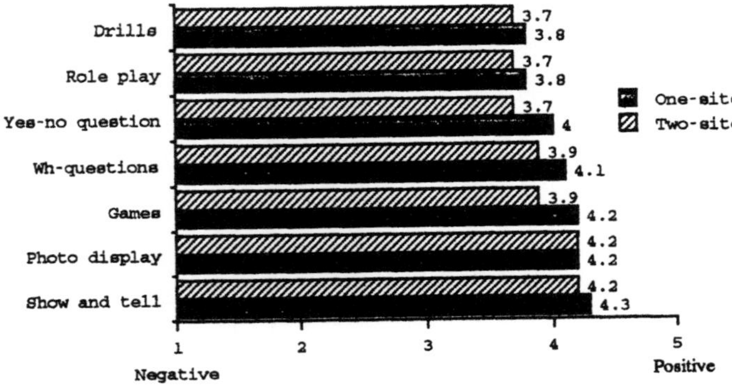

FIGURE 9: TEACHING TECHNIQUES

5.3 Individual Issues

In assessing the success or suitability of this instructional medium, the students' level of ability in English was a crucial factor. Students with higher TOEFL listening scores showed higher evaluation scores for teaching techniques. The age of students was not a factor affecting the evaluation of the interactive video classroom.

5.4 Overall Evaluation

Figure 10 shows that students felt that an interactive video class was quite different from a traditional class. They were less relaxed than in a traditional class. However, they felt that they could concentrate better in an interactive video class than in a traditional one, and that an interactive video class motivated them more to practice English. We believe this last factor is largely dependent on the international nature of this experiment. New technology seems attractive. The novelty of an interactive video may help students' concentration and may make students more motivated in class.

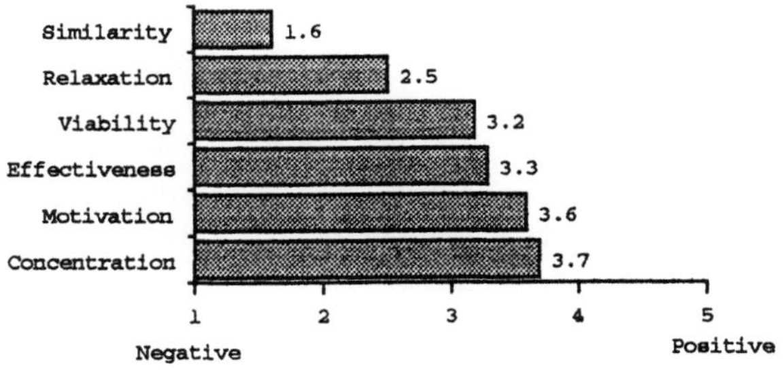

FIGURE 10: COMPARISON WITH TRADITIONAL CLASSROOM

5.5 Observers

Evaluation by observers showed a very similar profile to that given by students. There was a tendency for the observers to give slightly higher evaluation scores than the students. In particular, Australian observers rated the viability of interactive video, as a complement to an actual face-to-face class, more highly than their Japanese counterpart. This could be because the Australian observers were more experienced with the medium.

6. Conclusion

In summary, the results of the experiment were as follows: (a) that there were no significant differences between 64 kbps and 128 kbps; that the layout of seats and the quality of microphones affected learning to a considerable degree; (b) that the individual differences of the instructors in terms of pitch and speed of speaking did not affect the evaluation; that there was no difference between one-to-one site and one-to-two site teaching settings; that some presentation techniques were more suitable than others; (c) that the English ability of the students correlated with the evaluation of the presentation techniques; and that there was no difference in evaluation according to the age of the students. In comparing their experience with a traditional class students reported that they were less relaxed with the new technology. However, they felt that they could concentrate better on learning in an interactive video class, which also motivated them more to practice English.

It is expected that technological developments will improve the quality of sound and image transmission, because they are the most crucial factors for the optimal use of this system, particularly for interactive small-size classroom instruction such as foreign language courses. On the pedagogical side, there should be more case studies and experiments in this area of high-tech teaching, in which we should test various teaching techniques, different media for different purposes, as well as conduct a comparative survey of the educational effectiveness of the two instruction modes, namely, an ordinary face-to-face class and an interactive video conference class.

Although we admit that there are many problems that we should solve before actually installing the system for educational use in our university, our experimental project has indicated that given appropriate settings, face-to-face instruction by the low-bit rate video conference system is a viable alternative to direct classroom teaching. At the same time, it has been shown that international distance education has the potential to assist foreign language education "in a highly motivated way". This clearly anticipates an educational community without borders which transcends the constraints of time and space.

REFERENCES

Arger, G. (1990). *The evolution of a videoconferencing policy for Australian distance education*. Research and development division working papers, 015-E90. Chiba City, The National Institute of Multimedia Education.

Hiraga, M.K. & Wilkinson, V.A. (1988). Teaching English through telecommunications: Chiba to Kumamoto. *The Journal of the University of the Air* 6, pp. 1-16.

Wakamatsu, S. et al. (1989). *Application of low bit rate videoconferencing to teaching at a distance*. Report on multimedia education 8. Chiba City, The National Institute of Multimedia Education.

Wakamatsu, S. et al. (1991). Experimental international language teaching between Japan and Australia using 64/128 kbps compressed video via ISDN. *Bulletin of the National Institute of Multimedia Education* 6, pp. 149-156.

APPENDIX: QUESTIONNAIRE FOR STUDENTS

1. Evaluation (conducted after each experimental session)

Please answer by marking one of the five degrees, 1, 2, 3, 4, or 5 (1=strongly disagree, 5=strongly agree).

A. Technology

(1) Sound
- a. It was easy to use the microphone.
- b. I was satisfied with the clarity of sound.
- c. I was satisfied with the lack of echo.
- d. I was satisfied with the lack of sound interference.
- e. I was satisfied with lip synchronization.
- f. The time delay was not a problem.
- g. The teacher's voice was clearly heard (please disregard Australian accent).
- h. The other students' voices were clear (series II only).

(2) Picture
- a. The screen was large enough to see the teacher and materials presented.
- b. I could see a clear picture of the teacher.
- c. I could see clearly the words and pictures the teacher presented.
- d. I could see a clear picture of the other students (series II only).

(3) Room
- a. The size of the room was suitable.
- b. The layout of the desks and chairs was suitable.
- c. The room was suitable for an interactive TV session.

(4) Camera
- a. I could see the right picture on the monitor at the right time.
- b. The document camera for display of student material was suitably located.

B. Pedagogy

(1) Script and audio tapes prior to TV session
- a. The Japanese translation was helpful.
- b. I enjoyed the listening part of the tape.
- c. The speaking activities in Part 2 of the tape were easy.
- d. The tapes helped me to speak English with better rhythm and intonation.
- e. The drawings were helpful.

(2) Situation
- a. The number of students in the TV session was suitable.
- b. The duration of the interactive TV session was suitable (not too long nor too short).

(3) Psychology
- a. It was easy for me to learn with this kind of technology.
- b. I did not feel under pressure in front of many people.
- c. It was easy to ask questions or give opinions in this type of interactive TV session.
- d. It was easy to concentrate in this type of interactive TV session.
- e. The technology motivated me to study English.
- f. The Australian cultural content made the study of English more relevant.

(4) Content
- a. The grammar was easy to follow.
- b. There was not too much new vocabulary.
- c. The content of the materials was interesting.
- d. The content of the materials was useful.

e. The meaning was clear.

(5) Teacher
a. The teacher seemed to have a good command of this kind of technology.
b. The teacher spoke clearly.
c. The teacher spoke at a suitable speed.
d. The teacher's instructions were clear.
e. The teacher presented the materials in an effective order.
f. The communication between the teacher and the students was smooth.
g. The teacher was good at motivating the students to participate in the sessions.
h. The session was well-organized.

(6) Teaching Techniques
a. Yes/No questions were effective for interactive TV sessions.
b. Wh-questions were effective for interactive TV sessions.
c. Substitution or repetition drills were effective for interactive TV sessions.
d. Show & Tell was effective for interactive TV sessions.
e. Role play was effective for interactive TV sessions.
f. Games were effective for interactive TV sessions.
g. Talking about the photos was effective for interactive TV sessions.
h. Which of the techniques above was most effective in today's session a.b.c.d. or e.?

(7) Follow-up Activities
a. There were enough activities.
b. The activities were easy.
c. The activities helped me participate in the next TV session.

2. Overall Evaluation (conducted after the whole series of experimental sessions)

I. Compared with a traditional class, please answer the following (by marking one of the five degrees).
a. It was just like being in a face-to-face classroom.
b. I felt more relaxed in the interactive TV class than in a face-to-face class.
c. It was easier to concentrate in the TV class than in a face-to-face class.
d. Interactive TV motivated me to practice English more than a face-to-face session.
e. Interactive TV is more effective for foreign language learning than face-to-face classes.
f. Interactive TV is viable as a complement to an actual face-to-face class.

II. Which of the following if any should be improved? Please rate them according to the need for improvement.
a. Sound
b. Picture
c. Room
d. Camera
e. Content
f. Teaching techniques

III. How many students could be taught at the one time by interactive TV sessions?
How many sites could be connected at one time for interactive TV sessions?

IV. What were the merits of interactive TV sessions?

V. What were the demerits of interactive TV sessions?

VI. What were the main differences between interactive TV sessions and traditional face-to-face teaching?

VII. Please feel free to write any suggestions, comments, criticisms, etc.

COMPUTER CONFERENCING:
A FORUM FOR WRITTEN INTERACTION

Paula Kalaja and Sirpa Leppänen
University of Jyväskylä

This paper describes an experiment with computer conferencing in the L2 context: instead of meeting in class, a group of EFL university students discussed topics related to a content-area course via computer writing. Transferring ordinary classroom discussions into the computer-conferencing mode had interesting effects on the interactions. This paper is an attempt at developing a framework for the analysis of the goals and roles the students pursued, adapting ideas from classroom research.

1. Introduction

Computer conferencing provides an electronic network for carrying out group discussions, either in real or non-real time (see, for example, Kaye 1989, Murray 1990). It thus provides a forum where participants can interact - exchange opinions, argue, debate and joke - with each other in writing. Recently, computer conferencing has been used in higher education in the context of educational science courses and graduate seminars (see, for example, Konttinen and Sajavaara 1990, Marttunen 1992). In language teaching, computer conferencing has so far been used primarily in the L1 context, with only a few applications in L2 with secondary school students (e.g. Bee-Lay and Yee-Ping 1991, Tella 1991). In this article we will report on an experiment where we used non-real time computer conferencing in the L2 context with university students (see also Leppänen and Kalaja, in press). We will first describe the set-up of the experiment, in other words, how we turned ordinary classroom discussions into ones carried out via computers in writing. To demonstrate the interactive nature of computer conferencing discussions, we will attempt to identify the kinds of interactions that take place between students and the teacher, applying ideas from classroom research, especially by Ellis (1984). We will illustrate this by an analysis of one specific discussion round and two messages sent off during the course of the discussion.

2. Background: The set-up of the experiment

Out of 60 first-year students, we selected a group of five to participate in the experiment. They were all attending a course on British and American Institutions, a two-term content-area course consisting of a series of lectures and readings, discussions in small groups, and writing assignments on relevant topics. Unlike the other students, the experimental group did not meet in class for discussions. Instead, they had discussions via computers (on topics based on lectures or required readings).

The five advanced EFL students and the teacher had access to a number of terminals and micro computers on campus, and these were hooked up with the University's host computer. They wrote messages on-line in non-real time. The structure of this network is shown in Figure 1.

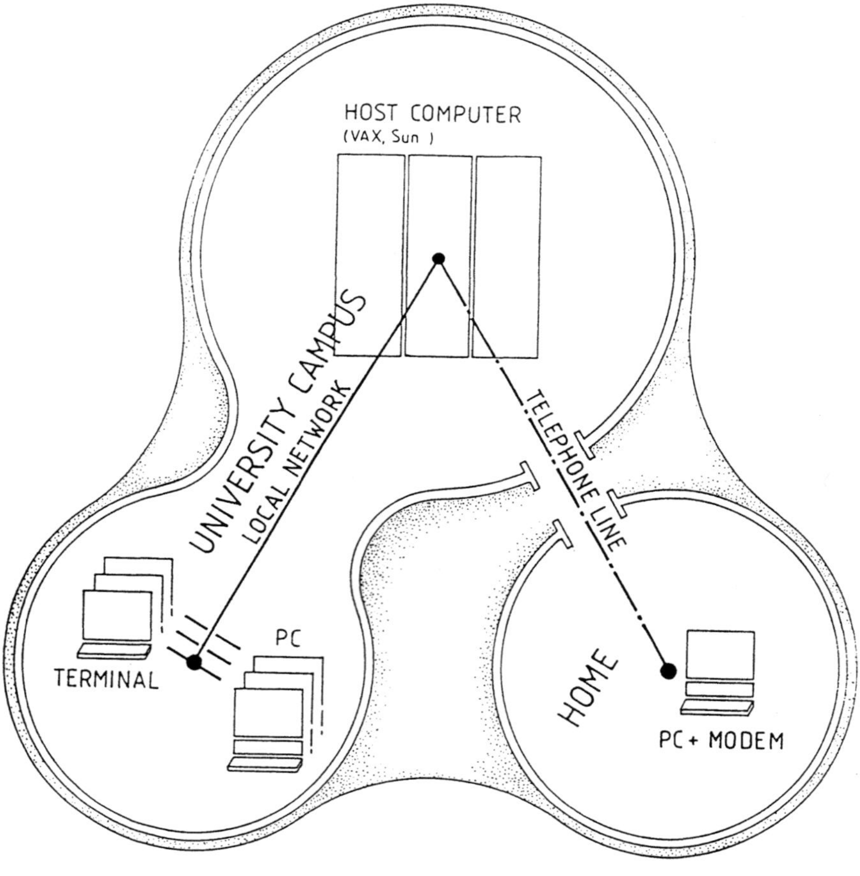

FIGURE 1: THE COMPUTER CONFERENCING SYSTEM

With these arrangements, the group had ten discussion rounds in the course of one term. As a rule, the teacher opened a round by providing a topic for discussion, and the students responded by sending a minimum of two messages per round. This was the "deal", as they put it.

3. Findings

Technically, these arrangements made the running of a discussion class more flexible. Instead of meeting, for example, in Classroom 123 two o'clock every Monday afternoon for an hour, the students and the teacher could work when and where they wanted to. In other words, they could work free of the constraints of a specific time or place. Furthermore, they could devote as many hours as they wished to the task (and it turned out that they indeed made use of these opportunities).

Linguistically these arrangements meant turning weekly teacher-led discussions into written ones. As in classroom discussions, the discussions evolved in time, one message following another, like turns in a conversation. However, they differed from classroom discussions in that the responses to a message were not immediate. This meant that the group's interaction was characterised by mediacy (of time and space) and, as the discussions were in non-real-time, by one-sidedness (similar features are typical of telephone answering machine messages, see, for example, Dingwall 1992). Furthermore, as the discussions were carried out in the written mode, the group obviously could not make use of all the interactional resources that participants in spoken discussions have (such as gestures, facial expressions, intonation, tone, back-channel cues). Instead, the group had to rely on other means, for example, in showing their affective responses to each other's contributions (such as capitals, underlining and exclamation marks for emphasis).

The ten discussion rounds and the individual messages turned out to be very complex. What actually took place in a discussion round was, however, to some extent constrained by the teacher's initial instructions as to how the students were to use the computer-conferencing system: each student had to log onto the computer at least twice a week. Secondly, the rounds were constrained by the teacher's instructions with regard to the content of the discussions: the topics were provided by the teacher, and these were based on lectures or required readings on the course.

3.1 Discussion rounds

Let us have a look at one fairly typical discussion round. The topic of this discussion is freedom of speech in the U.S.A. and Finland. Message 1 shows how the teacher initiates the discussion:

MESSAGE 1

> Welcome back
>
> As you read the article, what did you think of the controversy over freedom of speech vs. [the flag as] a sacred object? As an outsider, do you think this type of discussion is important or a waste of time? Please comment on the question in general and any point brought up in the article. You may also bring finland into the discussion if you choose.
>
> Alan

The teacher refers to his first message as a *question*. The form and content of his contribution is, in fact, not unlike a question we could find in an exam paper, or an essay topic. The implication here may be that the teacher expects his students to give an essay-like answer to his question. This expectation is further emphasised by the fact that he gives no specific instructions how he expects the students to build up a written discussion. In spite of the lack of instructions, a kind of written discussion does evolve during the following day or two. Figure 2 gives a schematic description of the discussion, and shows the kinds of goals that the students pursue in its course.

Figure 2 shows how the discussions do indeed take place free of time constraints. It also shows how the students do most of the "talking": out of the total of 15 messages, only 3 are by the teacher. In spite of the teacher's stereotypical initiation, the students end up as active participants. In particular, they not only act as Responders, but also as Elaborators and Initiators of interactions of various kinds, thus pursuing a number of goals in the discussions.

In this round, the students pursue (at least) four different kinds of goals: message-oriented, medium-oriented, framework and social goals (see Ellis 1984 on this terminology).

(1) Message-oriented goals in this context refer to the ways in which students deal with the question and/or topic given by the teacher. It seems that, in our data, students have two kinds of message-oriented goals. On the one hand, when their goal is to give an answer to the teacher's question, they simply state their own opinions about the topic given by the teacher. The other message-oriented goal they have is to hold a discussion with the group, in which case they make an effort to relate their contributions to other messages by, for example, referring to or commenting on earlier messages, asking questions, and expressing agreement or disagreement.

(2) Medium-oriented goals refer to the ways in which the students and the teacher deal with problems related to language.

#	DATE & TIME	SENDER	GOALS PURSUED
1	Thu Jan 17 08:43	T(eacher)	provides MESSAGE-ORIENTED GOALS for the students by asking a Q(uestion) and/or by introducing a discussion topic.
2	Fri Jan 18 11:18	S(tudent)1	MESSAGE-OR. GOALS: (1) Q-A: answers T:Q: expresses opinions. (2) DISC.: asks a general question. MEDIUM-OR. GOALS points out a spelling mistake made by the teacher.
3	Sat Jan 19 10:07	T	MEDIUM-OR. GOALS: DISC.: responds to 2:S1: corrects and apologises for his mistake.
4	Mon Jan 21 10:40	S2	MESSAGE-OR. GOALS: Q-A: answers T:Q, expresses opinions.
5	Mon Jan 21 12:02	S3	MESSAGE-OR. GOALS: Q-A: answers T:Q, expresses opinions.
6	Mon Jan 21 17:16	S1	MESSAGE-OR. GOALS: DISC.: comments on 4: S2 and 5:S3 and asks questions from them, clarifies opinions. FRAMEWORK GOALS: encourages S4 and S5 to contribute.
7	Mon Jan 21 18:04	S4	MESSAGE-OR. GOALS: Q-A: answers T:Q, expresses opinions.
8	Tue Jan 22 12:28	S3	MESSAGE-OR. GOALS: DISC.: responds to 6:S1, clarifies opinions. MEDIUM-OR. GOALS: asks for confirmation for her choice of a word.
9	Tue Jan 22 14:21	S5	MESSAGE-OR. GOALS: (1) Q-A: answers T:Q, (2) DISC.: asks a general question. FRAMEWORK GOALS: asks a technical question.
10	Tue Jan 22 14:45	S5	MESSAGE-OR. GOALS: DISC.: asks a general question from the group, comments on 2:S1, clarifies opinions.
11	Tue Jan 22 15:18	S4	MESSAGE-OR. GOALS: DISC.: responds to 6:S1: clarifies opinions, agrees with 6:S1 and clarifies opinions.
12	Tue Jan 22 16:16	S2	MESSAGE-OR. GOALS: DISC.: responds to 6:S1: clarifies opinions.
13	Wed Jan 23 09:57	T	MESSAGE-OR. GOALS: DISC.: gives feedback on the discussion so far. FRAMEWORK GOALS: answers with length 9:S5 technical question and gives technical instructions.
14	Wed Jan 23 10:26	T	FRAMEWORK GOALS: gives another answer to 9:S5 technical question.
15	Wed Jan 23 11:41	S1	MESSAGE-OR. GOALS: DISC.: clarifies opinions. FRAMEWORK GOALS: responds to 8:S5, 11:S4, 12:S2, comments on own role as a catalyst and explains her extra turn.

FIGURE 2: A SCHEMATIC DESCRIPTION OF ONE DISCUSSION ROUND

(3) Framework goals refer to the ways in which the students deal with the conditions of the discussions (the terms of the discussion as set by the teacher, and by the computer conferencing system itself).

(4) Social goals refer to the ways in which the students establish and maintain rapport with each other.

As may be expected, at the beginning of a round, the students interpret the teacher's first message as a question to which they give an answer by using such expressions as *I think ...*, *in my opinion ...* In this round examples of this are Messages 2, 4, 5, and 7. In these messages the students do not appear to be in control of the discussion: they respond, but do not initiate or elaborate. We could argue that their role is that of a stereotypical student answering the teacher's question. However, there is no feedback from the teacher, which means that this interaction is, in fact, impoverished in comparison with classroom question-answer interaction.

Figure 2 shows further how the students pursue the message-oriented goal of conducting a discussion within the group. In other words, they have written conversations. For example, they comment on each other's contributions (Message 6), ask questions (Messages 6, 9, and 10), and show agreement (Message 11). In these messages the students appear as active elaborators and initiators. It could be argued that their role is therefore no longer that of a stereotypical student who simply responds to what the teacher asks them to do.

Figure 2 also contains examples of the students' medium-oriented goals: for instance, Messages 2, 3 and 8 show how the students deal with problems of language. Message 2 shows how a student points out a spelling mistake made by the teacher; in Message 3 the teacher corrects the mistake. Message 8, in turn, is a typical example of how the students seek confirmation for and/or clarify their lexical choices by code-switching.

In addition, there are in Figure 2 examples of the students' framework goals. On the one hand, they discuss their interactional deal (in Message 6, for example, one of them encourages others to participate). On the other hand, as illustrated by Message 9, they ask questions about the computer conferencing system. In this connection it is particularly interesting to note that the only messages that the teacher sends off during this discussion round, Messages 13 and 14, are mainly concerned with framework goals. In these messages he answers a student's technical question and includes a great deal of technical instructions. In contrast, he gives practically no feedback on content (the message-oriented goals of the course). The closest he gets to giving feedback is his brief post scriptum in Message 13: *I have enjoyed the discussions so far*. On the whole, the teacher is thus relatively inactive, leaving the floor to the students. He more or less assumes the role of a by-stander or an eavesdropper in the discussions.

3.2 Messages

Let us now have a closer look at two messages in the discussion round we just described. These two were selected in order to show the potential of computer-conferencing systems to provide discussion practice. These messages also illustrate the complexity of the student interactions: the great number and variety of roles adopted and goals pursued by the students in each e-mail message, despite the constraints set by the teacher.

The message below is the 6th message in the discussion round and was written by Kaija (S1). This is her second contribution to the discussion:

MESSAGE 6

> Hi,
>
> I'm using the group reply now, but I'm not sure whether it is working or not. I found it quite interesting to read both Maija's and Saija's opinions on burning the flag. They were similar, weren't they.
>
> I mean you both think it is okay to burn some other's flag but when it comes to our honoured Finnish flag well then you have other rules. Isn't that a bit unlogical? And how would you react when a foreigner was burning our flag and on the other hand is it as bad as if a Finn was burning the flag. And is it okay if the troups in the Gulf go around burning Iraqi flags just because the United Troups are the good guys and Mad Dog Saddam's men are the bad guys?
> So, what I'm trying to say is that to me burning a flag is just a way of expressing one's mind. You can call me non-patriotic if you want, this is however my opinion. But I still kind of miss Reijo's and Taija's writings, it's already Monday evening. But at least I have written two times. I hope you don't hang me saying what I think. These just happen to be the things I like to quarrel about.
>
> So, that's it! Your own anarchist (?)
>
> ens05 Kaija

In the core of the message, Kaija first comments on some points made by two other students, Maija and Saija, challenging them by asking them some questions, and then elaborating on the points herself. This is message-oriented interaction between power equals, discussants, and consequently, Kaija acts here as Elaborator of this kind of interaction. At the same time, Kaija provides (indirectly) an answer to one of the questions asked by the teacher in his first e-mail message. This is also message-oriented interaction, but now between two participants, the teacher and the student, where the student acts as Responder.

A little later, Kaija reminds another two participants, Reijo and Taija, of their obligations as discussants (they were to send off a minimum of two messages per week). Kaija is thus taking an active role in running the discussion in pursuing framework goals. She is quite successful in doing this, for a number of messages follow from the others in response to her message (see Figure 2).

Finally, as a sender of e-mail messages, Kaija frames the core with a salutation, and an opening, and finishes it off with a closing and a signature of a kind. In other words, she uses the opening and the closing of the e-mail message for establishing and maintaining a friendly relationship with the group, thus pursuing social goals.

The following message is the 8th in the very same round, and it was sent off by Maija (S3) as her second turn in the discussion:

MESSAGE 8

> Hello!
>
> First I'd like to make some things clear to Kaija, you commented on my opinion on burning flags. You claimed that I said that it is all right to us to burn flags of other countries but nobody is allowed to burn our flag. That's not what I meant at least [all]. What Idid mean was that I would be irritated if you, for example, burned the flag but still you have the right to do so, I couldn't deny it. After all, a flag is only a piece of cloth and you can treat it how ever you like. The feelings I feel towards the values that the flag represents (edustaa?) they are in my mind and heart and you can't destroy them by burning or otherwise destroying the symbol.
> Well, I guess that's all that comes to my mind about this subject but I'm eagerly waiting for [looking forward to] the next one.
>
> We'll meet again ...
>
> Maija
>
> P.S. To err is human, but to really foul things up requires a computer. (Murphy's law)

In the core of the message, Maija clarifies a point which she has made earlier, making sure that another discussant, Kaija, has not misunderstood her. So Maija is acting as a discussant. At the same time, she indirectly provides an answer to one of the questions asked by the teacher. This is message-oriented interaction with the student as Elaborator and Responder, the roles being (actually) difficult to tell apart.

Unlike Kaija, Maija is not active in pursuing framework goals. But interestingly, in clarifying her previous points, she is not quite sure of her choice of a word, and therefore she switches codes from English into Finnish (followed by a question mark). Here Maija acts as Initiator of yet another kind of interaction, that is, medium-oriented interaction, by asking a linguistic question, and probably expecting a response from the others, if only from the teacher, a native speaker of English. (It turns out, however, that Maija fails to get confirmation for her choice of an English word. This may be explained by the nature of computer conferencing, its mediacy, see Figure 2.)

Like Kaija, Maija frames the core of her message with a salutation, and an opening, summarising a point made by Kaija earlier in the discussion round before clarifying her own points. She wraps up her message with a preclosing, and a closing quoting a song, followed by a signature of a kind. After this, she adds a postscript. It appears that Maija uses the closing, especially, to pursue social goals: to establish rapport with the others (and, we feel, she is bound to be successful in this, getting smiles or chuckles in response from the others, even though these do not show up in our written data!)

4. Conclusion

In this article our main purpose was to describe an experiment where we used computer conferencing as a forum for written EFL discussions and, in particular, to point out the potential it has for the foreign language development of the students.

Transforming classroom discussions into computer conferencing discussions had a number of important pedagogical advantages. Firstly, the discussions could be carried out free of the limitations of a specific time and place. Secondly, it affected the quantity of student contributions, as, in comparison with the teacher, the students did most of the 'talking'. Thirdly, the students acted in a number of roles: they not only responded to what the teacher asked them to do, but also actively performed as elaborators and initiators in the discussion in respect of all of the goals they pursued in the course. Fourthly, in addition to pursuing message-oriented goals (i.e. answering the teacher's questions and discussing a topic with others), the students also pursued medium-oriented goals (dealt with problems of language) and framework goals (most important of which was discussing the terms of the discussion). Fifth, the students were also concerned with establishing and maintaining social relationships within the group. Lastly, the teacher had a relatively passive role. After his initiation of the discussions, he gave the floor to the students. This may create a problem because, while the students enjoyed the freedom and independence, they might also have benefitted from feedback from the teacher. It could have been valuable for them if he had commented on the content and language of their contributions, urged them to be more active as discussants, and organised and monitored the discussions. One explanation why the teacher, who had a great deal of experience in leading ordinary classroom discussions, was passive may be that he was somewhat at a loss with the computer conferencing discussions. They seemed to require from him that he find a new role as a teacher. Instead of acting as a discussion leader, he would have had to find a way of helping the students without dominating them and the discussions too much. It may be that with this first attempt he did not fully succeed in finding this role.

Our analysis attempted to show how the students actively pursued a number of goals in the discussions. We managed to do this to a certain extent. However, our analysis may have its limitations as it did not take into account the fact that the students may pursue several goals simultaneously. For example, in Message 8 Maija's post scriptum *To err is human, but to really foul things up requires a computer. (Murphy's law)*, can be interpreted in (at least) two ways. On the one hand, by attempting to amuse the group, Maija is pursuing social goals. On the other hand, she may also be pursuing framework goals, by commenting indirectly on the group having to use computer conferencing in their discussions. A systematic analysis of the discussions would obviously have to find a way of dealing with multiple interpretations of this kind. It should be sensitive to the participants' potentially numerous and overlapping goals.

Another issue that was not addressed in our analysis was the variation in the linguistic and textual strategies that the participants used. The discussion rounds varied to some extent from round to round in their overall organisation and style, as did the messages. At times, the openings and closings could be compared with those in an informal letter or a short note; at other times, they resembled those found in everyday conversations or phone calls. As the students did not have any prior experience with computer conferencing, they seem to have adopted conventions from other written or spoken genres that they were familiar with. A systematic analysis of this variation, even though it certainly would be an interesting task, was, however, marginal to the main aim of this article. (But see, for example, Ferrara et al. 1991 for a discussion of electronic texts as a new register that uses resources typical of both spoken and written registers selectively.)

Despite these reservations, it seems to us that the potential value of computer conferencing for EFL learners became evident in the experiment. Even with an interactively passive teacher, computer conferencing no doubt managed to make students more active and autonomous as discussants. It seems that their various interactions with each other also made them aware that writing, just like speaking, is social and interactive in nature in that it is carried out with a particular/potential audience and its expectations and possible responses in mind (on the view of all writing as social and interactive see, for example, Nystrand 1989). It is this potential value that makes computer conferencing useful in language teaching, too. It can be used to make students more active, autonomous, and sensitive to writing as multi-levelled social interaction.

REFERENCES

Bee-Lay, S. & Yee-Ping, S. (1991). English by E-mail: creating a global classroom via the medium of computer technology. *ELT Journal* 45, 287-292.

Dingwall, S. (1992). Leaving telephone answering machine messages: who's afraid of speaking to machines? *Text* 12, 81-101.

Ellis, R. (1984). *Classroom second language development: a study of classroom interaction and language acquisition*. Oxford, Pergamon Press.

Ferrara, K., Brunner H. & Whittemore, G. (1991). Interactive written discourse as an emergent register. *Written Communication* 8, 8-34.

Kaye, A. (1989). Computer-mediated communication and distance education. In: Mason, R. & Kaye, A. (eds.). *Mindweave: communication, computers and distance education*. London, Pergamon Press.

Konttinen, R. & Sajavaara, K. (1990). Towards an electronic campus - utopia or reality? *Life and Education in Finland* 1, 48-54.

Leppänen, S. & Kalaja, P. (in press). Experimenting with computer conferencing in English for Academic Purposes. *ELT Journal*.

Marttunen, M. (1992). Commenting on written arguments as a part of argumentation skills - comparison between students engaged in traditional vs on-line study. *Scandinavian Journal of Educational Research* 36, 289-302.

Murray, D.E. (1990). CmC. *English Today* 23, 42-46.

Nystrand, M. (1989) A social-interactive model of writing. *Written Communication* 6, 66-85.

Tella, S. (1991). *Introducing International Communications Networks and Electronic Mail into Foreign Language Classrooms: A case study in Finnish secondary schools*. Research Report 95. Helsinki, University of Helsinki: Department of Teacher Education.

THE USE OF PHONE-IN RADIO PROGRAMMES IN TEACHING ENGLISH AS A FOREIGN LANGUAGE

Eileen Vick

University of Bayreuth

For the last four semesters, students at the Language Centre of the University of Bayreuth have had the opportunity to prepare and present a one-hour radio programme in English on the local commercial radio station at the end of each semester. We decided on live, monolingual programmes, which included phone-ins. I will give the reasons for these decisions and ask what benefits such programmes bring for language learning. I will then suggest ways of using the material with students who did not take part in the programme themselves. Finally, a speculative look will be taken at possible future applications of similar techniques on a wider scale.

1. Introduction

In the last fifteen years various foreign language radio programmes have been prepared and broadcast by L2 learners, ranging from bilingual programmes on local radio to an intercontinental chat-show in French by means of a NASA satellite. Examples of German language programmes in France described by Schlemminger (1986) and Bartholomé & Zschachlitz (1988) took a bilingual approach in order to make their programmes accessible to a wider audience. A similar project with second to fourth year pupils of Spanish in the United States described by Alsop (1984) was pre-recorded and then played back on the radio because "students felt more at ease making a tape-delayed broadcast than a live one". Making a broadcast in this way enables students to edit out mistakes and to avoid having to react on the spur of the moment. However, it excludes a possible learning experience for the students: that of preparing stategies for reacting appropriately under the pressure of making a live programme.

During the last two years the Language Centre at the University of Bayreuth has had the opportunity to make four English programmes and one in French which were broadcast on the local radio station at the end of each semester. Most of the students participating were students of Business Administration who had chosen English as their language option.

We decided to make monolingual, live broadcasts. In addition, we wanted to make possible interactive communication between the programme makers in the studio and the listeners at home. Thus we chose to make phone-in programmes.

2. Preparation

In preparation, a course was offered during the semester, with twelve to fourteen weekly ninety-minute meetings, culminating in the programme at the end. In these classes we tried to create a balance between structured practice and freer practice, between encouraging students to speak fluently and correcting their mistakes. This was difficult in the case of more introverted students who were unwilling to do without written texts for fear of making mistakes. Thus we felt it was important to provide useful phrases and to practise strategies for using them. Below are some examples of exercises we used in class to prepare students to deal with a live, phone-in programme.

2.1 Listening and vocabulary

In the first two classes we listened to two phone-in programmes of differing styles from BBC radio, *The Johnsons* and *Tuesday Call*. Both are regular programmes in which topical subjects are discussed, albeit in very different styles. *The Johnsons* programme we listened to, for example, about the repossession of homes from owners who could not keep up their mortgage repayments, was presented in a chatty way, listeners phoned in with home truths and tended to be middle-aged or retired people. In the case of *Tuesday Call*, the subject was the care of retarded people in the community, presented in complex language and carefully researched by the presenter, Kate Adie, and included expert studio guests. While listening to these programmes the students selected useful vocabulary and phrases with the help of a gap-fill exercise (see extract below).

1. How is the phone-in introduced?
   It's our Wednesday night phone-in and we're _______ ___ ____ ____.
   (Answer: *waiting for your call.*)
2. How is the number repeated?
   ____ ______ _____*: 071 3060222.*
   (Answer: *That number again*)
3. How does James ask listeners to phone in?
   ____ __ _ ____*: 071 3060222.*
   (Answer: *Give us a call.*)

(From *The Johnsons*, BBC Radio 2, 6 January, 1993).

In the case of *Tuesday Call*, students found the gap-fill exercise very difficult, due to the mass of unfamiliar information and vocabulary and the speed of delivery. It therefore would be necessary to give students some background information on the subject matter and the technical vocabulary used before playing the recording of the phone-in, or to restrict the selection of recordings to easier ones, such as *The Johnsons* quoted above. After completing the gap-fill exercise, we grouped the useful vocabulary according to function and added our own ideas (see below).

Functions and Phrases for phone-in programmes

(1) To introduce studio guests

(a) *With me in the studio is/are ...*
(b) *Sitting next to me is ...*
(c) *I'd like to introduce to you ...*
(d) *I'm very happy to have with me ...*
(e) *Our studio guest today is ...*

(2) To give the phone number

(a) *That phone number again: 071 306 0222.*
(b) *Give us a call: 071 306 0222.*
(c) *I'll say it again: 071 306 0222.*
(d) *Are you on the line? 071 306 0222.*

(3) To tell listeners the subjects they can call in on

(a) *We are happy to discuss any subject you care to raise, but nothing offensive, thank you.*
(b) *The subject of our programme today is...*

(4) To encourage listeners to phone in:

(a) *We're waiting to hear your views.*
(b) *It's your programme, so don't be shy, we're waiting to hear from you.*
(c) *Have you any good suggestions? Let's hear them, if you please.*
(d) *Share the story with us.*

(5) To introduce a caller

(a) *Let's take a caller...*
(b) *Elizabeth Smith's on the line.*
(c) *We have a caller from South London...*
(d) *Could I bring in the next caller...*
(e) *We've a call coming in.*
(f) *Who am I talking to?*
(g) *Who's on the line?*
(h) *And the first caller tonight in our phone-in: Frank, down in Norfolk.*

(6) To encourage someone to speak

(a) *How can we help you?*
(b) *What do you want to tell us then?*

(7) To ask an opinion

(a) *Can I just bring up this point with Roy Lilley?*
(b) *What do you think (about this/that)?*
(c) *Do you agree with that?*
(d) *Could I have your comment on this question?*
(e) *What's your opinion?*

(8) To interrupt (to give someone else the chance to speak)

(a) *Can I just bring Roy Lilley in there?*
(b) *Marjorie Wallis.*
(c) *It would be interesting to hear Mr. X's views on this.*
(d) *Now let's come back to Miss Y.*

(9) To interrupt (to speak oneself)

(a) *I wonder if I can come in there?*
(b) *May I interrupt you ...*

(10) To give someone the chance to reply to criticism/questions

(a) *Would you like to come back on that?*
(b) *Would you like to give a comment on this criticism?*
(c) *Does this criticism worry you?*
(d) *Does this criticism concern you?*
(e) *What do you think when you hear this criticism?*

(11) To give examples:

(a) *for instance*
(b) *for example*
(c) *First/second/third*

(12) To end a call

(a) *Thank you for your call.*
(b) *It was nice talking to you.*
(c) *We'll see what other callers have to say.*
(d) *Thank you, Gwen, I'm sure everyone will agree with you.*

(13) To say goodbye

(a) *take care*
(b) *bye-bye*
(c) *night-night*

2.2 Deciding on our target group and on suitable topics for the programmes

We had certain in-built disadvantages in comparison to such programmes as *The Johnsons* or *Tuesday Call*. Unlike the BBC programmes, which are both well-established and have their regular listeners, a once-per-semester programme does not have this infrastructure. Added to this was the fact that our programme was in a foreign language - this in itself made our phone-in a programme for minority tastes, although there are some native English speakers living in or around Bayreuth, for example, American soldiers. In the Alsop example mentioned above, the children presented a mixed bag of items as a sort of advertisement for learning Spanish. The presenters tried to teach listeners the days of the week in Spanish, for example. In our planning we presupposed that our listeners would be students with some knowledge of English, as the programme was scheduled to follow a regular weekly students' programme. Thus we chose topics either of general interest or of particular interest to a student audience, and, wherever possible, topics on which native speakers of English living locally could be invited to comment as studio guests. Topics chosen have included the withdrawal of Allied troops from Germany (interview with an army spokesman), sport in Bayreuth (interview with an American player for the local basketball team) and impressions on arriving in Bayreuth and on leaving (interviews with British and Irish exchange students).

2.3 Practising interviews

In pairs, students had interviews to prepare in class. The "studio guest" was given either a picture of an unusual personality or situation or a slip of paper stating his/her "achievement" and the pair worked together on an interview. These were then repeated for the whole class.

2.4 Expressing opinions

In groups of three, student A presented a point of view, then student B disagreed, then student C raised an objection and finally student A justified his or her point of view (see Jones 1983: Participant's Book, 16-17). Another idea was for each student to record on cassette at home a two-minute presentation of his/her point of view on a controversial topic. In the language lab, students then passed on their cassettes to another student who listened to the first opinion and added his/her own view. This continued until five or six opinions were on each cassette (Murphey 1992: 96-97).

2.5 Dealing with incoming phone calls

In small groups, one student was the "presenter" and called on each of the others to give their opinions on a topic (the topics in the exercise above could be used). He/she introduced the other students as "studio guests" or listeners calling into the programme and linked their ideas. Each student took a turn at being the "presenter".

2.6 Simulating a whole news programme

The preparation is, to a greater or lesser extent at different stages, a simulation of the final presentation on the air. One simulation of a whole programme which we used for practice was the *World News Magazine* (Jones 1983: Controller's Book 28-51 and Participant's Book 9-14). This was written specifically for EFL students. It takes from 90 minutes to 4 hours, depending on how much time is available. The group is divided into sub-groups, each of which is a "radio news team" with a brief to produce a 10-minute radio news broadcast to be recorded live at the end of the session. At the beginning of the simulation and then at 15-minute intervals until just before the "broadcast", groups are given copies of newspaper articles from Jones' book, supplemented with interesting up-to-date newspaper cuttings. Rather than simply summarizing the articles, people mentioned in the articles can be "interviewed" for their point of view on the events. The simulation is followed up by written work (including a critical "review" of the programme the student was involved in making) and in a later class by playing back the recorded programmes and discussing the content and presentation and doing any necessary remedial language work.

2.7 Outside class time

Contact with native speakers who were willing to talk to students was helpful (for example, with American exchange students or others in the university's "twinning programme", where a native speaker of the foreign language and a German practise together). It gave students the chance to practise speaking with a critical listener, improving not only their fluency, but also motivating them to see English as a medium of communication.
They also practised more specifically for the programmes. Meeting interview partners before going on air, putting faces to names, and discussing suitable questions with them made the atmosphere in the programmes themselves more relaxed than it otherwise might have been. Preparation outside class time also involved a visit by the students to the studio to watch the regular presenter in action and to have their questions answered.

2.8 Feedback

To encourage fluency, mistakes were noted down as they occurred for later correction by the whole class. Another method was to tape activities and give students a tapescript and a list of their mistakes, again for correction by the class. Although this was useful, it was extremely time-consuming - a quicker variation is to just note down the mistakes for correction by the class as they listen to the tape again.

3. The programmes themselves: lessons to be learnt

There are lessons to be learnt about how class preparation can help students to deal more effectively with phone calls and about how to encourage more listeners to phone in. In the third programme a trivial technical problem led to panic on the part of the presenter and confusion on the part of the caller and listeners.
Here is an excerpt from the conversation:

Presenter:	*OK, here on the phone, a girl. OK. What's your name?*
Caller:	*I'm Carol.*
Presenter:	*Hello?*
Caller:	*Hello.*
Presenter:	*Hello.*
Caller:	*Hello. Yes?*
Presenter:	*I can hear you.*
Caller:	*I can hear you.*
Presenter:	*Hey?*
Caller:	*Don't you hear me?*
Presenter:	*I can hear you.*
Caller:	*Yes, I'm Carol.*
Presenter:	*Ah, OK. We have some problems here. OK, what's your name first?*
Caller:	*I'm Carol.*
Presenter:	*You're Carol (...)*

In this example the presenter was thrown into confusion at the beginning of the call by a simple technical problem: the fact that he had not put on his headphones and could not hear the caller at first. Their conversation thus only begins on line 5. However, the presenter is still so nervous that he cannot concentrate on what the caller is saying and does not take in her name. Until line 13 radio listeners at home have received no explanation of what is happening, though by line 3 it should have been clear to the presenter that something was amiss and that he should provide some explanation for the listeners. A simulation of such "technical problems" in class might have helped the presenter to deal more competently with the situation.
On the question of encouraging listeners to phone in, we need to do more in future to mobilize potential callers. This can be done by informing local native speakers of English, schools, and particularly other students about the programme. Word of mouth was not effective enough as a medium of information; the local press and the radio station itself

should make announcements and handouts should be distributed, perhaps advertising a competition which listeners can enter by calling into the programme. Last but not least, the studio number should be clearly repeated several times in the programme itself. In our second programme the presenters did not feel willing to deal with phone calls, had prepared material for the whole hour and were intent on presenting all of it. As a result, listeners were given the phone number only once and were not given encouragement to call in. The studio was in effect sealed off from its listeners.

As long as the presenters feel confident to deal with phone calls and the programme has been well publicized to potential callers, the programme should be a success.

4. Feedback from the students by questionnaire

In their answers to a questionnaire students generally responded very positively to the experience of participating in a radio phone-in. They felt very motivated, especially because they had a specific goal to work towards and because they felt personally responsible for the programme:

(a) *We got everything worked out because we had the responsibility - not a teacher...*

(b) *...the participants were interested in making the programme, the motivation was good. That all made talking so effective, you could see the improvements we made.*

(c) *Knowing that one will be on air motivates (participants) to prepare for the sessions.*

The participants who had already spent longer periods of time in English speaking countries generally felt confident in using the language and said that the experience of participating in the making of the programme did not make much difference to their confidence in speaking English. However, in the case of students who had not spent any great length of time in an English speaking environment, the programme was a confidence boost:

(a) *...confidence grew, because one just had to talk in English. Only by talking you get more confident.*

(b) *I never talked as much and as easily in an English course*

5. Using the programmes with students not themselves involved in making them

A common objection to the making of radio programmes with language students is that the activity is elitist as only those students who are involved in the studio benefit from the exercise (Wicke 1991). However, particularly in the case of a phone-in programme, it is possible to involve others who did not themselves take part in the preparation of the programme themselves. Some activities used in the preparation of a phone-in can be integrated into other courses, such as a course we offered on Telephone Skills, and students in other courses can be invited to take part by calling into the programme. Even if students do not phone in themselves, they may still be actively involved as listeners. After the programme itself is over, a recording can be used in lessons with another class, either to analyse mistakes or as a basis for discussion.

6. Conclusion

In conclusion I would like to sketch future prospects in our use of phone-in programmes for foreign language teaching. One future possibility is a link-up between Bayreuth and other Bavarian universities by radio, again with listeners being invited to call in.

Our next concrete project, however, will be to take up an offer from Bavarian radio to make a ninety-minute telephone link-up with Georgetown University, Washington, DC, which will be broadcast on Bavarian radio on November 20th 1993. Our discussion topic will be the idea of multiculturality as seen from opposite sides of the Atlantic.

REFERENCES

Alsop, T.W. (1984). Planning a radio broadcast - an opportunity to increase interest in foreign language courses. *Foreign Language Annals* 17 (3), 191-194.

Bartholomé, P. & Zschachlitz, R. (1988). Radioarbeit im DaF Unterricht in Frankreich. *Info DaF* 15 (3), 324-334.

Basaille, J.-P. (1983). Réaliser/simuler une émission radiophonique. *Le Français dans le Monde* 180, 90-92.

Boulanger, L. & Pavet, J.-R. (1989). France/Pays-Bas: l'Europe en direct. *Le Français dans le Monde* 224, 31-32.

Carlisle, C. (1993). English talk show in Poland: the lighter side of being "on the air". *English Teaching Forum* 31 (2), p. 54.

Jones, L. (1983). *Eight Simulations*. Controller's Book and Participant's Book. Cambridge, Cambridge University Press.

Keil, E. (1991). *Hörerbeteiligung am Radio*. Vom sprachlosen Ich zum eloquenten Du. Bern, Peter Lang.

Leitner, G. (1983). *Gesprächsanalyse und Rundfunkkommunikation*. Die Struktur englischer phone-ins. Hildesheim. Georg Olms.

Murphey, T. (1992). *Music and Song*. Oxford, Oxford University Press.

Schlemminger, G. (1986). Radio selbst machen - in der Fremdsprache! Anregungen und Erfahrungen mit Deutschsendungen auf 'Freien Radios' in Frankreich. *Neusprachliche Mitteilungen aus Wissenschaft und Praxis* 39, 91-94.

Vick, E. & Jung, U.O.H. (1993). You're tuned in to Eszett radio: Phone-In-Sendungen im Fremdsprachenunterricht. *Der fremdsprachliche Unterricht (Englisch)* 27 (4), 46-48.

Wicke, R.E. (1991). Conference Call. Interkulturelles Lernen durch Rundfunkkontakte. *Der fremdsprachliche Unterricht (Englisch)* 25 (4), 39-41.

RADIO NEWS REVISITED: INVESTIGATIONS INTO THE STRUCTURE AND COMPREHENSION OF BBC RADIO NEWS

Gerlinde Hardt-Mautner

Vienna University of Economics and Business Administration

Radio is a traditional teaching medium which lacks both the glamour of TV and the high-tech appeal of computers. Yet it continues to be popular, both inside and outside the classroom. This paper provides a semiotic profile of radio, as a news medium in particular, and reports on an empirical study of the comprehension of BBC radio news. Against this background the use of radio in foreign language teaching is discussed.

1. Introduction

Talking about radio in this day and age is an act of 'revisiting' because radio can now look back on more than 70 years of history. In the meantime, a series of communications revolutions has swept the media landscape in quick succession. Each innovation is more than just an addition, though, but affects those media that are already there. This is precisely why 'revisiting' makes sense. After all, the radio that is competing with satellite television, viewdata systems and the CD player is not the same semiotic and cultural entity as it was in the 1920s.

Section 2 of this paper outlines what I have termed a 'semiotic profile' of radio, and in particular, of radio news. This will comprise, first of all, questions of message content and message structure. Secondly, I shall discuss the use or uses that radio news is put to, as well as its status and social impact; and thirdly, the issue of comprehension will be addressed. How is radio news processed by listeners, and what evidence is there that comprehensibility can or cannot be improved? Lastly, Section 3 finally raises questions related to the use of radio in English language teaching.

2. Semiotic Profile

2.1 Message Structure / Message Content

In the face of multimedia technology, perhaps the most salient characteristic of radio is its restriction to the auditory channel. Radio communication is entirely acoustic and basically one-way. Although phone-in programmes admittedly give listeners a chance to respond to what they have heard, the fact remains that the bulk of radio output is non-interactive.

The question now is what implications does this have for radio discourse, and more specifically, for radio news discourse, if, that is, we apply a comprehensive view of discourse that includes text *production*, the textual *product*, and textual *processing*.

2.1.1 Production

Because all that has to be produced and transmitted is sound, the production process is comparatively straightforward. By modern standards, radio is a low-tech medium. It makes fewer demands on logistics, manpower, finance and script writing than its most obvious rival, television. This makes radio very flexible and very fast; when news breaks, especially in distant and inaccessible locations, radio is likely to be the first medium to carry news on the event straight from the spot.

2.1.2 The Product

For the radio programmes, the restriction to acoustic signals means that not only the messages as such but also the meta-linguistic signposting has to be done acoustically. Stations are identified, programmes introduced and concluded by the spoken word, by music, or by a combination of both (cf. Hardt-Mautner 1991 and Hardt-Mautner 1992a).
News formats vary according to the degree of diversity which they permit in the use of the acoustic mode. The classical news format features only one newsreader reading off a script written by someone else; the news is generally introduced by a time signal and perhaps a gong. Increasingly, this has given way to news which provides more variety, and which at the same time makes the borderline between news and other programmes fuzzier. 'Infotainment' is beginning to make headway in radio, too. On many stations, it has become common practice to use introductory and concluding jingles, which sometimes merge imperceptibly into the preceding or following music programme. Frequently, pre-recorded correspondents' pieces or on-the-spot reportage are inserted into the news. An example of this technique, referred to as 'actuality' in newsmen's jargon, would be the presentation of a report about a demonstration against a background of demonstrators' shouting. By the same token, 'traditional' stories may be livened up by brief extracts from the speech or interview reported in the story. Such inserts not only add variety but also (supposedly) authenticate the story, because the news item then, at least superficially, ceases to be merely a 'story'. It would, however, be naive to assume that 'actuality' really 'authenticates' news reports; after all the mere selection of a certain recorded piece as well as the devices used for embedding it in the surrounding news item carry considerable manipulative potential.

2.1.3 The Listeners' Perspective

Radio confronts listeners with a string of ephemeral sound. Unlike a daily paper, a day's radio output cannot be scanned before deciding what to process in detail. (Of course there are programme listings, but one cannot actually listen to any of the programmes before they have been broadcast.) Skimming and pre-selecting are not possible; nor can one go back and re-process items, unless, of course, one extends the possibilities of the medium proper by making a recording.

One may of course argue that all language is basically linear, but with radio this linearity is compounded. Other monologic genres, such as newspaper discourse, get round this through the written mode; dialogic genres, on the other hand, beat linearity through being interactive. Conversation, for example, is also ephemeral, but although it is not possible to re-read a previous turn, one can at least ask for it to be repeated. Neither of these mechanisms for coping with linearity works with radio. The onus is entirely on the text producers to help listeners with the decoding. As we shall see later on, different radio stations fulfil this task with varying success.

To round off this section, I would like to say a few words about the content of radio news. As in other news genres, items are included or excluded on the basis of their relative newsworthiness. The higher a 'story' scores on a scale of several so-called 'news values', the more likely it is to qualify for inclusion (cf. Galtung & Ruge 1973; Hetherington 1985: 1-21; van Dijk 1988: 119-124). Aspiring journalists acquire an intuitive grasp of these criteria in the course of their professional socialization. This intuition in designating some stories as 'newsworthy' and rejecting others becomes part and parcel of editors' discursive practice and each generation is instrumental in handing it down to the next, which may or may not wish to challenge established conventions. Currently, radio news is still mainly of the 'hard news' type, dealing with the politics of élite people in élite nations, with the economy, with natural disasters, accidents, and so on. There is a tendency, in more popular programmes, to include human interest stories, but a public service broadcaster like the BBC will generally position them at the end of bulletins.

Editors like to cultivate the myth that they report 'the facts, and nothing but the facts'. Radio news is indeed non-evaluative on the surface of discourse, and this is why the myth about objectivity is more difficult to expose than in the case of tabloid newspapers, for example. However, radio, too, as a medium, can offer only mediated reality. Broadcasters carry out this process of mediation according to conventionalized techniques of discourse production. Listeners, in turn, have acquired conventions for decoding. They know what to expect of news and process the texts against the backdrop of these expectations. Both on the encoding and the decoding side, a case can thus be made for the existence of news schemata, in van Dijk's sense (van Dijk 1988). The use of a schema can explain why news stories of similar content also end up with very similar macrostructures. Let me just quote one example from my corpus, two BBC-Radio-4-bulletins of the 12th and the 31st October '89 respectively (see page 106).

Testing recall with informants reveals that listeners resort to inferencing to compensate lapses of memory (Hardt-Mautner 1992, Ch. 3). This inferencing is partly guided by people's knowledge of the world and partly by their knowledge of those recurring patterns of discourse structure.

*BBC Radio 4, 12/10/89	BBC Radio 4, 31/10/89
(1) Later this morning the Chancellor of the Exchequer Mr Nigel Lawson will deliver his speech to the Conservative Party conference.	(1) This afternoon Mr John Major will make his first appearance in the Commons as Chancellor during a debate on the economy.
(2) He's expected to defend the government's handling of the economy.	(2) He's expected to stress that the government's policies will not be altered.
(3) Our financial staff say that both the pound and share prices have rallied a little this morning as a result of optimism over what Mr Lawson might say.	(3) Ahead of the Commons debate the financial markets this morning are quiet.
	(4) The pound is little changed and share prices are up.

2.2 Use and Social Impact

A semiotic profile of a medium would be incomplete if it failed to include information on the social context in which the medium is used. In the early days of radio, so few sets were available that people would gather around one set and listen as a group (McLuhan 1987 [1964]: 306; Pegg 1983: 197). Nowadays many households have several radio sets. In 1987, for example, 77% of radio listeners in the UK said they had more than one set (Gunter & Svennevig 1988: 12). The sets are usually spread around the house so that it is possible to listen in different rooms without having to carry a set around.

Radio is commonly referred to as a *secondary medium* (Crisell 1986: 15-17), which means that listening tends to be an accompanying activity. As the following extract from an interview with a British informant shows, the level of attention may vary considerably, and occasionally listening still is (almost) 'the sole purpose':

> "... usually in the morning I'll be — erm — getting and having breakfast at the same time — er — it might be the sole purpose in an evening though I could well be glancing through the evening pa — newspaper at the same time and — er — it's a kind of background to pick up anything that er — might be interesting. So I'm split — doing two things nearly all the time" (quoted in Hardt-Mautner 1992a: 222).

Listening is often a solitary activity, with radio as a substitute for human company. But it does not have to be. There was one informant, a metal worker, who described the situation in the factory where he worked, where the workers gather for their teabreak and make a

* As anyone with access to the BBC's domestic service will be aware, Radio 4 is a 'serious' station concentrating on the spoken word, with a predominantly middle class, older audience, whereas Radio 1 is a pop-music network aimed primarily at the under 20s. The two stations have different news formats which fit the style of their programmes.

point of listening to the news bulletin that comes on at the time of their break; everybody is shushed and has to listen. (Actually, this is one scenario which comes pretty close to the original group listening referred to above.)

Given the massive competition from television, it is quite surprising that radio is obviously holding its own so well. According to UK figures published in Gunter & Svennevig (1988: 22), 45% of radio listeners said they listened for more than two hours per day. Under deregulation, new stations proliferate, posing a major competitive threat to the established public service broadcasters.

Yet the social impact of radio has clearly diminished. Figures compiled by the IBA show that it is television not radio which is people's preferred source of world news (Gunter & Svennevig 1988: 38). Radio has a reputation for being more objective than television, but this does not prevent people from considering TV their main source of news. It might be argued, on a somewhat speculative note, that this is entirely in keeping with the growing visualization of culture. The moving image simply carries the day.

The question now is, what do people make of what they hear? In particular, how much of the news do they process? This brings me to issues of comprehension, to be considered in the following section.

2.3 Comprehension

In this section, I shall briefly summarise an empirical study investigating the comprehension of BBC radio news by native speakers of British English.* The tests involved two different news bulletins, one from BBC Radio 4 and one from Radio 1. These were played to over four hundred subjects, of varying social backgrounds, who were then asked to write a summary of each bulletin in free recall. For practical reasons, the tests were carried out in schools, with 16- to 18-year-olds. There was a second group of informants, however, namely 23 older subjects who were interviewed on their listening habits, language attitudes, etc., and who also did the tests.

The data thus gathered were analysed both quantitatively (with the help of computer-aided statistical procedures) and qualitatively. The quantitative analysis involved (i) counting the length of the summary of each news item, and (ii) the number of 'keywords' recalled (with a list of previously drawn up keywords functioning as a yardstick). In the qualitative analysis the summaries were scrutinized for evidence of text processing strategies as outlined by van Dijk (1980).

The quantitative results may be summarized as follows:

(1) Noticeable differences emerged in the amount and the nature of text processing by

* The study has been published as Hardt-Mautner (1992a). A summary in English is given in Hardt-Mautner (1992b).

various groups of subjects. These differences were not idiosyncratic, but were related to the social and socio-psychological characteristics of the recipients.

(2) The most decisive extralinguistic factors to influence comprehension were gender and school type (mainly Grammar Schools vs. Comprehensives) in the case of the written tests, and gender and social class in the case of the oral tests.

(3) In general, informants understood Radio 1 better than Radio 4. There were older informants, however, who were irritated by Radio 1's presentation style, and this seemed to have a negative effect on the immediate retrieval from memory. However, a few prompts usually sufficed to jog the interviewees' memory so that eventually they would again remember more of Radio 1 than of Radio 4.

(4) Female subjects generally coped better with Radio 1 than with Radio 4 news. In the oral comprehension tests, the poorest results were achieved by the non-graduate female subjects, many of whom were clearly insecure and betrayed a lack of background knowledge about current political and economic developments — unlike their male counterparts, who were often self-confident, talkative and well-informed politically.

(5) For both the Radio 1 and the Radio 4 bulletins, Grammar School pupils' recall rates were higher than those of Comprehensive School pupils. However, the difference between the two school types was much greater with Radio 4 than with Radio 1. The Radio 1 news format thus helped to narrow the gap between those who did well and those who produced poor results.

In sum, the BBC's policy of integrating news into different networks can be said to positively affect comprehension.

3. Radio News in (E)LT

Against the background of the 'semiotic profile' sketched in Section 2, I shall now take a brief look at radio from a language teaching perspective.

(1) The continued popularity of radio is clearly a justification for continuing to use it in the classroom, too, especially in conjunction with other media.

(2) For classroom applications, the low level of technical sophistication of radio means two things. Firstly, no complicated and cumbersome machinery and no intricate logistics are needed. It is cheap and easy to integrate into classroom work spontaneously — much more so than video (not to mention computers). Secondly, a live radio bulletin will invariably be more up-to-date than that day's paper or than the TV news recorded the night before. This competitive advantage in terms of topicality is likely to be appreciated by students.

(3) Two points that are probably not in its favour as a teaching medium are these: the strict linearity of radio discourse and its restriction to the acoustic channel. Here care must clearly be taken not to make demands of learners that even native speakers find difficult to

meet. Playing and re-playing tape-recordings is the obvious answer here; on the other hand, it is important that learners should get used to fast and efficient on-line processing, because this is precisely one of the language skills they will be expected to master later on.

(4) My next point relates to the critical appraisal of radio, and particularly of radio news, as pieces of culture-bound discourse. In spite of the so-called 'communicative revolution' in language teaching a great deal of it is still immensely system-centred and behaves as if text linguistics, discourse analysis and critical linguistics had never happened. Moreover, classical cultural studies, or what is referred to as 'Landeskunde', is often little more than the trite, supposedly 'factual' description of the geography, politics and institutions of the country concerned. As Martin Montgomery observed in a talk he gave in Vienna recently, the study of media language provides an opportunity to marry the two traditions: that of the type of classical cultural studies just described and that of a more critical approach which takes account of the pivotal role that language plays in building and maintaining social relations. If we agree that students should learn to appreciate the full communicative impact of language then why should we forever talk only about polite requests, apologies, and friendly greetings? One does not have to adhere to a 'conspiracy theory' to acknowledge that language has manipulative potential, and that some groups of society have more means at their disposal to exploit this potential than others. Media language is an obvious case in point, and I think it would be a great challenge to make students aware that even such innocuous-looking texts as radio news bulletins may be as ideologically loaded as newspaper articles, for example.

(5) Finally a few remarks about comprehension. One of the assets of radio news as language input is that it is presented in studio quality (i.e. without distracting background noises). Also, it is an entirely natural occurrence of standard pronunciation, and teachers need not worry about the mismatch, so common in many recordings of textbook dialogues, of social situation, stylistic register and pronunciation.*

On the other hand, the comprehension problems encountered by native speakers are likely to be compounded for non-native speakers. Even with native-speaker informants it is obvious that knowledge about political and economic matters is a crucial factor affecting the processing of news texts. Unless a listener can fit the information into an already existing cognitive structure it remains meaningless, which is why the educated middle class generally does much better. Depending on the kind of foreign language news one uses ('domestic' or 'international'), there may be greater or lesser comprehension problems related to learners' deficiencies in the relevant background knowledge. Working with young people we may also face the problem that they are not very interested in current affairs at

* In parts of the world where special news aimed at non-native speakers is available (e.g. Voice of America Special News Reports or the BBC's Slow News), teachers obviously need to decide when and how to help their students master the transition from slow and simplified news to "the real thing".

all, in whatever language, and that not all faults in text processing are due to strictly linguistic factors. Apart from the usual preparation to listening, activities involving radio news thus call for a thorough exploration of the respective current affairs background.

4. Conclusion

By way of conclusion, let me once again adopt a wider purview. The media scene is expanding so rapidly that there is a persistent danger of educators jumping on the bandwagon before they know where it is heading. Media cannot be used effectively and responsibly in teaching unless their social and cognitive impact has been assessed critically. For each new medium that arrives on the scene we need the kind of semiotic profile that I have sketched for radio — and of course, in the case of a new medium many of the observations would not seem as self-evident as they perhaps do with radio. Preferably that critical assessment of the potential and the limitations of new media should also be done by the very people who are at the forefront of the technological innovation process, such as software specialists, for example, rather than only by 'professional' critics such as philosophers, anthropologists or linguists.

The use of technology invariably changes human communication. That, in itself, is not a bad thing. But unless we are prepared to dig a bit deeper we do not have even a fighting chance of making sure that these changes are not all changes for the worse.

REFERENCES

Chrisell, A. (1986). *Understanding radio*. London/New York, Methuen.

Galtung, J. & Ruge, M. (1973). Structuring and selecting news. In: Cohen, S. & Young, J. (ed.). *The manufacture of news*. Deviance, social problems and the mass media. London, Constable, pp. 62-72.

Gunter, B. & Svennevig, M. (1988). *Attitudes to broadcasting over the years*. London, John Libbey.

Hardt-Mautner, G. (1991). Look with thine ears: A reappraisal of radio as a teaching medium. *CALL Austria* 15 (Sondernummer, Oktober 1991), 49-60.

Hardt-Mautner, G. (1992a). *Making sense of the news: Eine kontrastiv-soziolinguistische Studie zur Verständlichkeit von Hörfunknachrichten*. Frankfurt a. M., Peter Lang.

Hardt-Mautner, G. (1992b). Absorbing news? Investigating the production and comprehension of radio news from a sociolinguistic and contrastive point of view. In: Mair, C., Markus, M. & Wallmannsberger, J. (eds.). *New departures in contrastive linguistics*. (= Innsbrucker Beiträge zur Kulturwissenschaft, Anglistische Reihe Band 5). Innsbruck, Vol 2, pp. 33-41.

Hetherington, A. (1985). *News, newspapers and television*. London/Basingstoke, Macmillan.

McLuhan, M. (1987 [1964]). *Understanding media*. London and New York, Ark Paperbacks.

Pegg, M. (1983). *Broadcasting and society. 1918 - 1939*. London and Canberra, Croom Helm.

van Dijk, Teun A. (1980). *Textwissenschaft*. Eine interdisziplinäre Einführung. Tübingen, Niemeyer.

van Dijk, Teun A. (1988). *News as discourse*. Hillsdale, NJ, Lawrence Erlbaum Associates.

ENTWICKLUNG VON RADIOSPRACHKURSEN FÜR DEUTSCH ALS FREMDSPRACHE

Hubert Eichheim

Goethe-Institut München

Between 1988 and 1994 the *Goethe-Institute*, *InterNationes*, *Deutsche Welle* and *Deutschlandfunk* cooperated to produce a new radio language course called "Deutsch - warum nicht?". It consists of a total of 104 fifteen-minute broadcasts divided into 4 series and will be aired in 35 different language versions. Each of the language versions is supported by an accompanying textbook. When the first series was broadcast in 1991 about one hundred and five thousand of these textbooks were mailed to listeners around the world. Despite such encouraging demand the authors of "Deutsch - warum nicht?" know only very little about their listeners' learning profiles. For this reason, research projects have been set up in Indonesia, Poland and Turkey to find out about the listeners' modes of learning and the degree to which the teaching modules have been successful. In addition to this, experiments are being made in a number of countries in connection with broadcasts from local stations. These are supported by contact phases to overcome listener isolation. The paper deals with the planning, development and evaluation of the radio course.

1. Bedarfslage

Fremdsprachenkurse im Radio sind keineswegs eine der großen medialen Neuerungen. Die ersten dieser Art wurden schon bald nach dem Krieg in Deutschland ausgestrahlt, um dem großen Bedarf nach Englisch gerecht zu werden. Und dann wurden auch die ersten Schallplattenkurse über Hausierer vertrieben. Deutsch als Fremdsprache tauchte erst spät auf diesem Markt auf. Es hatte ja auch niemand Lust, in den Jahren nach dem Krieg die Sprache zu lernen, mit der die große Vernichtung verkündet worden war. Der Kalte Krieg ließ jedoch bald die Wunden vergessen und richtete das Augenmerk der Menschen auf den Ost-West-Konflikt. Das Radio konnte Botschaften weit in das gegnerische Gebiet hinein unzensiert über Kurzwellensender verbreiten. Dieser Aufgabe haben sich zahlreiche Sender wie BBC, Radio Free Europe, RIAS, Sender Freies Berlin, Deutschlandfunk und Deutsche Welle angenommen. Als das Goethe-Institut Mitte der sechziger Jahre den Bedarf an Deutschkenntnissen weltweit im Steigen sah, lag es nahe, sich eines weitverbeiteten Mediums zu bedienen. So entstand eine Arbeitsgemeinschaft aus Deutscher Welle, Deutschlandfunk, Inter Nationes und Goethe-Institut. Das Goethe-Institut verantwortet das pädagogische Konzept und besorgt das Manuskript, die Deutsche Welle produziert die Sendungen, Inter Nationes betreibt die Herstellung des Begleitbuchs, und die Sendeanstalten strahlen den Kurs über ihre Kurzwellensender aus; der Deutschlandfunk für die europäischen Länder, die Deutsche Welle für die übrige Welt. Die Finanzierung geschieht durch das Auswärtige Amt.

Der hier vorgestellte Radiosprachkurs "Deutsch-warum nicht?" von Herrad Meese ist die

dritte Produktion dieser Arbeitsgemeinschaft. Er besteht aus vier Serien von je 26 Sendefolgen zu 15 Minuten. Dazu gibt es ein Begleitbuch und eine Tonkassette mit den deutschen Texten.
Der Erklärteil jeder Sendung ist in die Ausgangssprache übersetzt. Der Kurs wird nach Fertigstellung in 35 Fassungen von Albanisch bis Urdu vorliegen und ausgestrahlt werden.

2. Aufbau der Sendefolgen und des Begleitbuchs

Bei allen Alleinlernmaterialien ist die gleichmäßige Steuerung des Lerners von großer Bedeutung. Der Lerner muß einen festen formalen und, wenn man will, rituellen Rahmen vorfinden, der immer gleich ist. Darin findet er sich sofort zurecht und erhält Sicherheit für die Planung seines Lernprozesses. Nach diesem Prinzip sind Sendefolgen und Begleitbuch aufgebaut.
Jede *Sendefolge* beginnt mit einer Einführung. Dann folgt eine kurze Wiederholung der wichtigsten Elemente der vorangegangenen Sendung. Vor der Einführung des neuen Textes wird kurz auf das empfohlene Lernverfahren aufmerksam gemacht, das jeweils von der Textsorte oder der angestrebten sprachlichen Fertigkeit abhängig ist. Der neue Text (meist ist es ein Dialog) wird in zwei Teilen dargeboten, gefolgt von einer Erklärphase, in der jede Äußerung semantisiert wird. Anschließend kommt eine knappe Darstellung und Erklärung eines morphosyntaktischen Phänomens. Zum Schluß wird der gesamte Text mit unterlegter "suggestopädischer" Musik wiederholt. Dem Lerner wird dabei empfohlen, sich den Text noch einmal entspannt anzuhören und sich dem Klang der Musik und der Sprache hinzugeben, ohne sich dem Zwang des Verstehenmüssens auszusetzen.
Wegen der 35 verschiedenen Sprachfassungen, der damit verbundenen hohen Entwicklungs- und Druckkosten ist das *Begleitbuch* außerordentlich spartanisch ausgestattet. In jeder Lektion wird zunächst eine Darstellung der Grammatik oder anderer Lern-, bzw. Handlungsziele gegeben, dann folgt der Lektionstext auf Deutsch mit einer anschließenden Auflistung der Wörter und Wendungen in beiden Sprachen. Am Ende stehen jeweils 3 bis 6 Übungen der herkömmlichen Art. Außerdem enthält das Begleitbuch einige wichtige landeskundliche Informationen (Landkarten, Abbildungen von Geldscheinen etc.), ein zweisprachiges Wörterverzeichnis, die Texte und Dialoge in Übersetzung sowie einen Lösungsschlüssel für die Übungen.

3. Voraussetzungen

Der Arbeitsgemeinschaft war von vornhinein bewußt, daß ein für die ganze Welt konzipierter Sprachkurs auf bestimmte Ansprüche, wie sie für autonomes Lernen bestehen, verzichten muß, daß darüber hinaus das Medium Radio weitere Einschränkungen verlangt. Aus früheren Hörerbefragungen wußte man wenigstens, daß der durchschnittliche Hörer-Lerner

(a) ein junger Erwachsener ist,
(b) über einen akademischen Hintergrund verfügt,
(c) bereits eine Fremdsprache gelernt hat,
(d) bisher kein oder nur wenig Deutsch gelernt hat.

In einem Werkgespräch im Jahr 1988 wurden die Grundprinzipien für den neuen Kurs aufgrund der Erfahrungen mit den Vorläufern festgelegt. Der Kurs sollte

(a) Strategien für eigenständiges Lernen vermitteln;
(b) den Schwerpunkt auf die Fertigkeit Hörverstehen legen;
(c) trotzdem auch die produktiven Fertigkeiten (Sprechen, Schreiben) nicht ganz vernachlässigen;
(d) einen sehr eingeschränkten Wortschatz von nicht mehr als 400 lexikalischen Einheiten pro Serie vermitteln;
(e) eine sehr flache Progression im formalen Bereich verfolgen;
(f) breit gestreute Informationen zur Landeskunde, Geschichte und Literatur liefern;
(g) unterschiedliche Textsorten in teils authentischen Texten anbieten;
(h) Elemente der Suggestopädie verwenden, soweit es das Medium Radio zuläßt.

4. Vom Handlungsgerüst bis zur fertigen Sendung

Aufgrund dieser Vorgaben lag es nahe, die einzelnen Lektionen nach einem inhaltlichen Gliederungsprinzip zu gestalten, d.h. jede einem anderen Thema oder Teilaspekt eines Themas zu widmen ohne eine verbindende Geschichte. Doch zeigte sich bald, daß das Fehlen eines Handlungsstranges und der diesen tragenden Personen ein erhebliches Kohärenzproblem aufgeworfen hätte. Die Zusammenhänge hätten erst durch umständliche Erklärungen oder ergänzende Informationen geliefert werden müssen, was den zeitlichen Rahmen der Sendung und den räumlichen im Begleitbuch gesprengt hätte. So wurde wie schon in den früheren Radiosprachkursen für Deutsch als Fremdsprache ein Handlungsgerüst errichtet, das mit fünf Personen ausgestattet wurde, die alle 104 Sendungen hindurch auftreten und die Stichwörter für die landeskundlichen Informationen und unterschiedlichen Texte (Dialoge, Briefe, Ansagen, Gedichte, Lieder etc.) liefern, bzw. sie selbst sprechen.
Die Entwicklung eines Radiosprachkurses in diesem Umfang stellt alle Beteiligten vor außerordentliche Schwierigkeiten:

(1) Die Suche nach den Autoren gestaltet sich besonders schwierig, da von ihnen nicht nur didaktische und auch eine gewisse literarische Kompetenz verlangt wird, sondern auch noch eine Professionalität in der Arbeitsdisziplin. Sie müssen über vier Jahre

hinweg alle zwei Wochen ein sendereifes Manuskript mit der entsprechenden Lektion für das Begleitbuch liefern.

(2) Gleichzeitig müssen die Bearbeitungen der Erklärtexte in 35 Sprachen erfolgen.

(3) Zwischen den vier Partnern muß eine ständige Abstimmung stattfinden, die zu Kompromissen führt, die aber der Attraktivität der Sendungen keinen Abbruch tun dürfen.

(4) Die Fertigstellung der Sendung (Aufnahme, Tonmischung) wird erschwert durch die Berücksichtigung der Empfangsbedingungen. Die Störungen bei Kurzwellenempfang erlauben es nicht, die Szenen als Hörspiel zu inszenieren; Hintergrundgeräusche und Überblendungen sind nur in sehr geringer Dosierung möglich. Und gerade diese wären notwendig, um die Dekodierung der Texte zu erleichtern.

5. Ausstrahlung und Betreuung der Hörer

Nach Fertigstellung einer Serie wird der Sprachkurs in das Programm aufgenommen. Die Hörer werden durch Informationsblätter über die Sendezeit und die Möglichkeit, das Begleitbuch kostenlos zu beziehen, informiert. Von August 1991, als die Serie 1 erstmals ausgestrahlt wurde, bis Ende 1992 wurden von der Deutschen Welle 67 154 und vom Deutschlandfunk 37 760 Begleitbücher versendet.

6. Evaluierung

Trotz des scheinbaren Erfolgs ist den Produzenten nicht bekannt, inwieweit damit Deutsch gelernt wird. Obwohl fast jeder Besteller des Begleitbuchs eine Karte oder einen Brief an die Sendeanstalten schreibt, erfährt man daraus nur selten etwas über die Lernmotivation und den tatsächlichen Bedarf.

Einer Hörerbefragung haben wir folgende Informationen zu verdanken:

(1) Etwa 60% aller Hörer-Lerner, die den Fragebogen zurückgesendet haben, sind Nullanfänger.
Wir wissen aber nicht, ob sie das Tempo der Ausstrahlung in ihrem Lernprozeß mithalten konnten.

(2) Etwa 40% der Hörer-Lerner verfügten schon über Deutschkenntnisse.
Wir wissen aber nichts über Quantität und Qualität dieser Kenntnisse.

(3) 47% der Hörer-Lerner lernen Deutsch aus reinem Vergnügen.
Wir wissen aber nicht, wann das Vergnügen erschöpft ist.

(4) 38% der Hörer-Lerner beabsichtigen eine Reise nach Deutschland, und 26 % lernen Deutsch aus Gründen, die mit ihrer beruflichen Laufbahn zu tun haben.
Wir wissen aber nicht, ob ihre Vorstellungen realistisch sind und ob ihnen tatsächlich durch den Kurs Hilfe zuteil wird.

(5) Nur 42% der Hörer-Lerner hören regelmäßig die Sendungen.
Wir wissen aber nicht, ob sie auch die Folgeserie verfolgen.

(6) 69% lernen die Wörter auswendig.
Wir wissen aber nicht, ob sie sie im Gedächtnis behalten, ob sie sie innerhalb eines Textes wiedererkennen und ob sie sie angemessen verwenden können.

Angesichts der zahlreichen offenen Fragen hat sich die Arbeitsgemeinschaft entschlossen, ein Forschungsprojekt durchzuführen, die fehlenden Daten zu Lernverhalten und Lernerfolg zu erheben und daraus Schlüsse zu ziehen für den weiteren Einsatz des vorliegenden Sprachkurses die Entwicklung neuer Projekte dieser Art. Mit dem Forschungsprojekt wurden zwei Gruppen beauftragt, von denen die eine sich mehr des Marketings und des Vertriebs, die andere der didaktischen Seite annimmt. In einem Vorprojekt wird eine Schwachstellenanalyse in Indonesien, Polen und der Türkei durchgeführt, um zu erfahren, wo es sich lohnt, weiteren Fragestellungen nachzugehen. Dabei werden Interviews mit Lernern verschiedenen Profils und Vertretern von Institutionen, die sich mit Fremdsprachenunterricht befassen, gemacht. Auch wird die Frage untersucht, in welcher Weise das Material nach der ersten Ausstrahlung konfektioniert und vertrieben werden muß, um eine breitere Lernerschicht und größere Effizienz zu erreichen. Am Ende des Vorprojekts werden die Forschungsziele des Hauptprojekts formuliert und ein detaillierter Projektplan entwickelt.

7. Anschlußprojekte

Während der Entwicklung von "Deutsch-warum nicht?", die Ende 1988 einsetzte und erst Mitte 1994 abgeschlossen sein wird, mußte durch die politischen Ereignisse und die technologische Entwicklung immer wieder das ursprüngliche Konzept verändert werden. Durch verbesserte Satellitentechnik und durch das Entstehen von unzähligen kleinen Radiosendern in fast allen Ländern der Welt, ergab sich die Notwendigkeit, von dem Prinzip der zentralen Ausstrahlung abzugehen und den Kurs kleineren Anbietern zu überlassen. In Brasilien und Griechenland finden die ersten Versuche mit lokaler Ausstrahlung und Betreuung der Lerner in Kontaktphasen statt. Darüber hinaus werden nach Abschluß der Produktion aus dem Material Lernpakete zur individuellen Nutzung in Lernerzentren oder für die häusliche Arbeit zusammengestellt. Diese sollen individuelles Lernen ermöglichen unter Verwendung neuester Technologie wie Computer, CD-Rom, Hypertechnik und Multimedia.

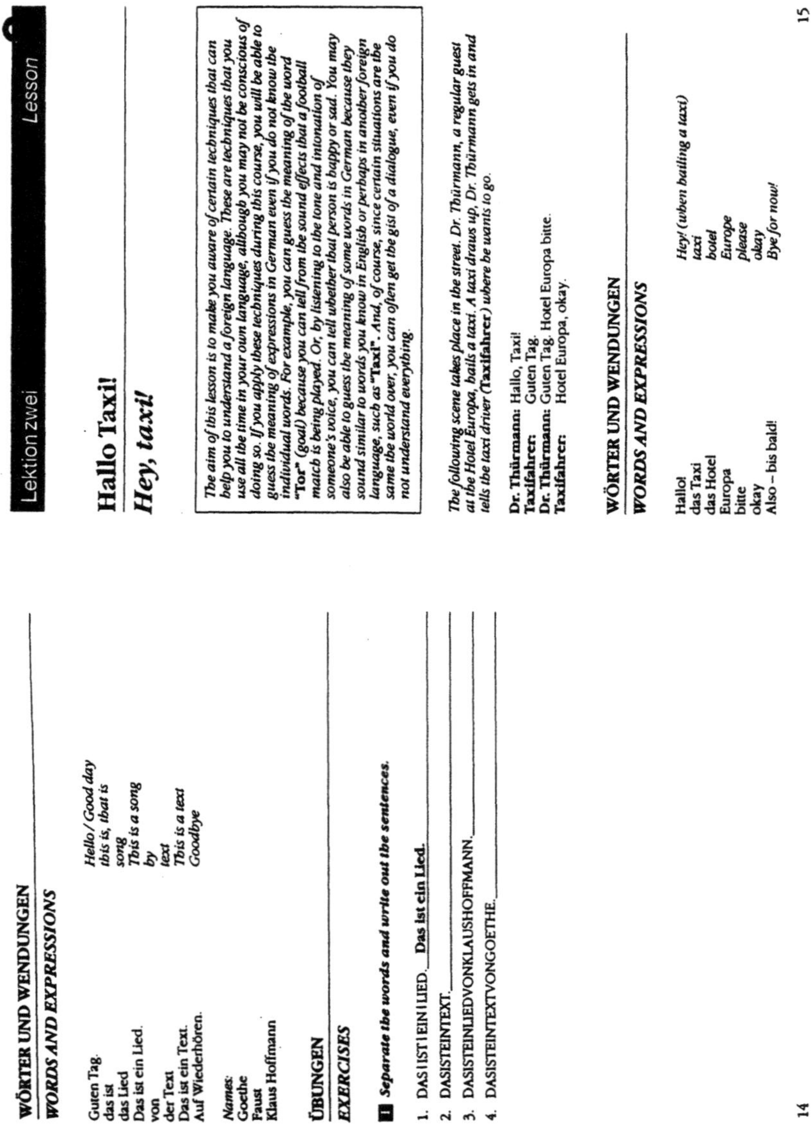

Lektion zwei — Lesson

Hallo Taxi!

Hey, taxi!

The aim of this lesson is to make you aware of certain techniques that can help you to understand a foreign language. These are techniques that you use all the time in your own language, although you may not be conscious of doing so. If you apply these techniques during this course, you will be able to guess the meaning of expressions in German even if you do not know the individual words. For example, you can guess the meaning of the word **"Tor"** *(goal) because you can tell from the sound effects that a football match is being played. Or, by listening to the tone and intonation of someone's voice, you can tell whether that person is happy or sad. You may also be able to guess the meaning of some words in German because they sound similar to words you know in English or perhaps in another foreign language, such as* **"Taxi"**. *And, of course, since certain situations are the same the world over, you can often get the gist of a dialogue, even if you do not understand everything.*

The following scene takes place in the street. Dr. Thürmann, a regular guest at the Hotel Europa, hails a taxi. A taxi draws up, Dr. Thürmann gets in and tells the taxi driver **(Taxifahrer)** *where he wants to go.*

Dr. Thürmann: Hallo, Taxi!
Taxifahrer: Guten Tag.
Dr. Thürmann: Guten Tag. Hotel Europa bitte.
Taxifahrer: Hotel Europa, okay.

WÖRTER UND WENDUNGEN

WORDS AND EXPRESSIONS

Hallo!	*Hey! (when hailing a taxi)*
das Taxi	*taxi*
das Hotel	*hotel*
Europa	*Europe*
bitte	*please*
okay	*okay*
Also – bis bald!	*Bye for now!*

15

WÖRTER UND WENDUNGEN

WORDS AND EXPRESSIONS

Guten Tag.	*Hello / Good day*
das ist	*this is, that is*
das Lied	*song*
Das ist ein Lied.	*This is a song*
von	*by*
der Text	*text*
Das ist ein Text.	*This is a text*
Auf Wiederhören.	*Goodbye*

Names:
Goethe
Faust
Klaus Hoffmann

ÜBUNGEN

EXERCISES

1 ***Separate the words and write out the sentences.***

1. DAS I IST I EIN I LIED. **Das ist ein Lied.**
2. DASISTEINTEXT. ____
3. DASISTEINLIEDVONKLAUSHOFFMANN. ____
4. DASISTEINTEXTVONGOETHE. ____

14

Abbildung von zwei Seiten des Begleitbuchs aus der Lektion 2 der Serie 1. Hier wird die starke Betonung der rezeptiven Fertigkeiten innerhalb des Radiosprachkurses deutlich. Der

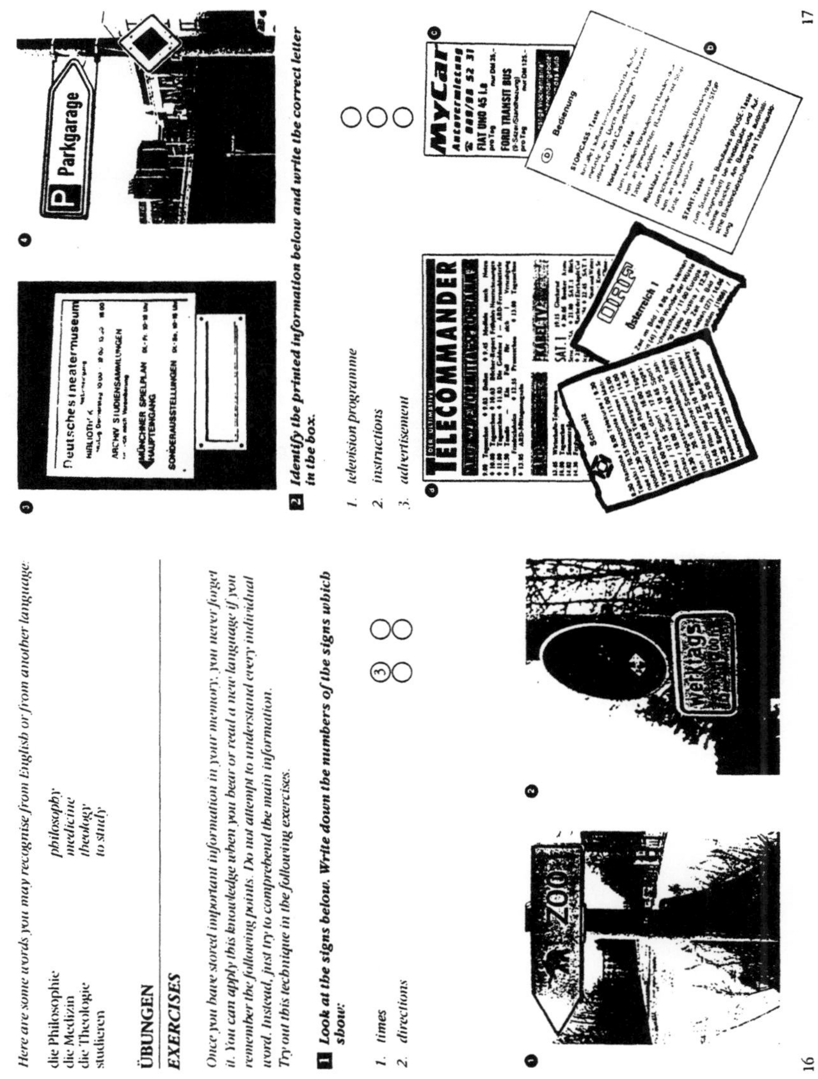

Here are some words you may recognise from English or from another language:

die Philosophie	*philosophy*
die Medizin	*medicine*
die Theologie	*theology*
studieren	*to study*

ÜBUNGEN

EXERCISES

Once you have stored important information in your memory, you never forget it. You can apply this knowledge when you hear or read a new language if you remember the following points. Do not attempt to understand every individual word. Instead, just try to comprehend the main information. Try out this technique in the following exercises.

1 Look at the signs below. Write down the numbers of the signs which show:

1. *times* (3)
2. *directions*

2 Identify the printed information below and write the correct letter in the box.

1. *television programme*
2. *instructions*
3. *advertisement*

16 17

Lerner wird mit unerwarteten Texten (in diesem Fall mit einer Stelle aus Goethes Faust) konfrontiert und erhält gleichzeitig Hilfen, wie er damit umgehen kann.

Herrad Meese: Radiosprachkurs Serie III 1
Lektion fünf: Ich verteile mal die Getränke
endg. Fass. Juni 1992 [220 16]

Erkennungsmelodie

Moderator
Liebe Hörerinnen und Hörer!
Heute hören Sie die fünfte Lektion aus Serie III. Die Lektion hat den Titel:'Ich verteile mal die Getränke' - Ich verteile mal die Getränke.
In der letzten Sendung haben Sie gehört,wie ein Ehepaar nach Aachen gekommen ist.Hören Sie noch einmal, wie sich das Ehepaar am Informationszentrum nach einem Stadtplan erkundigt. Achten Sie bitte auf die Artikel -wie der, die,das und ein.

Angestellte
Guten Tag. Kann ich Ihnen helfen?
Herr Frisch
Ja,gern. Haben Sie wohl einen Stadtplan?
Angestellte
Ja,sicher. Sehen Sie:Hier ist der Hauptbahnhof. Da sind Sie jetzt. Das hier ist die Innenstadt. Haben Sie denn schon ein Hotel?
Frau Frisch
Ja, das Hotel Europa.

Moderator
Heute ist ein besonderer Tag: Andreas feiert seinen Geburtstag. Und - wie es in Deutschland üblich ist- hat er dazu ein paar Freunde zu sich nach Hause eingeladen.
Hören Sie nun den ersten Teil der Geburtstagsparty:Die Freunde gratu-

Manuskriptseite, wie sie von der Autorin an die Rundfunkanstalt geliefert wird. Die linke Seite stellt den deutschen Text dar, der in der jeweiligen Lektion Lernstoff ist. Auf der rechten Seite werden die Erklärungen gegeben. Dieser Text wird von ausländischen Mitarbeitern der Deutschen Welle in 35 Sprachen übertragen.

RESOLVING INHERENT CONFLICTS: AUTONOMOUS LANGUAGE LEARNING FROM POPULAR BROADCAST TELEVISION

Robert Vanderplank
Heriot-Watt University, Edinburgh

The autonomous language learner might consider that the television documentary is potentially a rich and powerful resource for both language and content learning. However, while difficulties arising from linguistic inaccesibility may be resolved through the addition of closed captions/teletext subtitles, difficulties arising from the programme structure and from the intentions and goals of programme producers are more problematical and call for resolution at an affective level. The autonomous learner needs not only conscious and reflective control over the dynamic stream of speech which closed captions/teletext subtitles help to provide, but also a specifically educational orientation to viewing which may be assisted by active tutoring, task setting and an integration of activities using different media.

1. Introduction

Television and video have traditionally either been neglected in the literature of applied linguistics or have been regarded as being a teacher resource for presentation and stimulation. The mainstream view for over thirty years has seen television as primarily a visual medium with largely negative effects on learner-viewers unless there is substantial teacher mediation (Duke 1980; McGovern 1983; Lonergan 1984; Cooper et al. 1991). However, evidence from fields such as educational psychology (Salomon 1979; Salomon & Leigh 1984), adult and continuing education (Gallagher 1978; Bates 1980, 1984), and media and communication studies (Robinson & Levy 1986; Katz & Liebes 1986; Hart 1988), as well as from applied linguistics (Vanderplank 1990), suggests that problems associated with content learning are quite separate and different from problems associated with language learning from television. Difficulties for learners arising from the inaccessibility of the language spoken on television lie largely within the cognitive domain of learning and may be resolved through technological solutions such as closed captions / teletext subtitles, which are now widely available on English language broadcast television and on videotaped films. Difficulties arising from the intentions and methods of programme makers, however, are largely affective in nature and more difficult to resolve.

In this paper, I want to focus on the problems encountered by autonomous learners in self-access and home environments in using popular scientific documentary programmes as resources for language learning, and describe how the very structure of such programmes may contribute to the difficulties experienced by learners. The autonomous learner might naturally consider that the popular scientific documentary is a rich resource for learning both language and content, and for developing such skills as listening and note-taking, and reading rapidly in English. Evidence from studies carried out in Britain and Denmark confirms this (Vanderplank 1992). However, analysis of the discourse and structure of several documentary programmes indicated that the language and content was structured within a framework of expressive language and images, much of which would be characterised as belonging to the affective domain of learning: raising awareness, expressing values, integrating values into current systems of beliefs, ideas and attitudes (Kratwohl et al. 1964). Programme producers seek not only to impart information, but also to achieve acceptance and integration of their information within our value system. Not surprisingly, the goal appears to induce a mental set towards viewing (an authentic native speaker response) rather than towards language learning (the desired response of the autonomous language learner).

2. Four axioms

I strongly recommend that readers who have not seen a programme with closed captions /teletext subtitles should try to see one before reading any further. These "same language" subtitles are intended as an aid to viewing for the deaf and hearing-impaired. They are available as an optional adjunct via the teletext system in Britain and many European countries and via the dedicated closed-caption system in North America. Closed captions / teletext subtitles provide a near-verbatim text of the spoken discourse as it is spoken and their value to language learners has been reported widely in language learning literature (Price 1983; Bean & Wilson 1989; Neuman & Koskinen 1990; Vanderplank 1988, 1990, 1993).

I have worked with teletext subtitles for a number of years and have set out below what I believe to be the four axioms of the value of teletext subtitles (and closed captions) for language learning:

(1) Teletext subtitles transform general output programmes such as documentaries and situation comedies into a rich language resource for learners.

(2) Teletext subtitles redress the balance of visual and verbal elements in a television programme.

(3) Teletext subtitles have a liberating effect on both teachers and learners in terms of choice, control and responsibility.

(4) Teletext subtitles enable learners to watch programmes in a native- speaker-like way.

3. The Inherent Conflict and the Educational Challenge

It is the fourth axiom which is in many respects the most controversial and most problematical and which forms the main theme in this paper. Once we solve the problems of inaccessibility caused to learners by the rich, dynamic and complex spoken language of television, we are faced with the same problems as those faced by all who hope to exploit the educational potential of television. If autonomous language learning viewers can laugh in the right places and for the right reasons, and can understand and appreciate the language of sophisticated documentary programmes, then we must ask ourselves the same questions as those educationalists who seek to use television for native-speaker education and learning.

The key problem for those of us interested in the challenge of using popular television programmes for educational purposes is that TV is universal - illiterates can watch it. It can be watched and enjoyed with a very low level of mental effort, it can appeal just to emotions and sentimentality. In this respect, it is quite unlike print which requires a far higher level of decoding skill to begin with, that is, it requires a cognitive effort using cognitive skills (Salomon & Leigh, 1984).

For television and language learning, the factors we need to understand if we are to meet the educational challenge are:

(a) How TV programmes and the messages they convey are structured.
(b) What language and messages language learners are receiving.
(c) How we can encourage learners to watch programmes not just for information and interest but also for language development and learning.
(d) How we can maximise intentional language learning in addition to incidental learning.

4. Cognitive and Affective Objectives in Two Documentaries

How can we meet the educational challenge and resolve the inherent conflict between an orientation to TV viewing and an orientation to language learning? One method is by looking carefully at the language and structure of two TV science documentaries and at what objectives they serve. These two documentaries were shown on normal broadcast TV in the UK as part of the "Horizon" series, not as part of any educational programme or course.

4.1 Documentary 1. "The Battle of the Merozoites"

The theme of this programme is that Dr Patarroyo, a Colombian chemist and researcher, claims to have developed a vaccine against malaria. Parts of the transcript of the programme are given in the Appendix.

A fairly standard set of questions to orientate a class of language learners in the first few minutes of the programme might be:

"As you watch, I should like you to note words and phrases for talking about malaria, and be ready to answer these questions:

(1) What is malaria?
(2) How is it caused?
(3) Why are preventative measures ineffective?"

In fact, these questions could probably have been answered by most learners without watching the programme, even if they lacked the precise terminology, which, of course, the programme provided (see Transcript 1). The average autonomous learner would almost certainly have turned on the programme with the answers to these questions as "given" knowledge, that is, the general background knowledge that the viewer brings to a programme.

4.2 Cognitive objectives

Those of us who know and use documentaries with teletext subtitles know that they are a rich and powerful resource for learning both language and content in a wide range of subject areas. For the most part, I would argue, we tend to think of documentaries as being factual and informative. In using documentaries, we seek to teach and encourage our learners to learn cognitive skills and to achieve cognitive objectives:

Cognitive Objectives

1. Recall and recognition of knowledge
2. Comprehension of knowledge
3. Skill in application of knowledge comprehended
4. Skill in analysis of situations involving this knowledge; skill in synthesis of this knowledge into new organization
5. Skill in evaluation in that area of knowledge to judge value of materials and methods for given purposes

(Kratwohl et al. 1964: 49-50)

In language learning terms, we are all familiar with what this taxonomy means:

(a) Knowledge of facts and language, vocabulary building
(b) Reading and listening comprehension, understanding how the facts and language fit together
(c) Demonstrating knowledge and understanding, generating one's own language, transferring and adapting language to new situations and uses
(d) Seeing patterns in discourse, being critical about one's own speech and writing, editing, proof-reading, checking, evaluating other people's language

I also think that it is quite clear how we can use a documentary to practice these skills and help achieve the objectives listed.

4.3 Affective Objectives

However, as the programme progresses, its cognitive orientation becomes less evident and its focus shifts, as Transcript 2 in the Appendix illustrates. While we are first of all being given facts and are being expected to use our cognitive skills, the latter part of this sequence calls for other skills and serves other objectives: skills of appreciating the problem, of valuing the research done, of having one's awareness and attention raised, of having one's attitude sharpened or shaped, of asking if the programme has meaning for oneself.

The skills called for generally fall into what is known as the Affective Domain, and a much neglected domain it is, in spite of the fact that it is at least as important as the cognitive domain. Just as we cannot be all emotion and attitude, so we cannot be all reason and logic. Both domains must be addressed in any complete learning situation.

There is much more to the affective domain than simply a "filter" or "attitude" and "motivation" (cf. Schumann 1993). The notion of affect covers a great deal more than "expressive language" and a more detailed breakdown of levels within the affective domain following Kratwohl et al.'s taxonomy is given below:

The Affective Domain

1. Receiving and attending
   1.1 Awareness
   1.2 Willingness to receive
   1.3 Controlled or selected attention
2. Responding
   2.1 Acquiesence in responding
   2.2 Willingness to respond
   2.3 Satisfaction in response
3. Valuing
   3.1 Acceptance of a value
   3.2 Preference for a value
   3.3 Commitment (conviction)
4. Organization
   4.1 Conceptualization of a value
   4.2 Organization of a value system
5. Characterization of a value or value complex
   5.1 Generalized set ("attitude cluster")
   5.2 Characterization

(Kratwohl et al. 1964)

Common terms used to express the affective domain are interest, appreciation, attitude, belief, value, adjustment. Under each level of the domain, we can specify learning objectives, for example:

1.2 Willingness to receive
- assumption that awareness of stimulus already achieved
- at best, willing to take notice of phenomenon and give it attention: "this programme is interesting" vs "I'm indifferent to this"
- no implication of degree of mastery at this level

Objectives/skills in relation to programme
- attends (carefully) when watching programme
- listens to views expressed with respect
- appreciates and tolerates cultural patterns exhibited by individuals and groups
- sensitivity to problems presented

2.2. Willingness to respond
- importance of cooperation at this level

Objectives/skills in relation to programme
- voluntarily listens to and looks at language of programme
- voluntarily seeks new language to build up own competence in both known and new areas
- engages in viewing tasks that will help develop ability
- contributes to group work and discussion on programme

3.1. Acceptance of a value (belief)
- emotional acceptance
- varying degrees of certitude

Objectives/skills in relation to programme
- continuing desire to develop linguistic skills and ability
- sense of responsibility for development of own performance
- appetite for good, informed NS-standard English in variety of registers as means of self-expression

In language learning terms, the implications of 3.1 might be:
- copying up notes and vocabulary in notebook
- reading more on subject in English
- discussing topic voluntarily with others
- re-watching programme with/without closed captions
- looking up words
- reviewing specific scenes of programme

4.1. Conceptualization of a value
- process of abstraction and generalization
- ability to defend choices and attitudes if challenged

Objectives/skills in relation to programme
- finding out and crystalizing basic assumptions underlying issues and attitudes expressed in programme and how expressed
- forming and expressing own judgements
- relating own attitudes to those in programme
- using programme to derive ideas and expressions about conduct and life

5.1. Generalized set
- "attitude cluster"/common thread
- does the programme speak directly to you? (examples of ozone depletion/skin cancer; smoking and cancer)

4.4 Putting Cognitive and Affective Objectives Together

Levels within the taxonomy are not fixed or hard-and-fast but seek to capture the progression of learning and also to express the essential links between cognitive and affective development in learning. If we progress, learn, and are able to receive and process information along only one dimension, our potential for educational development is limited and our ability to use different sources and resources is also limited. Kratwohl et al.'s taxonomy combines the cognitive and affective dimensions of learning in the following hierarchical pattern.

	Cognitive Objectives		Affective Objectives
1.	Recall and recognition of knowledge	1.	Receiving and attending to stimuli
2.	Comprehension of knowledge	2.	Responding (on request, willingly or enthusiastically)
3.	Skill in application of knowledge apprehended	3.	Valuing what has been responded to so as to respond voluntarily and seek ways of responding
4.	Skill in analysis of situations involving this knowledge; skill in synthesis of this knowledge into new organization	4.	Conceptualization of each value responded to
5.	Skill in evaluation in that area of knowledge to judge value of materials and methods for given purposes	5.	Organization of these values into a system and finally organizing the value complex into a single whole; a characterization of the individual

To summarise, skills and objectives within the Cognitive Domain deal with the recall and recognition of knowledge and the development of intellectual abilities and skills. Skills and objectives within the Affective Domain describe changes in interest, attitudes and values; the development of appreciation and adequate adjustment. In other words, the Affective Domain encompasses our ability to think through new information which perhaps contradicts long-held beliefs, and arrive at a satisfactory synthesis which integrates new values into old.

One helpful aspect of such a taxonomy is that it helps us identify the levels at which we are working and expect our students to work. All too often, we find that we are just not demanding enough of our learners. Let us take the example of "attending". As we know, TV can be attended to at a very low level, barely conscious some might say. Even active attention is really not high enough to match cognitive objectives in learning from TV programmes. We really need to be aiming at least at Level 3, at Valuing. Only from this level, do learners begin to take control and responsibility for their performance and development.

It also shows us that much of our experimentation is at too low a level to be of real value. We insist on testing for recall and recognition, when altogether more challenging goals await learners. In ESL/EFL terms, the communicatively competent learner is the one who has achieved not only a certain level in terms of psycho-motor and cognitive skills, but also in terms of affective skills.

4.5 Orientating the Learner-Viewer through Discourse

As I have already argued, a scientific documentary such as "The Battle of the Merozoites" contains many discourses, cognitively- and affectively- orientated. To put it another way, the language and images of sequences and scenes may appeal to either our reason or to our values, beliefs and attitudes, or to both domains at once.

In the sequence given in Transcript 3 in the Appendix, we see that there are in fact three distinct discourse types that are being interwoven to form a rich, complex and interesting sequence:

Expository discourse:	Presenting and explaining information and facts
Narrative Discourse:	Telling stories, giving case studies
Argumentative Discourse:	Presenting issues, making "statements"

However, for the language learner, the rich mix is likely to be far too heady a concoction for conscious and reflective language learning to take place. The cognitive dimension (information, facts, understanding) is likely to be supplanted by the narrative and argument - we follow the story and are struck by the emotional appeals "millions will die if something isn't done". Content is, as it were, wrapped up (or perhaps buried) in a framework of narrative and argument designed to engage viewers affectively. What can be done? Firstly, raising awareness of the multi-dimensional and multi-discoursal nature of scientific documentaries can help orientate the mental set of learner-viewers towards intentional language learning as distinct from the incidental language learning of "normal" television watching. For example, awareness-raising tasks for the sequence of Transcript 3 might be:

(1) What facts do you learn about malaria and its treatment from watching this sequence? What expressions and language are used to present and explain these facts? Who presents and explains them? (Orientation to expository discourse)

(2) What stories are told in this sequence? Who tells them? (Orientation to narrative discourse)

(3) What issues and questions does the sequence try to deal with? How are these expressed? Who expresses them? (Orientation to argumentative discourse)

(4) Does this sequence have any "special" and direct meaning for you? (Orientation to level 3 of Affective Domain)

Typical answers for Task 4. might be:

The learner-viewer is Colombian/ is from a malarial area/ knows someone with malaria/ is a doctor/ a medical researcher/ has been to a malarial area and taken pills/ has been to Atlanta/ etc.

The view held in this paper is that the very affective engagement of a learner-viewer in a programme or sequence - the "special" or personal meaning - can be turned to cognitive advantage in language learning terms through simple awareness-raising and orientating tasks. With my own students at Heriot-Watt University who watched this documentary as part of a self-study programme, it was enough to provide them with the theme of the programme: "A Colombian doctor claims to have developed a vaccine against malaria" to obtain "meaning" for them in the sense of value and attitude and to orientate their viewing towards both cognitive and affective educational objectives. I might add that they themselves were quite shocked at their own prejudices towards claims made by doctors and researchers from Third World countries, when these were made explicit.

5. Ordering Discourses: Documentary 2. "The Transplanted Brain"

Transcript 4 given in the Appendix gives the opening sequence of this programme on Parkinson's Disease and new approaches to its treatment. An analysis of the structure of the discourse of this sequence shows that the order of information presented is:

(1) Examples of symptoms and physical effects of Parkinson's Disease.

(2) Social effects of Parkinson's Disease.

(3) Clinical description and suggested treatment.

Apart from the voiceover, the order of people speaking about the disease is from those who are least expert but most affected to those who are most expert but least affected. Case studies and stories are followed by issues and arguments which are in turn followed by the facts about Parkinson's disease. This may make for very good and engaging television - it is, of course, the human dimension that most attracts us as viewers - but the viewer who is also a language learner and who may need a more "content"- and information-orientated programme in order to achieve cognitive language learning objectives may face considerable difficulties in using such a programme for language learning as the programme is not structured towards such objectives. Were it to have such objectives, we might expect the order:

(1) Exposition: What is Parkinson's Disease? How is it caused?

(2) Narrative: Case Studies.

(3) Argument: What are the social, medical, ethical and racial issues and implications of the disease and the proposed treatments?

As with the programme on malaria, the programme makers in this case are not seeking simply to impart information on Parkinson's Disease and on new methods of combatting it in the same way that such information might be given to medical students. They are telling human stories about the physical and social effects of Parkinson's Disease, about the ethical questions surrounding its treatment, and about attitudes to Third World medicine and research. They are also seeking to make controversial statements about issues on which people have strong feelings, beliefs, attitudes and responses. In other words, they are seeking to engage viewers not at a cognitive level but at an affective level. We all know something about Parkinson's Disease and the stories of its victims are frequently in the news. We therefore bring both knowledge and attitudes to the programme. The programme builds on our knowledge very little but challenges or reinforces our attitudes and beliefs a great deal. Taken together with the sheer pace and dynamic construction of interwoven discourses, for language learning-viewers this must mean the strong likelihood of a mental set towards impressionistic viewing rather than conscious and reflective language learning.

6. Towards Resolving the Conflict

I have found with my own students that the strong affective pull of good, engaging television documentaries is to some extent counterweighted by the very presence of the teletext subtitles, which do provide a degree of conscious and reflective control over the dynamic stream of speech. With subtitles, the autonomous learner watching a videotaped documentary can, in effect, freeze speech, check it, analyse the language, look up words, and so on. Reading and discussing related articles also helps in setting up not only a raised level of given information and vocabulary, but also helps in forming a critical mental set so that ideas, values and beliefs expressed in a programme are met with an active response, active on both cognitive and affective levels, rather than with rather passive reception - the "interesting programme" response. There are parallels with this approach in our daily lives in the way in which reading newspapers, listening to radio news, and watching television news are all integrated activities. Research (Robinson & Levy, 1986) confirms that the most knowledgeable, critical and responsive of viewers are those who are able to integrate other media sources with their viewing.

What I seek, above all, in my work with learners using subtitled programmes to learn language outside the classroom, at home or in self-study, is to raise the effort that they put into watching and to encourage a critical and self-critical, interactive approach to viewing: conscious and reflective in terms of language and content, aware and appreciative in terms of opinions and ideas. It has seemed to me that understanding how the very structure of programmes has contributed to the difficulties faced by learners in using television programmes as a language learning resource is an essential step in resolving conflicts and improving autonomous language learning.

I have suggested that there may be two useful ways of looking at and understanding programme language and structure:

(1) In terms of the messages received by learner-viewers and the cognitive and affective goals of a programme.

(2) In terms of the way in which expository, narrative and argumentative functions are structured within a programme to optimise the achievement of these goals.

In this paper I have only touched the surface of problems facing the autonomous language learner who wishes to draw on television and video as resources. I have found a focus on the programme itself and on the goals of programme makers surprisingly productive. I would encourage all those who are interested in the problems of language learning from television to look carefully at the programme as well as at the learner and the teaching methodology.

7. Next Steps

I began researching the value of teletext subtitles for language learning seven years ago. For the first few years I concentrated on the learner as the key variable: language level, attitude, motivation, attention. I then turned my focus to the role of the teacher as mediator and context-setter, as learners on the whole found intentional language learning from television programmes difficult. It seemed to me that much of the difficulty for learners lay in a paradox: the learning problem was caused not in spite of the fact that a particular programme was interesting and engaging, but more often because a programme was interesting and engaging. The present paper has been a first attempt to build a framework for understanding how the programme itself, its structure, its discourses and its messages, may work against the linguistic and cognitive goals that autonomous learners set themselves. The next steps will be to investigate how we may best resolve the paradox and exploit the engaging qualities of television programmes for rapid linguistic development.

REFERENCES

Bates, A.W. (1980). Towards a better theoretical framework for studying learning from educational television. *Instructional Sciences* 9, 393- 415.

Bates, A.W. (1984). *Broadcasting in education: an evaluation*. London, Constable.

Bean, R.M. & Wilson, R.M. (1989). Using closed-captioned television to teach reading to adults. *Reading Research and Instruction* 28 (4), 27-37.

Cooper, R., Lavery, M., & Rinvolucri, M. (1991). *Video*. Oxford, Oxford University Press.

Duke, J. (1980). How not to use the video. *Modern English Teacher* 8, 14- 15.

Gallagher, M. (1978). Good television and good teaching: some tensions in educational practice. *Educational Broadcasting International* 11 (4), 203-206.

Hart, A. (1988). *Teaching television: the real world*. Cambridge, Cambridge University Press.

Katz, E. & Liebes, T. (1986). Mutual aid in the decoding of Dallas: preliminary notes from a cross-cultural study. In: Drummond, P. & Paterson, R. (eds.). *Television in transition*. London, British Film Institute, pp. 187-198.
Kratwohl, D.R., Bloom, B.S., & Masia, B.B. (1964). *Taxonomy of educational objectives: the classification of educational goals*. Handbook 2: Affective Domain. London, Longmans Green.
Lonergan, J. (1984). *Video in language teaching*. Cambridge, Cambridge University Press.
McGovern, J. (ed.) (1983). *Video applications in ELT*. Oxford, Pergamon Press & The British Council (ELT Documents 114).
Neumann, S.B. & Koskinen, P.S. (1990). *Using captioned television to improve the reading proficiency of language minority students*. Falls Church, VA, National Captioning Institute.
Price, K. (1983, Fall). Closed-captioned TV: an untapped resource. *MATSOL Newsletter*.
Robinson, J.P. & Levy, M.R. (eds.) (1986). *The main source: learning from television news*. London, Sage.
Salomon, G. (1979). *The integration of media, cognition and learning*. London, Jossey-Bass.
Salomon, G. & Leigh, T. (1984). Predispositions about learning from print and television. *Journal of Communication* 34 (2), 119-135.
Schumann, J.H. (1993). Some problems with falsification: an illustration from SLA research. *Applied Linguistics* 14 (3), 293-306.
Vanderplank, R. (1988). The value of teletext subtitles for language learning. *ELT Journal* 42, 272-281.
Vanderplank, R. (1990). Paying attention to the words: practical and theoretical problems in watching television programmes with uni- lingual (CEEFAX) subtitles. *System* 18 (2), 221-234.
Vanderplank, R. (1992). Non-native speakers viewers' use of teletext subtitles in English: some exploratory studies. In: Davies, G. & Hussey, M. (eds.). *New technologies in language learning*. Frankfurt a.M., Peter Lang, pp. 89-102.
Vanderplank, R. (1993). A very verbal medium: language learning through closed captions. *TESOL Journal* 3 (1), 10-14.

APPENDIX

Transcript 1

Voiceover (VO): Despite the propaganda, more soldiers are killed by malaria than by armed combat. One bite from a mosquito carrying the malarial parasite is enough to kill.

The malaria parasite infects 300 million people a year, killing nearly 2 million worldwide.

Now the enemy within is gaining strength with increased resistance to drugs designed to combat it.

But one scientist claims to have developed the world's first effective vaccine and to be winning the battle against malaria. Any malaria vaccine would help protect the armed forces. Over the years they've been recruited by researchers to help in the fight against malaria. An effective vaccine would also transform the lives of millions of people in the developing world.

And tourists travelling to countries where drug resistant strains of the parasite are common are now more than ever in greater need of protection.

The most deadly form of malaria is caused by a parasite called plasmodium falciparum. The infected mosquito injects the parasite when sucking blood.

Colonel Jerald Sadoff (Walter Reed Army Institute of Research): One of the reasons it's so hard to make a vaccine is that the parasite uses a lot of tricks to fool the immune system to prevent effective immunity from occuring. One of the tricks it does is to change from one thing to another pretty quickly. You're immune against one part of it but then it's something else. Also at certain stages, like at the first stage, there's very little of it there.

VO: (accompanying diagram) The first stage of the parasite is called the sporozoite. If these sporozoites aren't attacked by the immune system, they go on to the liver.

Col. Sadoff: Pretty soon they get inside liver cells - there is very little ability to recognise them. And when the body first starts recognising them, then they change into merozoites and they're bursting out of those liver cells and into the bloodstream.

VO: The next form of the parasite, the merozoite, is able to invade red blood cells. Once inside the cell, the merozoites rapidly divide and burst out to release more merozoites to invade more red blood cells. Every 48 hours thousands of merozoites are ejected from the red cells in waves causing symptoms of malaria. Fever interspersed with periods of shivering which can be fatal. The cycle gets repeated again and again.

Col. Sadoff: The mosquito comes in and bites the person that's infected and the cycle starts again when the mosquito bites and infects another person and then infects someone else.

Transcript 2

Col. Sadoff: The main weapons that we've used in the past have been insecticides. Unfortunately the bugs got smart or resistant and insecticides are not as useful as they were, or as with DDT, the residuals are more toxic for humans then we care to use to kill off these insects. Walter Reed have taken 10 to 15 years to develop a drug and the parasite can become resistant to in 2 to 3 years. We're becoming quite discouraged about drugs as it takes so long to develop them and parasites are becoming resistant very rapidly. Our great fear is that we won't have any drugs for the treatment of malaria and people will be dying from malaria and there won't be any drungs to treat them and we'll have no effective control.

And just think about that. We have 300 milion cases and 2 million children dying as it is - what would it be if we had no drugs? We're really almost desperate to develop a vaccine.

Transcript 3

VO: (the scene is Dr Patarroyo's clinic) There were now two areas of controversy over the vaccines - the peptides chosen and the precise control over its production. In the West he would not have been able to proceed without some formal review of his vaccine and its safety. Without such regulation, Patarroyo was able to move quickly from monkeys to man.

Dr Patarroyo: In a human being if you just by chance damage the kidneys, the lungs, the heart, the brain, that's a serious issue. Besides that there were ethical considerations. I was very scared. I hesitated and I'm not ashamed to say that. For 9 months I could not take that step. But there were several situations that forced me to do that. Having succeeded with the monkeys, also I had the other question. What if it works in humans also? Then I would have the other doubt - that I spent too long not making the decision.

VO: The first human trials using the new polymer were carried out in the new military hospital in Bogota. 13 soldiers took part in this trial. 9 got vaccine, 3 got saline and one was deliberately injected with malaria to act as the source of the parasites. After they were infected, blood samples were taken to check the presence of the parasite. In spite of Dr Patarroyo's doubts, the trial was a success. The vaccine partially protected the volunteers from malaria.

When these results were published, the World Health Organisation in Geneva asked the malaria team at the Centers for Disease Control in Atlanta to repeat Dr Patarroyo's work on monkeys.

Dr Bill Collins: Dr Patarroyo came to our laboratory to prepare the peptides as close as possible to what he was doing in Colombia for our monkeys. We challenged the animals two weeks after the last immunisation and then followed them daily to see how the disease was progressing. After 10 to 12 days it became obvious that the vaccine as given here did not give protection. 30 monkeys were challenged even though we didn't know which were immunised. 29 became sick and needed treatment with drugs. Only one animal was protected.

VO: So in Atlanta neither the polymer version of Patarroyo's vaccine nor the peptides were able to protect the monkeys as they had done in Colombia. These negative results fuelld doubts and speculation about the vaccine.

Back in Colombia, Patarroyo had already started a massive series of human trials with the marines.

Dr Pat.: The military forces of Colombia allowed us to perform the first trial which involved 63 vaccinees and 122 placebos. And these people were told that we didn't know exactly who were the conditions for vaccination. And we didn't know how much and how often to give them the vaccine. We explained them every single thing and they decided to participate. We asked them to give blood samples every 15 days in order to look at clinical laboratory tests like blood chemistry, blood count and urine analysis in order to find out if the vaccine was safe in a large group of people.

VO: Other studies with the marines tested the safety of the vaccine and established that 3 doses would be needed and in what doses they would be effective. The commander of the marine base was happy to volunteer his men to take part in the trials to boost his force's effectiveness.

Transcript 4

From the first scenes of "The Transplanted Brain"

VO: The population is getting older as people live longer and longer. Many have active lives well into old age.

In control of their faculties, they're able to enjoy their later years. But with increasing age, the chances of developing a degenerative disease get greater.

A few years ago this man was vigorous and active. He ran a clothing company very successfullly. Today he can no longer recognise his wife and can barely feed himself. He suffers from one of a number of degenerative brain diseases that afflict the elderly.

General MacArthur and Harry Truman both had one of the more common disorders, Parkinson's Disease. So did the actor Michael Redgrave. Right now, Mohammed Ali has the same symptoms. It's a disease that most often occurs in older people but not exclusively so.

At the age of 20 Don Burns was an amateur tennis champion. Today at 39 he can only sit on the sidelines and watch because Don is one of the youngest victims of Parkinson's Disease.

This disorder robs its victims of the ability to precisely coordinate their body movements. Don has come to Vanderbilt University in Nashville, Tennessee to take part in testing a new surgical technique that may offer hope to millions of victims of Parkinson's Disease. He will soon undergo an experimental operation that may help him control his involuntary tremors.

Don Burns: The symptoms really vary a lot. For me they start on the left side. There's a lot of achiness, muscle weakness, loss of small motor coordination. My face becomes like a mask, it's more frozen, I'm not as expressive. I don't blink as much. That's one of the things you really can't control. I can blink or wrinkle my face if I consciously think about it. Normally a person expresses themselves facially, but I can't any more. The first 3 or 4 years it didn't affect me very much. I had subtle symptoms I was aware of, but that other people weren't aware of. In the last 3 years particularly the last year, they've become more pronounced.

VO: A classic symptom is a shuffling gait. There is a drug treatment but the effectiveness wears off after a few years and the disease gradually gets worse. The handicap is not just physical.

Don Burns: I not only have to deal with this myself, but I also have to deal with others' reactions to it. It's very hard to see someone you love going through this. I think harder than to go through it yourself. It's been very hard for friends, the church, etcetera. Some try to protect me totally. If I'm slow they want to do it for me. People in my position want support, not people trying to take what they're doing away from me.

VO: Don and his wife Karen are both Presbyterian ministers and live in California with their two children. (phone rings) Karen and Don's mother are with him. Others call to wish him luck.

Don Burns: That's great. Let me tell Karen. Tom Kean the custodian arranged to have a private mass said for me. The Catholic Church is going ecumenical. As a Presbyterian, that's great.

VO: Don and Karen have not found everyone so understanding.

Karen Burns: It has had some significant implications for our careers. We're both Presbyterian pastors and had hoped we'd be co-pastors in a congregation. Almost 3 years ago we were being interviewed in that capacity and Don participated in a service in that area. Soon afterwards someone called our superior pastor and said "Does Don Burns have Parkinson's?" And he said "Yes, but it doesn't effect his ministry." The person said "We'll never have anyone with Parkinson's".

VO: All this is made no easier by the difficulties of doing the most mundane of daily tasks. To button his shirt, Don wills his fingers to make the right moves. The message doesn't arrive properly. With all Parkinson's patients, the problems start in the brain.

Dr Margaret Esiri (Neuropathology, Oxford University): The damaged part of the brain lies deep within it. The best way to show you is to slice through the brain.

I've done this to another brain. If we remove the rear half of the brain we can see the parts affected in Parkinson's Disease. There's a horseshoe- shaped area containg pigment. It appears blackish. This is the substantia nigra. It has fibres from nerve cells which travel to the caudate nucleus. This side to here and this side to here. These fibres secrete dopamine. It's the degeneration of the fibres that leads to the lack of dopamine in patients with Parkinson's. That gives rise to the symptoms of tremor, rigidity and poverty of movement.

VO: The black horseshoe is clearly visible in a normal brain. But in a Parkinson's brain it has virtually disappeared. Since the death of these cells results in the lack of dopamine, why not just replace the dopamine? One way was suggested. In the body, two other organs that make dopamine are the adrenal glands. The idea was to remove one adrenal gland surgically and implant some of its cells in the appropriate part of the brain. They could make dopamine and stop the symptoms...

LEARNER-DIRECTED VIDEO

William Savage
Asian Institute of Technology, Bangkok

This paper concerns the interactive use and production of video by language learners, highlighting learner-directed applications of video in task-based learning. Participants on our Talkbase program use video to document aspects of their work and to present research they undertake in the development of learner-defined pieces of work. Learner-directed video work facilitates language learning because of the linguistic discipline of the medium, specifically in terms of group interaction, understanding of content and meaning, and a critical approach to writing and the presentation of information.

1. Introduction

The development and discussion of video in second language education, as reviewed in Section 2, has progressed from the exploitation of ready-made video recordings to the use of the video camera in various ways. These include the recording of classroom activities and the production of video programs by learners, the latter being an integral, and integrated, component of the program on which this article is based. Section 3 provides a brief introduction to the language learning and teaching context, the Talkbase pre-master's program at the Asian Institute of Technology (AIT)* in Bangkok, Thailand. The process through which our students become competent at using video within the Talkbase framework is outlined in Section 4 with reference to the program's timetable.

Although motivation and visually contextualized language have been put forward as rationales for video, few practice-based accounts have related video use in language programs with current research in task-based language teaching nor mentioned how it affects language learning. Some ideas on this from our experience on Talkbase are presented in Section 5, concluding with comment on the notion that learners will only be able to take video use to its logical end, that is, using it themselves for their own purposes, if the language program itself is learner-centered and experiential.

2. Three Decades of Video and Language Teaching

> "...there can be very few practising (and journal-reading) teachers with access to video who still need to be told that 'video places language in context' or who are as yet unaware of the virtues of the freeze-frame button" (MacWilliam 1990: 157).

Indeed, many of the early accounts (Jensen & Vinther 1978; Kennedy 1978), and even more recent popular publications (Stempleski & Tomalin 1990), of video use in language teaching tended to focus on visually-contextualized language and techniques for using the buttons on a video-cassette player, usually in a 'how-to' description of bringing videotapes

---

*AIT is an international English-medium postgraduate institution established in 1959 with a present study body of 1000.

into language classrooms for learner viewing. At the same time, however, Jensen & Vinther (1978: 25) were prophetic in predicting that there would be a wide range of pedagogical possibilities to be explored over the ensuing years. MacWilliam's comment itself highlights the past and present reality that most video work in language education has remained within the confines of exploiting ready-made, typically commercially-produced, video programs for various predetermined purposes inside traditional language classrooms. As one reads through the following selective documentation of these purposes, it should be kept in mind that a logical evolution of video's potential is to "release the learner from classroom-bound activities" (Kennedy 1978: 139).

2.1 Using Ready-Made Video Materials

Most of the earlier publications on video use in language classrooms focused on identifying paralinguistic features, functions, and the actors' sociocultural traits, in addition to grammatical, lexical and phonological features of the language being presented (Silva 1984; Lonergan 1984). Descriptions of button manipulation and accompanying student exercises included being able to repeat sequences, silent viewing with students supplying explanation, and pausing a scene while students generated lists of vocabulary items or predicted what would happen next (Pike 1984; Lonergan 1984). Learners were brought more into the picture with videos providing note-taking practice (Lonergan 1984), language practice models, listening comprehension practice and as stimuli for discussions (Kelly 1985: 52).

A good example of these sorts of video programs are productions by the BBC, both commercial or taped television programs, and language teaching video packages produced by commercial concerns. In her review of purpose-made videos for ELT, Bevan (1986: 157) set out criteria for selecting videos for the language classroom including high technical standards, a sense of wholeness, relevant textbook exercises, accompanying audio materials, ease of teacher's manual use and a variety of purposes. Certainly much of what is commercially available meets these criteria. However, the range of pedagogical possibilities remains highly constrained, teacher-directed and often simply a translation of traditional media approaches to the television screen (Eisenstein et al. 1987: 209).

"Recipes" for using video recordings were a common theme as were operating instructions for cameras, video-cassette recorders and television monitors, even though the latter are more appropriately, and usefully, found in particular operating manuals of the wide variety of equipment types available (Smith 1987: 57). It should be acknowledged that in many formal language learning environments teachers and students do not have access to cameras. Thus, ready-made video recordings can provide a welcome and entertaining break from sole reliance on audio materials.

2.2 Recording Classroom Activities

In the early 1980's, video enthusiasts began writing about ways to record learners in various classroom activities (Lonergan 1984 and 1990), usually for the purpose of evaluating learner discourse and performance, typically with "tasks" set by the teacher, and most likely executed following instructions from a video "textbook" or "exercise" manual. For example, students could be given sketches, role plays or simulations to perform in front of the camera. This can be a motivating experience for learners engaging in what for many will be their first exposure "under the lights". Learner motivation is cited often as an important reason for taping students on video and viewing the results with the class. But as with most technology, the novelty soon wears thin as the "exercises" are worked through one by one, possibly at a regular time set aside for video. However, when the technology ceases to be the focus of activity and instead becomes a user's tool to accomplish some genuine purpose, then it is not the activity which motivates but rather the purpose itself. Here enters the question of when an activity is authentic, when a purpose is genuine. My colleague, Brian Kenny, has answered it like this:

> Because authenticity is found in the relationship between a learner and an activity, rather than in the activity itself (Widdowson 1981), it follows that a piece of work authored by the learners will be more authentic to them than one made by a teacher or materials designer (Kenny 1993b: 219).

Learners are doing a "piece of work" when they "[become] engaged by an activity, responding in a spontaneous, creative way" (Kenny 1993b: 219). Spontaneity and creativity demand that learners have an "author's" control over the content of an educational activity and choice of the means through which to present the activity's outcome. One response to this demand occurs when groups of learners choose video, among other media, as a way of documenting aspects of their self-defined and self-directed work while learning language through experience.

2.3 Learner Production of Video Programs

The idea that "student production of video recordings has a valuable contribution to make to language learning" (Sturtridge 1982: 101, quoted in L'Estrange & Revell 1984: 145) is one which underpins how one form of educational technology (in the hardware sense) can contribute to experiential learning (Jung 1994). This sentiment has been with video-prone teachers for a while and has found expression when the camera has been turned over to groups of learners (Bufe 1985 and 1992). Allan (1985: 80) lists the activities in which learners engage when producing video as including decisions about content, researching the topic, planning and writing scripts, and finally acting in and recording the presentation. Such activities involve learners in real communication tasks which cannot be completed unless they have mastered the necessary linguistic skills (Charge & Giblin 1988: 282). In order to prepare for such an undertaking, Charge & Giblin (1988) describe a video course offered to learners where they use the cameras and production facilities under the guidance and control of a teacher. In this scenario it appears requisite that learners attain a certain level of mastery over the language before they are able to tackle the linguistic and communicative demands of video production.

Properly integrated as a tool in a language program, it is inherent in the video production process that learners realize opportunities for improvement, both of language ability itself, and of educational potential, through the language being learned: "they start to learn what they can do, both individually and in a team, when offered a minimal task and a short time to fill with moving pictures" (Cooper et al. 1991: 5). Whether a learner is given or offered a "task" overlooks the learner's ability to define tasks, activities or whole pieces of work for themselves. In a learner-centered pedagogy where students are expected to do this, a goal of the language program will be to enable learners to communicate more competently. Hart (1992), for one, sees a "documentary" approach to video production as being more in line with this goal.

3. Talkbase

Talkbase* began in early 1985 as an eight-week intensive pre-sessional course held 3 times a year for AIT master's students in various fields of engineering, applied sciences and management. Over the past several years, AIT pre-master's students representing some 20 Asian countries have been joined by professional staff from regional organizations. Class sizes have ranged from 15-36 participants with 24 being a typical enrollment. Twenty-six Talkbase programs have been conducted to date for 495 participants, 371 of whom went on to study at AIT. The remainder, our "special" students, came to AIT solely to attend Talkbase for the two months and then returned to their work.

The Talkbase program is learner-centered and task-based, its pedagogical framework built around the research paradigm of field, problem and solution (see the Talkbase timetable in Appendix 2). The content of each program is determined by the fields of interest of its participants, their experiences and the particular academic demands facing them. During the first half of Talkbase, participants engage in a variety of tasks aimed at establishing fields of enquiry, identifying and clarifying problems to be solved, and approaching solutions. Tasks include large and small group text analysis, audio- and video-taped interviews, and pieces of writing. There are regular reportbacks on individual and group activities. Towards the second month, common fields of interest emerge among groups of students. These are developed through investigative research as pieces of work which are publicly presented at

*Hall and Kenny (1988) have described the Talkbase program at an earlier stage of its development as the AIT Pre-Master's course. More recently, Kenny (1993a and b) has put forward a practice-based theoretical foundation for the program by examining work in learner autonomy and task-based language teaching.

the end of the program during a poster session. The presentations take the form of poster boards, tape-slides, interactive computer programs and video documentaries.

4. Becoming Video Users: The Process on Talkbase

Video is just one of the media tools used by Talkbase participants to accomplish various program tasks. Documenting their pieces of work in a video program requires participants to employ a wide range of video techniques which necessitate acquiring the skills to do so. Since the participants typically have never used video prior to coming to AIT, we have built into the timetable a gradual process through which they become comfortable handling the camera and familiar with what is required to produce a completed program. The teachers provide the equipment, studio and editing facilities, and samples of captions and scripts. There is very little teacher-fronted instruction in the video production stages. Rather, participants work together on tasks with the teachers giving feedback and advice on their work as it develops. What follows is a brief description of each of the stages in the process headed by the entries from the Talkbase timetable.

4.1 Introduction to Media

On the Wednesday afternoon of Week 2, the classroom is arranged similar to a recording studio: two portable cameras on tripods connected to TV monitors with chairs facing the cameras and monitors. We explain to the group that there will be several opportunities over the subsequent weeks when they will be able to use video to record various activities, including the piece of work in the program's second half.

People are often taken aback by the presence of cameras, monitors and a caption stand but they become immediately involved as we invite them to come up and work the cameras. As students shoot different scenes in the classroom, we call out the sorts of shots they are taking and write them on the white-board, for example, a wide shot, a two-shot, panning from right to left. Once most of the shot variations have been identified, written on the board, and tried out by other camera operators, we introduce photo captions and the idea that written captions can also be superimposed onto the screen to add explanation to a video sequence.

We pass out a simple script for a short program about food in different countries which calls for a discussion between a presenter and three food "experts", introduced by prepared commentary read over photo captions. Students work the cameras according to the shot directions and then "cut" between camera shots as the panelists improvise the discussion. This practice program allows for comments to be made on caption timing, suitability of shots and speaking to the camera. At this point, we walk down the corridor to have the media technicians orient the students to the actual studio and editing facilities and practice with professional-grade equipment.

4.2 Field Trip

At the end of the second week Talkbase participants take either a day-long or overnight trip to tourist destinations near Bangkok, affording an opportunity for practice using the video camera. Upon returning to AIT, students view this record of the field trip and pick up where improvements could be made in shooting video.

4.3 Studio Practice

After the first introductory session, we explain that the following week they will be producing short video programs for practice. Without any interference from the teachers, the participants divide themselves into small groups and plan the program by deciding on an idea, writing a rough shooting script, recording any necessary outside footage (sometimes on the field trip), and then working in the studio to put the program together. We view these together on Friday afternoon at the end of Week 3.

4.4 Viewing Videos

Although we stress the amount of time required for recording voice-overs, captioning, and editing even the shortest of video programs, we are usually surprised with the sophistication students achieve on their first short video production attempt. These programs show how quickly the groups learn to put into practice what they had just been introduced to. Typical topics include "talk shows" in the studio, interviews with AIT personnel or invited outsiders, and variety-type programs complete with lip-synched popular songs. The videos also reveal the sense of humor of many students. By the end of the afternoon, people tend to be comfortable with having appeared on video in front of their colleagues and teachers, adept at the technical aspects of video use, and, at the same time, critical of their technique. It is at this point that video ceases to be the object of activity and becomes a means of documentation.

4.5 Field-Problem Solution on Video

As mentioned earlier, tasks in the first half of Talkbase are framed within the research paradigm of field-problem-solution. In each of the second, third and fourth weeks each of these elements is progressively developed: through analysis of the introductions of published research articles, interviews with AIT personnel about their fields of interest, and development of pieces of writing over the three weeks about students' own fields, problems within the fields and possible solutions. In the first two interviews, students record the discussions on cassette tapes to be presented, discussed and analyzed in a reportback session. The third interview focussing on solutions is recorded on videotape, either in the studio or outside with portable cameras, usually with an informant from a previous interview who the group found to be interesting.

4.6 Video Reportback

The comments made in this reportback are not about video technicalities, as in previous discussions, but rather are geared towards the content of the information recorded on the video and the message being communicated. This is at the end of Week 4 and just prior to the "poster session" during which the teachers pin up several dozen fields, problems, topics and other ideas which have emerged from the participants over the first four weeks. Many of these come from the video-taped activities. Students work for a couple of days to group themselves around a piece of work, by proposing a research rationale and getting feedback on it from colleagues and teachers during reportback sessions.

4.7 The Piece of Work

Once a piece of work is defined by a group, one that is feasible to investigate over the remaining four weeks, each group tentatively decides the medium through which they will present their research findings. Until about three years ago, all pieces of work were presented as poster boards, but as other media have become more accessible, students can now also decide whether their topic lends itself to a video program, synchronized tape-slide presentation, computer display or a combination of these. A list of pieces of work over the years is found in Appendix 1.

Student groups collect and analyze data to propose a solution to the problem they have identified within their field by interviewing specialists both on and off AIT's campus. They also collect written information from their informants. We have had groups of students collecting data and recording videotape at Thai government agencies, international organizations based in Bangkok, from farmers, fishermen and tourists, and from AIT secretaries, researchers, and professors. Reportback sessions are regularly scheduled when the groups return to AIT to up-date the teachers and other student groups on the progress of their investigation. We look at videotapes of the interviews and of other on-site scenes. We review written materials brought in by the students. And we discuss what needs to be done next in order to complete the piece of work.

By the beginning of Week 7, groups have returned to campus and begin shaping the presentation of their piece of work. They prepare draft scripts showing shot number, vision and sound instructions; they review and select shots from their recordings; they prepare captions from photographs or with computer graphics programs. The teachers work intensively with each group in turn as they explain what they are trying to show in their program, get feedback on the writing in the script and practice reading their voice-over commentary. As each group puts the finishing touches on their piece of work, they go into the studio to produce the video program.

4.8 Public Reportback

The culmination of any Talkbase program is the public reportback session held in the middle of the final week. Open to the public, this session draws people from the AIT community and many others from outside AIT: teachers at other institutions, student groups from other language programs in the area, and people with whom our own students came into contact during their investigations.

Visitors look at participants' poster boards and view their video programs, but more importantly, engage with the students in spirited and informed discussion about their pieces of work. The following day is for evaluation, first of the pieces of work and then of the Talkbase program as a whole.

5. Using Video and Learning Language

There are four recurring comments, among others, made by students in the spoken and written evaluation at the end of a Talkbase program: they are more confident and competent at using English to communicate; they have experienced and benefitted from learning how to work cooperatively; they know better how to initiate, plan, carry out and assess a piece of work; and they are equipped to incorporate media technology into research conduct and presentation. That these comments correlate with the Talkbase program objectives is no accident since they are discussed with participants at the beginning of the program and then serve as the basis for the evaluation. The objectives are for learners to:

(a) initiate, plan, organize and carry out pieces of work
(b) be able to explain why they are doing what they are doing
(c) be able to understand what other people mean when they talk and write about what they are doing
(d) elicit relevant information from other people
(e) clarify ideas in speech and in writing
(f) examine their own and other people's work critically
(g) use media in the process of clarifying ideas and carrying out pieces of work
(h) work and cooperate with other people

Legutke & Thomas (1991: 155) caution against implementation of a task-based approach which is not placed within a program's "thematic context or broader educational aims". Where a program's aims, or objectives, match the characteristic features of task-based learning, such caution can be heeded. Nunan (1991: 279) lists these features as:

(1) An emphasis on learning to communicate through interaction in the target language
(2) The introduction of authentic texts into the learning situation
(3) The provision of opportunities for learners to focus, not only on language, but also on the learning process itself
(4) An enhancement of the learner's own personal experiences as important contributing elements to classroom learning
(5) An attempt to link classroom learning with language activation outside the classroom

Legutke & Thomas (1991) again: "In a classroom where language is not an end in itself but the means for learners to pursue topics and work through tasks, this focus on 'experience' is as much concerned with the learner's interaction with materials, tasks and other learners as with the acquisition of formal knowledge" (p. 214). They see this pursuit of work through tasks as being a realization of experiential learning in practice.

The effect or benefit of using video in language learning is a frequent query in the video literature (O'Brien 1986: 169). We have found that learner-directed video work, when incorporated in a task-based, experiential language program that is learner-centered, facilitates language learning because of the linguistic discipline of the medium. Specifically, groups of learners interact intensively in the target language as they go about setting tasks to produce a video program. Their understanding of the linguistic content and meanings in their fields of enquiry is challenged and deepened as they determine how best to interpret the results of their pieces of work. A critical approach to writing and presenting information is necessitated by the restrictions imposed by concerns of video program duration and audience interest.

In a task-based program which happens to have video as one tool students use in the accomplishment of program objectives, it is not the video activity itself which is the focus of the task. With an inventory of media capabilities at hand, students are freed to explore the boundaries of task outcomes. To varying degrees, teachers are aware of advances in educational technology, both in the hardware (e.g. equipment and learning resources) and software (methodology). As hardware becomes more widely available and increasingly consumer-friendly, so should our teaching methods become more learner-friendly.

REFERENCES

Allan, M. (1985). *Teaching English with video*. Essex, Longman Group Limited.

Bevan, V. (1986). Purpose-made videos for English language teaching. *ELT Journal* 40 (2), 156-168.

Bufe, W. (1985). L'apprentissage de la civilisation en direct: l'interview vidéo sur le terrain. Aspects relationnels entre le natif et le non-natif. *Bulletin CILA* 42, 53-70.

Bufe, W. (1992). Der Einsatz der Videokamera im interkulturellen Fremdsprachenunterricht. In: Jung, U.O.H. (ed.) unter Mitarbeit von H. Jung. *Praktische Handreichung für Fremdsprachenlehrer*. Frankfurt a.M., Peter Lang, pp. 199-213.

Charge, N.J. & Giblin, K. (1988). Learning English in a video studio. *ELT Journal* 42 (4), 282-287.
Cooper, R., Lavery, M. & Rinvolucri, M. (1991). *Video*. Oxford, Oxford University Press.
Eisenstein, M., Shuller, S. & Bodman, J. (1987). Learning English with an invisible teacher: an experimental video approach. *System* 15 (2), 209-216.
Hall, D. & Kenny, B. (1988). An approach to a truly communicative methodology: the AIT pre-sessional course. *English for Specific Purposes* 7, 19-32.
Hart, I. (1992). Video, foreign languages teaching and the documentary tradition. *System* 20 (1), 1-13.
Jensen, E.D. & Vinther, T. (1978). Video in foreign language teaching. *System* 6 (1), 25-39.
Jung, U.O.H. (1994). Experiential learning: what educational technology can contribute. In this volume, pp. 1-14.
Kelly, R. (1985). Video and language learning: an approach to viewing comprehension. *RELC Journal* 16 (1), 52-67.
Kennedy, C. (1978). A video course for teachers. *System* 6 (3), 139-143.
Kenny, B. (1993a). For more autonomy. *System* 21 (4), 431-442.
Kenny, B. (1993b). Investigative research: how it changes learner status. *TESOL Quarterly* 27 (2), 217-231.
Legutke, M. & Thomas, H. (1991). *Process and experience in the language classroom*. New York, Longman Inc.
L'Estrange, H. & Revell, J. (1984). Some books on the use of video in ELT. *ELT Journal* 38 (2), 142-148.
Lonergan, J. (1984). *Video in language teaching*. Cambridge, Cambridge University Press.
Lonergan, J. (1990). *Making the most of your video camera*. London, Centre for Information on Language Teaching and Research.
MacWilliam, I. (1990). Video and language comprehension. In: Rossner, R. & Bolitho, R. (eds.). *Currents of change in English language teaching*. Oxford, Oxford University Press, pp. 157-161.
Nunan, D. (1991). Communicative tasks and the language curriculum. *TESOL Quarterly* 25 (2), 279-295.
O'Brien, T. (1986). Review of video in language teaching. *ELT Journal* 40 (2), 169-170.
Pike, H. (1984). Video as a teaching aid. *World Language English* 3 (3), 201-203.
Silva, T. (1984). Teacher-made videotape materials for the second-language classroom. In: Savignon, S. & Burns, M. (eds.). *Initiatives in communicative language teaching*. Reading, MA, Addison-Wesley Publishing Company, pp. 137-153.
Smith, M. (1987). Review of 'Teaching English with Video'. *ELT Journal* 41 (1), 57-58.
Stempleski, S. & Tomalin, B. (1990). *Video in action: recipes for using video in language teaching*. Hemel Hempstead, Prentice Hall International Ltd.
Widdowson, H.G. (1981). *Teaching language as communication*. Oxford, Oxford University Press.

APPENDIX 1

PIECES OF WORK ON TALKBASE

VIDEOS

Integrated Farming
The Effect of Tourism on Forest Environments
Traffic Snarls in Bangkok
Foreign Investment in Thailand
Safety on Construction Sites
The Seed Centre
Slum Solutions
A Break-Even Concern: The AIT Playschool
Why Farmers Do Not Cooperate
Impact of Dams on Fish Populations
Saving the River
Bridging the Gap
Motivation in Training
Changing Attitudes to Forests
Bicycling to the Future
Electricity in Thailand
My Experience on Talkbase
Construction Explosion in Bangkok
Planting Trees for the Future
Don't Upset the Neighbors
Making Progress in English
Coordinating Extension Work
Slum Areas in Bangkok
Thailand's Images
Lungs of the City
Micropower for Remote Areas
Pollution of Coastal Waters
The Traffic Pollution Crisis
Deforestation in Thailand
Traffic Noise Pollution
Ventilation in the AIT Cafeteria
The Chao Praya River: To Love It Is To Clean It!
Drinking Water at AIT
Wildlife Conservation in Thailand: Successful?
An Integrating Model of Rural Development
Computer Graphics in Entertainment
Education in the Klong Toey Slum
Bangkok Buses
Irrigation Structures
Labourers Living on Building Sites

TAPE-SLIDES

That Sinking Feeling
Packaging and Trucking
Channels of Communication
Agroforestry
Foreign Aid: A Necessary Evil
Women Working in a Man's World
Single Mothers: A Social Problem
Sick Building Syndrome
Smoking & Society
Integrated Duck-Fish Farming
Economical Electricity Consumption
Mosquitoes at AIT
Mass Transit in the Future
Problems of Teaching English
Koh Samet

APPENDIX 2

TALKBASE TIMETABLE

MON	TUE	WED	THUR	FRI
July 12 Orientation & Testing ------------- Grouping & Getting to work	13 Reportback 1 ------------ Further Investigation	14 Reportback 2 ------------ Word Processing & Listening Library	15 Further Investigation ------------ Reportback 3 Evaluating The Timetable	16 Writing (Week 1 evaluation) Talkbase Committee ------------ Feedback Consultations
19 Text Analysis (eliciting field) ------------ Library tour Text search Consultations	20 Text Analysis (small groups) ------------ Recorded Information: field	21 Reportback ------------ Introduction to Media	22 Writing (field) Committee Writing feedback ------------ Planning for studio practice	23 Field Trip
26 Text Analysis (eliciting problem) ------------ Text search Consultations	27 Text Analysis (small groups) ------------ Recorded Information: field-problem	28 Reportback ------------ Studio Practice	29 Studio	30 Writing (field-problem) Committee Writing feedback ------------ Viewing Videos
August 2 HOLIDAY	3 HOLIDAY	4 Text Analysis (eliciting solution) ----------- Text search Consultations	5 Text Analysis (small groups) ----------- Field-problem-solution on video	6 Field-problem-solution on video ----------- Video Reportback

TALKBASE TIMETABLE (Continued)

<table>
<tr><th>MON</th><th>TUE</th><th>WED</th><th>THUR</th><th>FRI</th></tr>
<tr><td>9
Poster Session (topics and pieces of work)</td><td>10
Writing (field-problem-solution)
Reportback: Thinking about a piece of work

Clarifying piece of work</td><td>11
Reportback: pieces of work</td><td>12
HOLIDAY</td><td>13
Data Collection
Reportbacks
Consultations</td></tr>
<tr><td>16</td><td>17</td><td>18</td><td>19</td><td>20</td></tr>
<tr><td colspan="3"><------------ Further data collection
Reportbacks
Consultations
Organizing piece of work -----------------></td><td colspan="2"><-------- Reportbacks ----------></td></tr>
<tr><td>23</td><td>24</td><td>25</td><td>26</td><td>27</td></tr>
<tr><td colspan="5"><------------ Further data collection
Reportbacks ---------------->
Consultations
Organizing piece of work</td></tr>
<tr><td>30
Final preparation</td><td>31
Preview of public reportback presentations</td><td>September 1
Public Reportback</td><td>2
Evaluation</td><td>3
Testing

Winding down</td></tr>
</table>

AN INTERNATIONAL BIBLIOGRAPHY OF COMPUTER-ASSISTED LANGUAGE LEARNING: THIRD INSTALMENT

Udo O.H. Jung
University of Bayreuth

In CALL, more often than not, yesterday's news is tomorrow's old hat. Information on the latest developments in computer-assisted language learning dates only too easily. And it takes a relatively long time to prepare a whole volume of bibliographic references: a year goes by before a new book sees the light of the day. When Gothild Lieber and I prepared the second volume of the *International Bibliography of Computer-Assisted Language Learning* we stopped collecting material towards the end of 1991. It took us a whole year to sort and reference the material, to assemble the indices and to laserprint the manuscript. When the finished product hit the market in the summer of 1993, the earliest entries stemmed from 1988, this being the date when volume I of the bibliography had appeared.* An interval of 5 years can cool down information to such a degree that it becomes practically worthless in some instances. The historian is then the only person to profit from such a compilation.

To avoid this danger altogether it was decided that any sequels to the two volumes should be published at shorter intervals. The more than 300 entries on the following pages constitute the *3rd instalment* to the *International CALL Bibliography*. They roughly cover the two-year period from 1992 to the present. On occasion, pre-1992 publications were included to stop gaps left in the preceding two volumes. A total of 42 journals are represented in this compilation. In addition a number of books were sifted to procure information. Access to the material contained in the bibliography is the same as in its two predecessors. The entries are computersorted and arranged alphabetically (first mode of access). There is, at the same time, a detailed subject index, which allows the user to thematically explore the contents of this collection. To indicate the continuity from the first two volumes to this third instalment we began counting entries where we left off at the end of volume II. This will also enable the compiler to reassemble this and subsequent instalments in a third volume, if and when there is a palpable need for such a publication.

---

*Udo O.H. Jung (1988). *An international bibliography of computer-assisted language learning with annotations in German*. Frankfurt a.M., Peter Lang.
Udo O.H. Jung & Gothild Lieber (1993). *An international bibliography of computer-assisted language learning with annotations in German*. Volume II. Frankfurt a.M., Peter Lang.

Descriptor Term	Frequency
Hypertext	41
Tertiary Education	40
Writing	32
Artificial Intelligence	30
Authoring System/Program	26
Concordance	21
Word Processing	21
Reading	19
Database	18
Telecommunication	16

Not counting the target languages - English continues to lead the way with 89 mentions followed by French (35) and German (20) - the frequency hierarchy of descriptor terms shows that *Hypertext* has clearly remained on the advance road since it first entered the charts,** and CALL has not turned into a grass roots movement either. It still is a top-down event which takes its origin in institutes of higher learning. However, with little more than 300 entries to base judgements on, it is hazardous to go any further. It must be left to the reader's hunches to corroborate or reject the truthfulness of the above piece of statistics. What is more, the bibliography which follows and especially the subject index with its 435 index terms provide him with an opportunity to do his own bit of research. On an average, each and every entry in this bibliography is characterized by five descriptor terms so that multi-angled research approaches become possible.

3052 Alexander, S. (1992). IconAuthor. *The CTISS File* 13, 24-26.

3053 Anderson, J. et al. (1991). *Technology and adult literacy*. London, Routledge.

3054 Anon (1992). Consortium for the development of computer-based learning materials for modern languages led by the CTI Centre for modern languages, University of Hull. *ReCALL* 7, 29-32.

3055 Arenhövel, F. (1993). Computer im Sprachunterricht der Grundschule. *Pädagogische Welt* 47 (12), 544-546, 536.

3056 Atkinson, T. et al. (1992). *Hands off - it's my go*. IT in the language classroom. London, CILT and NCET.

**See Jung, U.O.H. (1991). Galluping through the international CALLscape, or you can't teach an old dog new tricks. In: Holzmann, C. & Peters, K. (eds.). *Man and the Media*: Special Number (15) of *CALL Austria*. Vienna, Verein CALL Austria, pp. 101-115.

3057 Bailin, A. (1990). Skills-in-context and student modeling. *CALICO Journal* 8 (1), 7-22.

3058 Bationo, B.D. (1992). The effects of three feed-back forms on learning through a computer-based tutorial. *CALICO Journal* 10 (1), 45-52.

3059 Battenberg, W. (1993). "Broken Plot" - eine computergestützte Präsentation von Lehrbuchtexten. *Englisch* 28 (2), 64-67.

3060 Beauvois, M.H. (1992). Computer-assisted classroom discussion in the foreign language classroom: conversation in slow motion. *Foreign Language Annals* 25 (5), 455-463.

3061 Becker, D.A. (1992). Getting started with CD audio in HyperCard. *CALICO Journal* 9 (4), 33-48.

3062 Beilby, M. (1992). Asymetrix Toolbook 1.5. *The CTISS File* 13, 16-18.

3063 Benest, I.D. (1990). A hypertext system with controlled hype. In: McAleese, R. & Green, C. (eds.), pp. 52-63.

3064 Bertin, J.-C. (1992). Didactique et technologie: l'intégration version NEXT. *Les Cahiers de l'APLIUT* 46, 59-68.

3065 Bhatia, A. (1991). Kanji retrieval by recursive location of elements using Hypercard. *CALICO Journal* 9 (2), 4-25.

3066 Bleyhl, W. (1992). Englisch lehren und lernen mit dem Computer. In: Buttjes, D. et al. (eds.). *Neue Brennpunkte des Englischunterrichts*. Frankfurt a.M., Lang, pp. 316-329.

3067 Blomeyer, R.L. & Martin, C.D. (eds.) (1991). *Case studies in computer aided learning*. London, Falmer Press.

3068 Blommaert, M.R. (ed.) (1992). *Computerondersteund taalonderwijs*. Een verbefering in het taalverwervingsproces? Brussels, Vrije Universiteit Brussel: Instituut voor Taalonderwijs.

3069 Böger, J. (1993). Emanzipation durch Lernen der Technologie. EuroCALL 1993 in Hull/England. *Kielikeskustelua* 10, 20-25.

3070 Börner, W. (1992). Das Werkzeug "Textverarbeitung" im fremdsprachlichen Schreiben: Idealkonzeption und Realisierungen. In: Börner, W. & Vogel, K. (eds.). *Schreiben in der Fremdsprache*. Prozeß und Text, Lehren und Lernen. Bochum, AKS Verlag, pp. 297-313.

3071 Bolt, P. (1992). An evaluation of grammar-checking programs as self-help learning aids for learners of English as a foreign language. *Computer Assisted Language Learning* 5 (1/2), 49-91.

3072 Bolt, P. (1993). Grammar checking programs for learners of English as a foreign language. In: Yazdani, M. (ed.), pp. 140-197.

3073 Bolton, W. (1993). Checking the spellers. *English Today* 34, 45-50.

3074 Boucher, P. (1992). L'intelligence artificielle et l'apprentissage des langues: existe-t-il des tuteurs réellement intelligents? *Les Cahiers de l'APLIUT* 45, 9-23.

3075 Bowerman, C. (1992). Tutoring in an ITS for German writing: the student-tutorial module synergy. In: Thompson, J. & Zähner, C. (eds.), pp. 1-11.

3076 Boyle, C.D.B. & Snell, J.R. (1990). Intelligent navigation for semistructured hypertext documents. In: McAleese, R. & Green, C. (eds.), pp. 28-39.

3077 Braithwaite, K. (1992). Enseignement assisté par la communication internationale électronique. *Les Cahiers de l'APLIUT* 46, 51-58.

3078 Breese, C. (1993). Computers and the writing process: a memo to the Head. In: Monteith, M. (ed.), pp. 57-63.

3079 Brockett, A.A. et al. (1992). Development of a human-computer interface. *ReCALL* 7, 17-27.

3080 Brondmo, H.P. & Davenport, G. (1990). Creating and viewing the *Elastic Charles* - a hypermedia journal. In: McAleese, R. & Green, C. (eds.), pp. 43-51.

3081 Brücher, K.H. (1992a). Autorenprogramme im computerunterstützten Fremdsprachenunterricht. Ein Praxisbericht und eine Rezension der Eurocentres/Wida-Autorenprogramme. *Zielsprache Französisch* 24 (1), 22-29.

3082 Brücher, K.H. (1992b). Lückentexte - automatisch erstellt: Anleitung für ein Makro zur Erstellung von Lückentexten mit WORD 5.0. In: Jung, U.O.H. (ed.). *Praktische Handreichung für Fremdsprachenlehrer*. Frankfurt a.M., Lang, pp. 227-235.

3083 Buchholz, E. (1992). Factors influencing the acceptance of CALLware. *Literary and Linguistic Computing* 7 (2), 132-137.

3084 Bull, S. (1993). Towards user/system collaboration in developing a student model for intelligent computer assisted language learning. *ReCALL* 8, 3-8.

3085 Bump, J. (1990). Radical changes in class discussion using networked computers. *Computers and the Humanities* 24, 49-65.

3086 Burnett, L. (1993). Teacher off: computer technology, guidance and self-access. *System* 21 (3), 295-304.

3087 Burston, J. (1993). Exploiting available technology. *CALICO Journal* 11 (1), 47-52.

3088 Burston, J.L. (1991). Using Système-D in a classroom environment. *CALICO Journal* 8 (4), 51-57.

3089 Butler, C.S. (ed.) (1992). *Computers and written texts*. Oxford, Blackwell Publishers.

3090 Canto, H. (1992). Un didacticiel pour l'enseignement de l'intonation en français langue étrangère (FLE). *Les Cahiers de l'APLIUT* 44, 51-59.

3091 Cardey, S. & Greenfield, P. (1992). The 'Studygram' natural language morphology system: a first step to an intelligent tutoring platform for natural language morphology. In: Thompson, J. & Zähner, C. (eds.), pp. 42-59.

3092 Carter, L. (1992). Computer mediated discourse and student participation at Montpellier. *Les Cahiers de l'APLIUT* 45, 67-76.

3093 Chan, C. & Liu, L-C. (1992). Yu-Gong Yi Shan: exploring some possibilities of designing tomorrow's foreign language textbook. *CALICO Journal* 9 (4), 49-59.

3094 Charlot, M. (1992). Entraînement à la lecture et CDROM. *Les Cahiers de l'APLIUT* 45, 91-96.

3095 Chen, J.C. et al. (1990). Querying an object-oriented hypermedia system. In: McAleese, R. & Green, C. (eds.), pp. 231-238.

3096 Chenik, N. (1992). *L'enseignement assisté par ordinateur et son application à l'enseignement de l'anglais de spécialité*. Paris, Thèse pour le doctorat (Paris IV - Sorbonne).

3097 Chun, D.M. & Brandl, K.K. (1992). Beyond form-based drill and practice: meaning-enhancing CALL on the Macintosh. *Foreign Language Annals* 25 (3), 225-267.

3098 Civil, A. et al. (1992). CATACROC: computer-assisted learning of Catalan. *CALICO Journal* 10 (2), 59-68.

3099 Claydon, P. et al. (1992). A knowledge-based learner comparison for aspects of academic writing: problems or potential? In: Thompson, J. & Zähner, C. (eds.), pp. 12-21.

3100 Colbourn, C. & Cockerton-Turner, T. (1990). Using hypertext for educational "Help" facilities. In: McAleese, R. & Green, C. (eds.), pp. 105-113.

3101 Commission of the European Communities (ed.) (1993). *Foreign language learning and the use of new technologies*. Conference Proceedings London 1993. Brussels, Bureau LINGUA.

3102 Conoscenti, M. (1992). Keep smiling! The happy Hypertext. *Computer Assisted Language Learning* 5 (1/2), 41-48.

3103 Crookall, D. et al. (1992). Computer-mediated language learning environments. *Computer Assisted Language Learning* 5 (1/2), 93-120.

3104 Curtis, F. (1993). Computer discourse: language imprisoned or empowered? In: Monteith, M. (ed.), pp. 96-113.

3105 Dalgish, G.M. (1990). Teaching the computer Swedish: morphology and phonology. *CALICO Journal* 7 (4), 55-66.

3106 Dalgish, G.M. (1991). Computer-assisted error analysis and courseware design: applications for ESL in the Swedish context. *CALICO Journal* 9 (2), 39-56.

3107 Daud, N.M. (1992). Issues in CALL implementation and its implications on teacher training. *CALICO Journal* 10 (1), 69-78.

3108 Davidson, J. (1994). The evaluation of computer-delivered natural speech in the teaching of reading. *Computers & Education* 22 (1/2), 181-185.

3109 Davidson, L. (1992). Using large text data-banks on computers. In: Roach, P. (ed.), pp. 5-34.

3110 Davies, D. (1992). ELNET: the European learning network. In: Davies, G. & Hussey, M. (eds.), pp. 123-127.

3111 Davies, G. & Hussey, M. (eds.) (1992). *New technology in language learning*. Proceedings of the 1989 Man and the Media symposium. Frankfurt a.M., Peter Lang.

3112 Davies, G. (1992). Expodisc: an interactive videodisc for learners of Spanish. In: Davies, G. & Hussey, M. (eds.), pp. 103-110.

3113 Davies, P. et al. (1992). Authorware Professional: multiplatform icon authoring. *The CTISS File* 13, 7-11.

3114 Davis, J.N. et al. (1992). Assessing user needs in early stages of program development: the case of foreign language reading. *CALICO Journal* 9 (4), 21-27.

3115 Davis, S.B. (1993). Hypertext and multimedia. *English Today* 33, 17-24.

3116 Dechet, A. (1992). Démarche info-active pour dynamiser l'apprentissage de l'anglais de l'informatique. *Les Cahiers de l'APLIUT* 46, 23-50.

3117 Decoo, W. (1993). Customer satisfaction in CALL: queries from the users and our final impact. *CALICO Journal* 10 (3), 50-64.

3118 Deegan, M. (1992). Guide. *The CTISS File* 13, 27-29.

3119 Demaizière, F. & Dubuisson, C. avec la collaboration de Odile Blanvillain (1992). *De l'EAO aux NTF*. Utiliser l'ordinateur pour la formation. Paris, Ophrys.

3120 Denninghaus, F. (1992). Das Computerlehrsystem ILTIS und der Aufbau einer modularen Russischdidaktik an Hochschulen. *Fremdsprachen und Hochschule* 36, 121-135.

3121 Descamps, J.-L. (1992). Towards classroom concordancing. In: Arnaud, P.J.L. & Béjoint, H. (eds.). *Vocabulary and applied linguistics*. Basingstoke, Macmillan, pp. 167-181.

3122 Dhaif, H.A. (1990). Computer assisted language learning: a client's view. *CALICO Journal* 7 (4), 67-81.

3123 Diekneite, J. (1992). *Fehlermeldungen und Hilfestellungen im computerunterstützten Rechtschreibunterricht*. Frankfurt a.M., Peter Lang.

3124 Dodigovic, M. (1993). Interdisciplinary: computer assisted linguistic research and the development of LSP courseware. *CALICO Journal* 10 (4), 5-16.

3125 Dufresne, A. et al. (1990). Hypertext documents for the learning of procedures. In: McAleese, R. & Green, C. (eds.), pp. 96-104.

3126 Dyer, A. (1990). An examination of hypertext as an authoring tool in art and design education. In: McAleese, R. & Green, C. (eds.), pp. 130-135.

3127 Ebbecke, K. & Hartmann-Anthes, P. (1993). Korrekturhilfe ja - aber wie? Wie ein System individueller Serienbriefe helfen kann. *Praxis des Neusprachlichen Unterrichts* 40 (1), 81-87.

3128 Eck, A. & Multhaup, U. (1993). Der Computer als Werkzeug im fremdsprachlichen Unterricht: CD-ROM. *Fremdsprachen und Hochschule* 37, 99-124.

3129 Evans, M. (1993). NICOLAS: using HyperCard with intermediate-level French learners. *System* 21 (2), 213-229.

3130 Finke, W. (1992). Computergestützte Grammatikarbeit im Französischen (2). *Fremdsprachenunterricht* 45 (8), 468-470.

3131 Fletton, N.T. (1990). A hypertext approach to browsing and documenting software. In: McAleese, R. & Green, C. (eds.), pp. 193-204.

3132 Flowerdew, J. (1993). Concordancing as a tool in course design. *System* 21 (2), 231-244.

3133 Foelsche, O.K.E. (1993a). Konstruktion von Lernwelten für den Sprachunterricht. In: Röllinghoff, A. (ed.), pp. 29-46.

3134 Foelsche, O.K.E. (1993b). Von Drill und Kill bis Annotext. In: Röllinghoff, A. (ed.), pp. 7-20.

3135 Fox, G. (1991). Context dependency and transitivity in English. *ELR Journal* 4, 17-25.

3136 Furuta, R. & Stotts, P.D. (1990). Separating hypertext content from structure in Trellis. In: McAleese, R. & Green, C. (eds.), pp. 205-213.

3137 Fynn, J. (1994). La voix à la carte. *Les langues modernes* 88 (1), 55-63.

3138 Gallego, J.C. (1992). Tele-classes: the way of the future. A report on a language exchange via satellite. *Foreign Language Annals* 25 (1), 51-58.

3139 Garrigues, M. (1992). Traitement automatique et apprentissage des langues. *Le Français dans le Monde* 251, 68-73.

3140 Gartshore, P.J. (1990). Hypertext as a programming environment for the authoring and production of interactive videodisc training packages. In: McAleese, R. & Green, C. (eds.), pp. 214-222.

3141 Gauthier, M. (1992). L'image dans la pédagogie de l'expression libre et son application à l'ordinateur. *Les Cahiers de l'APLIUT* 45, 51-64.

3142 Geisert, P.G. & Futrell, M.K. (1989). *Teachers, computers, and curriculum.* Microcomputers in the classroom. Boston, Allyn & Bacon.

3143 Gillespie, J.H. & Gray, B. (1992). Hypercard and the development of translation and vocabulary skills. *Computer Assisted Language Learning* 5 (1/2), 3-11.

3144 Glencross, M. (1983). Grammar and CALL: a review of current practice in some French language programs. *ReCALL* 8, 21-26.

3145 Goh, I.S.H. (1993). A low-cost speech teaching aid for teaching English to speakers of other languages. *System* 21 (3), 349-357.

3146 Goodfellow, R. (1992). Lexical CALL: an approach to vocabulary processing and retrieval. In: Thompson, J. & Zähner, C. (eds.), pp. 28-41.

3147 Gormley, A. & O Néill, G. (1992). GFTR: a knowledge acquisition approach to the generation of CALL. In: Thompson, J. & Zähner, C. (eds.), pp. 22-27.

3148 Gray, E.F. (1992). Interactive language learning. "A la rencontre de Philippe". *The French Review* 65 (3), 499-507.

3149 Greenia, G.D. (1992). Computers and teaching composition in a foreign language. *Foreign Language Annals* 25 (1), 33-46.

3150 Groundwater-Smith, S. (1993). Beyond the individual: collaborative writing and the microcomputer. In: Monteith, M. (ed.), pp. 9-20.

3151 Grüner, M. & Hassert, T. (1992). *Computer im Unterricht*. Unterrichtsvorschläge. München, Goethe-Institut.

3152 Guillot, M-N. (1993). Computer information systems and learner independence - a word of caution. *ReCALL* 8, 16-20.

3153 Hagen, S. (ed.) (1993). *Using technology in language learning*. London, City Technology Colleges Trust in association with CILT.

3154 Handke, J. (1992). AI and CALL: some proposals towards the implementation of intelligent CALL software. In: Davies, G. & Hussey, M. (eds.), pp. 25-37.

3155 Hardman, L. & Sharratt, B.S. (1990). User-centered hypertext design: the application of HCI design principles and guidelines. In: McAleese, R. & Green, C. (eds.), pp. 252-259.

3156 Hatasa, K. (1991). Teaching Japanese syllabary with visual and verbal mnemonics. *CALICO Journal* 8 (3), 69-80.

3157 Hatasa, K. et al. (1992). Handling Japanese without a Japanese operating system. *CALICO Journal* 9 (3), 26-35.

3158 Hawisher, G.E. & Moran, C. (1993). Electronic mail and the writing instructor. *College English* 55 (6), 627-643.

3159 Hendricks, H.H. (1993). Models of interactive videodisc development. *CALICO Journal* 11 (1), 53-67.

3160 Henning, G. et al. (19939. Computer-assisted testing of reading comprehension: comparisons among multiple-choice and open-ended scoring methods. In: Douglas, D. & Chapelle, C. (eds.). *A new decade of language testing research*. Alexandria, VA, TESOL, pp. 123-131.

3161 Henry, G.M. (1991). Answer markup algorithms for Southeast Asian languages. *CALICO Journal* 9 (2), 27-38.

3162 Henry, G.M. (1992). Eliminating the keyboard: a new method for exotic L2 answer entry, feedback, and revision. *CALICO Journal* 10 (1), 53-68.

3163 Higgins, J. (1991). Looking for patterns. *ELR Journal* 4, 63-70.

3164 Higgins, J. (1992). Another look at artificial unintelligence. In: Davies, G. & Hussey, M. (eds.), pp. 15-23.

3165 Hirakawa, Y. et al. (1990). Hypermedia as a communication design software support. In: McAleese, R. & Green, C. (eds.), pp. 244-251.

3166 Hirata, K. (1990). SAIJIKI: Hyper-reading Japanese. *CALICO Journal* 8 (1), 51-63.

3167 Holland, V.M. et al. (1993). Parsers in tutors: what are they good for? *CALICO Journal* 11 (1), 28-46.

3168 Holzmann, C. (1994). Call for 4CALL. *TELL & CALL* 1, 46-49.

3169 Hooton, T. (1992). Hypermedia without the hype. *Computer Assisted Language Learning* 5 (1/2), 121-122.

3170 Hornbacher, R. (1992). Einsatz einer Textverarbeitung im Französischunterricht - gezeigt anhand eines konkreten Beispiels zum Einüben der Zeitenfolgeregeln des "style indirect". *CALL Austria* 17, 77-82.

3171 Howell, G. (1990). Hypertext meets interactive fiction: new vistas in creative writing. In: McAleese, R. & Green, C. (eds.), pp. 136-141.

3172 Hughes, H.E. (1993). Khorosho! An interactive videodisc survival Russian program. *Foreign Language Annals* 26 (3), 393-398.

3173 Hyland, K. (1993). ESL computer writers: what can we do to help? *System* 21 (1), 21-30.

3174 Ilse, W.-R. (1991). Concordancing in vocational training. *ELR Journal* 4, 103-113.

3175 Jahr, S. (1993). Eine computergestützte Übung zum Erwerb von kohärenzstiftenden Mitteln im fachsprachlichen Fremdsprachenunterricht. *Info DaF* 20 (1), 28-31.

3176 James, E.F. & Sherk, M.W. (1993). Project IVY (IIVVI): a CAI system. *International Review of Applied Linguistics in Language Teaching* 31 (1), 54-60.

3177 Jamieson, J. et al. (1993). Reliability of a computerized scoring routine for an open-ended task. *System* 21 (3), 305-322.

3178 Jappy, A. (1992). A quantitative approach to James Thurber's "Fables of Our Time". *Les Cahiers de l'APLIUT* 45, 78-89.

3179 Johns, T. (1991). From printout to handout: grammar and vocabulary teaching in the context of data-driven learning. *ELR Journal* 4, 27-45.

3180 Johns, T. (1991). Should you be persuaded: two examples of data-driven learning. *ELR Journal* 4, 1-16.

3181 Jonassen, D.H. (1990). Semantic network elicitation: tools for structuring hypertext. In: McAleese, R. & Green, C. (eds.), pp. 142-152.

3182 Jones, C.M. (1993). Computerizing language instruction: possibilities and pitfalls. *The IALL Journal of Language Learning Technologies* 26 (1), 19-25.

3183 Kaliski, T. (1992). Computer-assisted language learning (CALL). In Roach, P. (ed.), pp. 97-109.

3184 Kämper-van den Boogaart, M. (1992). Deutsch lernen mit dem Personalcomputer.

Lernen in Deutschland 12 (1), 62-74.

3185 Kappe, G. & Witthinrich, P. (1994). DFÜ (Datenfernübertragung) als Kommunikationsmedium im Bereich der modernen Fremdsprachen. *Neusprachliche Mitteilungen aus Wissenschaft und Praxis* 47 (1), 38-41.

3186 Kecskés, I. (1992). A multi-purpose authoring program. In: Davies, G. & Hussey, M. (eds.), pp. 51-59.

3187 Kelm, O.R. (1993). The use of synchronous computer networks in second language instruction: a preliminary report. *Foreign Language Annals* 25 (5), 441-454.

3188 Kempen, G. (1992). Language technology and language instruction: computational diagnosis of word level errors. In: Swartz, M.L. & Yazdani, M. (eds.). *Intelligent tutoring systems for language learning*. Berlin, Springer, pp. 191-198.

3189 Kibby, M.R. & Hartley, J.R. (eds.) (1994). *CAL into the mainstream*. Computer assisted learning. Selected contributions from the CAL 93 symposium 5-8 April 1993, University of York. Oxford, Pergamon Press.

3190 Kim, W-C.M. (1991). Conceptual design of an intellent Hypermedia language learning environment. *CALICO Journal* 8 (4), 25-36.

3191 King, T. & Huckbody, K. (1992). Routes into CAL at the University of Bradford. *The CTISS File* 13, 39-43.

3192 Klein-Braley, C. (1992). Sense and nonsense in CALL. In: Blommaert, M.R. (ed.), pp. 1-11.

3193 Knisbacher, A. (1991). Adventures in colloquial Hebrew. *CALICO Journal* 8 (3), 53-68.

3194 Knopik, T. & Ryser, S. (1990). AI methods for structuring hypertext information. In: McAleese, R. & Green, C. (eds.), pp. 224-230.

3195 Koh, T.-T. et al. (1990). On the design of a frame-based hypermedia system. In: McAleese, R. & Green, C. (eds.), pp. 154-165.

3196 König, E. & Müller, H.-H. (1993). Computerunterstützte Sprachanalyse für Einsteiger. *Info DaF* 20 (1), 3-15.

3197 König, E. & Müller, H.H. (1993). Vorbereitung von MS-Word-5.0-Texten für die Indizierung durch Word Cruncher (WC). *Forum Angewandte Linguistik* 25, 93-104.

3198 Kornum, L. (1993). Foreign language teaching and learning in a multimedia environment. *CALICO Journal* 10 (3), 65-76.

3199 Kowitz, J. & Carroll, D. (1991). Using computer concordancers for literary analysis in the classroom. *ELR Journal* 4, 135-149.

3200 Kukulska-Hulme, A. & Knowles, F. (1992). The computer as a tool for the writer: the quest for the "right" word. In: Davies, G. & Hussey, M. (eds.), pp. 39-49.

3201 Labrie, G. & Singh, L.P.S. (1991). Parsing, error diagnostics and instruction in a French tutor. *CALICO Journal* 9 (1), 9-25.

3202 Laing, D. et al. (1991). L'emploi du traitement de texte dans un cours universitaire de première année portant sur la littérature française. *The Canadian Modern Language Review* 47 (3), 477-485.

3203 Lawler, R.W. (1990). CASE: a case analysis support environment. In McAleese, R. & Green, C. (eds.), pp. 174-182.

3204 Lawler, R.W. (1993). Dual purpose learning environments. In: Yazdani, M. (ed.), 73-84.

3205 Leaver, B. (1992). PROPI authoring system. *The CTISS FILE* 13, 35-37.

3206 Legaleri, R. (1992). L'accès aléatoire. Application aux programmes de tests en turbo-pascal. *Nouveaux Cahiers d'Allemand* 3, 321-332.

3207 Legenhausen, L. & Wolff, D. (1992). Einsatzmöglichkeiten des Computers im Fremdsprachenunterricht. In: Jung, U.O.H. (ed.). *Praktische Handreichung für Fremdsprachenlehrer*. Frankfurt a.M., Lang, pp. 215-226.

3208 Levin, L.S. et al. (1991). The ALICE system. A workbench for learning and using language. *CALICO Journal* 9 (1), 27-56.

3209 Liou, H-C. (1991). Development of an English grammar checker. A progress report. *CALICO Journal* 9 (1), 57-70.

3210 Liou, H-C. et al. (1992). Can grammatical CALL help EFL writing instruction? *CALICO Journal* 10 (1), 23-44.

3211 Liou, H.-C. (1992). An automatic text-analysis project for EFL writing revision. *System* 20 (4), 481-492.

3212 Liou, H.-C. (1993). Investigation of using text-critiquing programs in a process-oriented writing class. *CALICO Journal* 10 (4), 17-38.

3213 Löhndorf, H. (1994). Computer im Fremdsprachenunterricht - ja oder nein: grundsätzliche Überlegungen. *Fremdsprachenunterricht* 38 (2), 81-87.

3214 Loritz, D. (1992). Generalized transition network parsing for language study: the GPARS system for English, Russian, Japanese and Chinese. *CALICO Journal* 10 (1), 5-22.

3215 Louw, B. (1991). Classroom concordancing of delexical forms and the case for integrating language and literature. *ELR Journal* 4, 151-178.

3216 Lunde, K.R. (1990). Using electronic mail as a medium for language study and instruction. *CALICO Journal* 7 (3), 68-78.

3217 Lutjeharms, M. & Hoogzand, A. (1992). Inzicht en automatisering bij het computerondersteund vreemdetalenonderwijs. In: Blommaert, M.R. (ed.), pp. 12-24.

3218 Lyman-Hager, M.A. (1990). Development of the Five College Foreign Language Resource Center. *CALICO Journal* 7 (4), 37-47.

3219 Maciejewski, A.A. & Leung, N.K. (1992). The Nihongo tutorial system. An intelligent tutoring system for technical Japanese language instruction. *CALICO*

Journal 9 (3), 5-25.

3220 Maes, J.-M. (1992). The intelligent dictionary project. In: Blommaert, M.R. (ed.), pp. 25-38.

3221 Mairesse, P. (1992). Pratique de l'autodictionnaire. *Le Français dans le Monde* 246, 59-64.

3222 Manning, P. (1992). Teaching strategies in ICALL. In: Thompson, J. & Zähner, C. (eds.), pp. 60-76.

3223 Marcus, S. (1993). Multimedia, hypermedia and the teaching of English. In: Monteith, M. (ed.), pp. 21-43.

3224 Matthews, C. (1992). Fundamental questions in ICALL. In: Thompson, J. & Zähner, C. (eds.), pp. 77-89.

3225 Matthews, C. (1992). Going AI. Foundations of ICALL. *Computer Assisted Language Learning* 5 (1/2), 13-31.

3226 Matthews, C. (1993). Grammar frameworks in intelligent CALL. *CALICO Journal* 11 (1), 5-27.

3227 Matthews, C. (comp.) (1992). *Intelligent CALL (ICALL) bibliography*. Hull, CTI Centre for Modern Languages.

3228 Mayes, T. et al. (1990). Signposts for conceptual orientation: some requirements for learning from hypertext. In: McAleese, R. & Green, C. (eds.), pp. 121-129.

3229 McAleese, R. & Green, C. (eds.) (1990). *Hypertext: state of the art*. Oxford, Intellect.

3230 McCarthy, B. (1992). Taking off with CALL. *ReCALL* 7, 6-9.

3231 McCarty, W. (1993). Das Texterschließungssystem TACT. *Forum Angewandte Linguistik* 25, 105-110.

3232 McGrath, W.T. et al. (1990). Computer programs developed by independent contractors: who owns the copyright? *CALICO Journal* 8 (1), 39-46.

3233 McKee, J. (1993). Computer-assisted vocabulary acquisition: an evaluation of the text analysis program. *ReCALL* 8, 9-15.

3234 McKnight, C. et al. (1990). A comparison of linear and hypertext formats in information retrieval. In: McAleese, R. & Green, C. (eds.), pp. 10-19.

3235 McMahon, H. & O'Neill, B. (1993). A story about storying. In: Monteith, M. (ed.), pp. 125-140.

3236 McVicker, J. (1993). Assisting English reading and vocabulary learning. In: Röllinghoff, A. (ed.), pp. 69-79.

3237 Mealing, S. & Yazdani, M. (1993). A computer-based iconic language. In: Yazdani, M. (ed.)., pp. 30-39.

3238 Mealing, S. (1993). Talking pictures. In: Yazdani, M. (ed.), pp. 40-58.

3239 Meißner, F.-J. (1993). Zukunftsmusik? Überlegungen zu einem elektronischen Lernerwörterbuch (I). *Fremdsprachenunterricht* 46 (1), 43-46.

3240 Meißner, F.-J. (1993). Zukunftsmusik? Überlegungen zu einem elektronischen Lernerwörterbuch (II). *Fremdsprachenunterricht* 46 (2), 104-106.

3241 Mendychowski, M. (1993). Multiple choice-testing or something more? *CALICO Journal* 10 (3), 41-49.

3242 Menzel, W. (1992). Constraint-based diagnosis of grammatical faults. In: Thompson, J. & Zähner, C. (eds.), 89-101.

3243 Meskill, C. (1993). ESL and multimedia: a study of the dynamics of paired student discourse. *System* 21 (3), 323-341.

3244 Metcalfe, P. (1992). CALL, the foreign-language undergraduate and the teaching of grammar: a linguistic and political battlefield. *ReCALL* 7, 3-5.

3245 Meunier-Cinko, L. (1992). Interactive French language curricula of the future: a study of computer and video potential. *The French Review* 66 (1), 147-153.

3246 Meyer, W. (1992). Computer mediated communication: Neue Werkzeuge für den Fremdsprachenunterricht. In: Jung, U.O.H. (ed.). *Praktische Handreichung für Fremdsprachenlehrer*. Frankfurt a.M., Lang, pp. 237-248.

3247 Meyer, W. (1993). Internationale Lernerkooperation durch elektronische Post. *Die Neueren Sprachen* 92 (4), 332-344.

3248 Michiels, A. (1992). Towards rule-governed computer-assisted language learning. In: Blommaert, M.R. (ed.), pp. 39-70.

3249 Miller, L. et al. (1994). An exploratory study into the use of CD-ROM storybooks. *Computers & Education* 22 (1/2), 187-204.

3250 Miller, P. (1992). Question Mark Professional and the multimedia extensions to it. *The CTISS File* 13, 30-33.

3251 Mindt, D. & Tesch, F. (1991). Computergestützte Forschungen zu einer didaktischen Grammatik des Englischen. *Fremdsprachen lehren und lernen* 20, 39-51.

3252 Monk, A.F. (1990). Getting to known locations in a hypertext. In: McAleese, R. & Green, C. (eds.), pp. 20-27.

3253 Monteith, M. & Monteith, R. (1993). Using HyperCard in writing narratives. In: Monteith, M. (ed.), pp. 141-156.

3254 Monteith, M. (ed.) (1993). *Computers and language*. Oxford, Intellect Books.

3255 Morawietz, H. (1992). Computer in der Grundschule? England und Frankreich als Vorbilder für ein Computerkonzept an deutschen Grundschulen und Orientierungsstufen? *Pädagogische Welt* 46 (9), 403-408.

3256 Motteram, G. (1992). Authoring tools and teacher training for CALL. *System* 20 (2), 151-160.

3257 Mparutsa, C. et al. (1991). Bringing concord to the ESP classroom. *ELR Journal* 4, 115-134.

3258 Müller, H.H. (1993). Stärken und Schwächen vier microcomputerfähiger Programme zur Textanalyse. *Forum Angewandte Linguistik* 25, 77-84.

3259 Mulligan, D. & Ryan, K. (1992). A prototype syntax checker for German learners of English. In: Thompson, J. & Zähner, C. (eds.), pp. 101-109.

3260 Murison-Bowie, S. (1993). Concordancing corner 1: what is concordancing and why should we do it? *TELL & CALL* 4, 42-44.

3261 Nagata, N. (1993). Intelligent computer feedback for second language instruction. *The Modern Language Journal* 77 (3), 330-339.

3262 Namenwirth, E. (1992). Tentative de mesure des effets de l'apprentissage de la grammaire par l'E.A.O. (enseignement assisté d'ordinateur). In: Blommaert, M.R. (ed.), 71-82.

3263 Nesbit, J.C. & Nakayama, K. (1990). Sequence comparison applied to correction and markup of multi-word responses. *CALICO Journal* 7 (4), 27-35.

3264 Nicolson, R.I. (1990). Towards the third generation: the case for IKBH (intelligent knowledge-based hypermedia) environments. In: McAleese, R. & Green, C. (eds.), pp. 166-173.

3265 Nielsen, J. & Lyngbæk, U. (1990). Two field studies of hypermedia usability. In: McAleese, R. & Green, C. (eds.), pp. 64-72.

3266 O'Brien, P. (1993). eL: using AI in CALL. In: Yazdani, M. (ed.), pp. 85-139.

3267 Oppenhuis, J. (1994). On forming and operating a CALL committee. *English Teaching Forum* 32 (2), 36-38.

3268 Pavanini, P. (1993). Computer e insegnamento delle lingue: lavorare con Arbeit mit Texten. *Scuola e lingue moderne* 31 (4), 115-123.

3269 Peacock, M. & Najarian, B. (1993). What is important in writing? Some differences in attitude between word-processing and handwriting pupils. In: Monteith, M. (ed.), pp. 64-74.

3270 Peng, Y-J.J. (1993). Answer markup on computer-assisted language learning. *CALICO Journal* 10 (3), 31-40.

3271 Perry, E. (1992). COMPULEARN and ESP: in defence of the authoring system. In: Davies, G. & Hussey, M. (eds.), pp. 71-82.

3272 Perry, E. (1992). COMPULEARN and ESP: in defence of the authoring system. *CALLBOARD* 13, 7-15.

3273 Perry, E. (1992). EAO et anglais de spécialité à l'université: attentes et réalisations. *Les Cahiers de l'APLIUT* 46, 9-22.

3274 Peters, K. & Schmid, K-H. (1994). Die Bildplatte ist tot, es lebe die Bildplatte! *TELL & CALL* 1, 16-25.

3275 Peters, K. (1992). WORDSTORE. Autorenprogramm zur Erstellung von Wortbanken. *CALL Austria* 17, 52-65.

3276 Peters, K. (1993). Wissen auf Knopfdruck - elektronische Multimedia-Lexika im Vergleich. *TELL & CALL* 4, 28-35.

3277 Peters, K. (1994). Neues von der Silberscheibe. *TELL & CALL* 1, 26-40.

3278 Pienemann, M. (1992). COALA - a computational system for interlanguage analysis. *Second Language Research* 8 (1), 59-92.

3279 Pollard, D. & Yazdani, M. (1993). A multilingual multimedia restaurant scenario. In: Yazdani, M. (ed.), pp. 1-13.

3280 Pople, A. (1992). Microsoft Visual Basic: a way to quick and easy courseware? *The CTISS File* 13, 13-15.

3281 Powell, B. (1992). The Computers in Teaching Initiative Centre for Modern Languages: an initial survey. In: Davies, G. & Hussey, M. (eds.), pp. 61-70.

3282 Pratt, J. (1993). Beyond the metaphor: breakdown and realignment. In: Monteith, M. (ed.), pp. 44-56.

3283 Rahtz, S. et al. (1990). Creating multimedia documents: hypertext processing. In: McAleese, R. & Green, C. (eds.), pp. 183-192.

3284 Räkel, H.-H.S. & Steinfeld, T. (eds.) (1992). *Dokumentation zum computergestützten Unterricht in Deutsch als Fremdsprache* (= Info DaF 19 (2), passim.

3285 Rautenhaus, H. (1993). Möglichkeiten der Integration von Telekommunikation in einen kommunikativen Englischunterricht - Bericht aus einem Seminar der anglistischen Fachdidaktik. In: Gienow, W. & Hellwig, K. (eds.). *Prozeßorientierte Mediendidaktik im Fremdsprachenunterricht*. Frankfurt a.M., Peter Lang, pp. 173-188.

3286 Rendall, H. (1993). Using the microcomputer to bridge the language gap. *CALICO Journal* 10 (3), 77-95.

3287 Reynolds, F.C. (1992). Bringing Minitel to the French classroom and integrating EDUTEL*CLASSE into the existing curriculum. *The French Review* 66 (1), 20-25.

3288 Rheinisch-Westfälische Auslandsgesellschaft e.V. (ed.) (1993). *Das RWAG-Hoesch Projekt*. Computergestützter und berufsorientierter Sprachkurs für ausländische Arbeitnehmer in der Metall [sic] und Stahlindustrie. Dortmund, RWAG.

3289 Riccioli, M.A. (1992). Desktop publishing: still a mystery? *Les Cahiers de l'APLIUT* 46, 99-113.

3290 Riccioli, M.A. (1993). What you scan is what you get. *Les Cahiers de l'APLIUT* 49, 80-92.

3291 Richmond, I.M. (1992). A hypertextual approach to teaching French business correspondence. *Computer Assisted Language Learning* 5 (1/2), 33-39.

3292 Ritter, M. (1993). "That's Us! A Book About Ourselves." An EFL project with intermediate learners, incorporating the computer as a tool. *CALICO Journal* 10 (4), 57-69.

3293 Rivas, M. (1992). Stratégies multimédia et acquisition de savoir-faire en langue de spécialité. *Les Cahiers de l'APLIUT* 45, 24-33.

3294 Roach, P. (1992). Fundamental concepts. In: Roach, P. (ed.), pp. 1-4.

3295 Roach, P. (ed.) (1992). *Computing in linguistics and phonetics*. Introductory readings. London, Academic Press.

3296 Roach, P. et al. (1992). Speech analysis and recognition. In: Roach, P. (ed.), pp. 35-49.

3297 Robinson, B. (1993). Collaborative writing using distanced electronic communications. In: Monteith, M. (ed.), pp. 75-82.

3298 Rogghe, G.L. (1992). Een multi-mediale cursus "Business English" in VULCO. In: Blommaert, M. R. (ed.), pp. 100-107.

3299 Röllinghoff, A. (1993). Moderne Lernstrategien fürs Wörterlernen. CALL Interface Design am Beispiel eines Wörterlernprogramms. In: Röllinghoff, A. (ed.), pp. 47-67.

3300 Röllinghoff, A. (ed.) (1992/1993²). *Latest developments in computer assisted language learning: CALL using Macintosh*. Lausanne, Ecole Polytechnique Fédérale de Lausanne: Centre de Langue.

3301 Roth, V.M. (ed.) (1992). *Computer in der Sprachtherapie*. Tübingen, Narr.

3302 Roussel, F. (1991). Parallel concordances and tonic auxiliaries. *ELR Journal* 4, 71-101.

3303 Rüschoff, B. (1992). Lernwerkzeug Computer: Möglichkeiten und Grenzen. *Französisch heute* 23 (3), 349-356.

3304 Rüschoff, B. (1993). Language learning and information technology: state of the art. *CALICO Journal* 10 (3), 5-17.

3305 Rüttinger, B. & Sourisseaux, A. (1992). Computergestützte Kommunikation in Gruppen. *Forum Angewandte Linguistik* 23, 51-59.

3306 Sampson, G. (1992). Machine translation. In: Roach, P. (ed.), pp. 85-96.

3307 Sanders, R. (1991). Error analysis in purely syntactic parsing of free input. The example of German. *CALICO Journal* 9 (1), 72-89.

3308 Schcolnik, M. & Rubin, H. (1991). The computer lesson as an integrated element in the academic EFL reading curriculum. *CALICO Journal* 8 (3), 81-92.

3309 Schlinkmann, D. (1994). Adam & Eve. Ein Computerprogramm (auch) zur Korrektur von Klassenarbeiten. *Praxis des Neusprachlichen Unterrichts* 41 (1), 48-56.

3310 Schmid, G. (1992a). Ein "PENFRIEND" für ganz Österreich. *TELL & CALL* 4, 9-14.

3311 Schmid, G. (1992b). Teacher training in CALL. In: Davies, G. & Hussey, M. (eds.), pp. 83-88.

3312 Schmid, G. (1993). Plädoyer für eine Re-Pädagogisierung von CALL. *TELL & CALL* 4, 12-15.

3313 Schmid, K.H. (1992). Schulische Telekommunikation. *CALL Austria* 17, 5-22.

3314 Schulz, R. (1992). Gedichte im computergestützten Englischunterricht. *Praxis des Neusprachlichen Unterrichts* 39 (1), 75-83.

3315 Schulz, R. (1993). What one has to know about methodology in computing. *CALICO Journal* 10 (4), 39-56.

3316 Scully, C. & Whiteside, S. (1992). Speech production modelling and speech synthesis. In: Roach, P. (ed.), pp. 73-84.

3317 Seedhouse, P. (1992). Communicative CALL: a contradiction in terms? *ReCALL* 7, 9-14.

3318 Seidel, C. (ed.) (1993). *Computer based training: Erfahrungen mit interaktivem Computerlernen*. Göttingen, Verlag für Angewandte Psychologie.

3319 Shires, N.P. (1992). Computer-mediated lists for foreign languages. *Foreign Language Annals* 25 (6), 533-539.

3320 Siegrist, L. (1992). LMC concordance program. *Neusprachliche Mitteilungen aus Wissenschaft und Praxis* 45 (4), 255-257.

3321 Simbruner, B. (1991). Interkulturelle Erziehung mit Apple Global Education. *Erziehung und Unterricht* 141, 848-855.

3322 Simpson, A. & McKnight, C. (1990). Navigation in hypertext: structural cues and mental maps. In: McAleese, R. & Green, C. (eds.), pp. 73-83.

3323 Siviter, D. & Brown, K. (1992). Hypercourseware. *The CTISS File* 13, 48-52.

3324 Slatin, J.M. (1990). Reading Hypertext: order and coherence in a new medium. *College English* 52 (8), 870-883.

3325 Smith, G.A. (1991). Tomorrow's foreign language textbook: paper or silicon? *CALICO Journal* 8 (4), 5-15.

3326 Soh Bee-Lay & Soon Yee-Ping (1991). English by e-mail: creating a global classroom via the medium of computer technology. *ELT Journal* 45 (4), 287-292.

3327 Sommerville, I. et al. (1990). The designer's notepad - a hypertext system tailored for design. In: McAleese, R. & Green, C. (eds.), pp. 260-266.

3328 Soula, J.-P. et al. (1992). ALGORD: outil d'apprentissage et analyseur de styles cognitifs? *Les Cahiers de l'APLIUT* 46, 69-79.

3329 Spaai, G.W.G. & Hermes, D.J. (1993). A visual display for the teaching of intonation. *CALICO Journal* 10 (3), 19-30.

3330 Stanton, N.A. & Stammers, R.B. (1990). Learning styles in a non-linear training environment. In: McAleese, R. & Green, C. (eds.), pp. 114-120.

3331 Stark, H.A. (1990). What do readers do to pop-ups, and pop-ups do to readers? In: McAleese, R. & Green, C. (eds.), pp. 1-9.

3332 Stenson, N. et al. (1992). The effectiveness of computer-assisted pronunciation training. *CALICO Journal* 9 (4), 5-19.

3333 Stenton, T. (1992). L'utilisation des hypertextes pédagogiques pour l'apprentissage de l'anglais: consommation ou apprentissage? *Les Cahiers de l'APLIUT* 46, 81-98.

3334 Stevens, V. (1991). Concordance-based vocabulary exercises: a viable alternative to gap-fillers. *ELR Journal* 4, 47-61.

3335 Stoks, G. (1993). Integrating new technologies into the modern languages curriculum. *CALICO Journal* 11 (1), 76-93.

3336 Stumpel, R. & Wesselo, M. (1992). COO-oefeningen bij CODE NEDERLANDS, een basisleergang NT2. In: Blommaert, M.R. (ed.), pp. 108-115.

3337 Swartz, M. & Yazdani, M. (eds.) (1992). *Intelligent tutoring systems for foreign language learning*. The bridge to international communication. Berlin, Springer.

3338 Teytaud, J.-P. (1992a). Traduction assistée par ordinateur en BASIC. *Les Cahiers de l'APLIUT* 45, 35-48.

3339 Teytaud, J.-P. (1992b). Traduction assistée par ordinateur en BASIC. Partie II: consultation et enrichissement des lexiques. *Les Cahiers de l'APLIUT* 46, 114-135.

3340 Teytaud, J.-P. (1993). Limiter la durée d'un test en BASIC. *Les Cahiers de l'APLIUT* 49, 66-79.

3341 Thibeault, T.F. (1993). A dynamic protocol for cooperative courseware development. *The IALL Journal of Language Learning Technologies* 26 (1), 7-18.

3342 Thomas, P.J. & Norman, M.A. (1990). Interacting with hypertext: functional simplicity without conversational competence. In: McAleese, R. & Green, C. (eds.), pp. 239-243.

3343 Thompson, J. & Chesters, G. (1992). *CALL for all*. Hull, University of Hull: CTI Centre for Modern Languages.

3344 Thompson, J. & Zähner, C. (eds.) (1992). *Proceedings of the ICALL workshop, UMIST, September 1991*. Hull, CTI Centre for Modern Languages.

3345 Thompson, J. (1992). *The CTI Centre for Modern Languages*. Hull, University of Hull: CTI Centre for Modern Languages.

3346 Thume, K.-H. (1992). *Studien zur Entwicklung und Effektivität von computergestütztem Fremdsprachenerwerb*. Regensburg, Roderer.

3347 Torikian, M. (1992). Watch your language!: an account of *SoundEdit* with reference to the validity of phonological rules. *System* 20 (4), 471-479.

3348 van Bodegom, M. (1993). Learn more in less time. In: Röllinghoff, A. (ed.), pp. 21-27.

3349 van der Neut, I. (1992). E-Mail Project Nederland-Frankrijk: Kenmerken en resultaten. In: Blommaert, M.R. (ed.), pp. 83-99.

3350 Vandewalle, J. (1992). P.A.R.A.D.I.S.E. Doelgericht computerondersteund taalleren op basis van uw favoriete teksten. In: Blommaert, M.R. (ed.), pp. 116-124.

3351 Vielau, A. (1992). Wirtschaftsenglisch per Computer - ein Beitrag zur Methodik des Schreibens. In: Börner, W. & Vogel, K. (eds.). *Schreiben in der Fremdsprache*. Prozeß und Text, Lehren und Lernen. Bochum, AKS Verlag, pp. 283-296.

3352 Waitzbauer, M. (1992). "Multimedia" und Sprachunterricht. *CALL Austria* 17, 27-35.

3353 Waitzbauer, M. (1994). CONTEXTS - ein Übungsgenerator auf der Grundlage von Text-Konkordanzen. *TELL & CALL* 1, 42-44.

3354 Walls, D. (1992). Survival or fluency? A general discussion on the application of technology to the teaching of foreign languages. *ReCALL* 7, 15-17.

3355 Warren, C. (1993). Computer-based information-stream simulations: their impact on language and thinking. In: Monteith, M. (ed.), pp. 83-95.

3356 Webster, J.J. (1993). Text processing using the Functional Grammar Processor (FGP). In: Ghadessy, M. (ed.). *Register analysis*. London, Pinter, pp. 181-195.

3357 Wernsing, A.V. (1992). Computer und fremdsprachliche Textproduktion. In: Bömmel; H.v. et al. (eds.). *Lernen und Lehren fremder Sprachen*. Tübingen, Narr, pp. 112-129.

3358 Whiskeyman, A.L. (1990). Development of IVD materials using non-native language mediation. *CALICO Journal* 8 (1), 75-86.

3359 Whistlecroft, L. (1992). HyperCard. *The CTISS File* 13, 20-23.

3360 Whitman, K.L. (1990). Development of interactive videodisc materials using non-native language remediation. *CALICO Journal* 8 (1), 65-74.

3361 Williams, N. (1993). Postwriting software and the classroom. In: Monteith, M. (ed.), pp. 114-124.

3362 Willis, T. (1992). Processing natural language. In: Roach, P. (ed.), pp. 51-71.

3363 Winter, F. (1992). De ontwikkeling van een gecombineerd testoefeningenprogramma voor computer-ondersteund taalonderwijs. In: Blommaert, M.R. (ed.), pp. 125-127.

3364 Wölfel, W. (1993). "CALL". Computer-assisted language learning im Englischunterricht. *Pädagogische Welt* 2, 75-61.

3365 Wolff, D. (1992). Einsatzmöglichkeiten von Computerprogrammen im Fremdsprachenunterricht: Psycholinguistische, lernpsychologische und didaktische Bewertungskriterien. In: Blommaert, M.R. (ed.), pp. 128-150.

3366 Wolff, D. (1993). Keynote address: state of the art, new technologies for foreign language teaching. In: Commission of the European Communities (eds.), pp. 17-27.

3367 Wolff, D. (1994). Der Computer als Forschungsinstrument im fremdsprachlichen Klassenzimmer. *TELL & CALL* 1, 4-14.

3368 Wright, P. & Lickorish, A. (1990). An empirical comparison of two navigation systems for two hypertexts. In: McAleese, R. & Green, C. (eds.), pp. 84-93.

3369 Wunsch, R. (1993). Tuning up the language classroom: how the computer can make writing more effective. *Die Neueren Sprachen* 92 (3), 228-249.

3370 Wyman, W.J. (1993). INTERNET and foreign-language instruction: a report from behind the front lines. *The IALL Journal of Language Learning Technologies* 26 (1), 26-33.

3371 Yazdani, M. & Pollard, D. (1993). Multilingual aspects of a multimedia database of learning materials. In: Yazdani, M. (ed.), pp. 14-29.

3372 Yazdani, M. & Uren, J. (1993). Generalising language tutoring systems. In: Yazdani, M. (ed.), pp. 59-72.

3373 Yazdani, M. (1992). LINGERing on! Steps towards an 'intelligent' language tutoring environment. In: Thompson, J. & Zähner, C. (eds.), pp. 109-118.

3374 Yazdani, M. (1993). An artificial intelligence approach to second language teaching. In: Yazdani, M. (ed.), 198-210.

3375 Yazdani, M. (ed.) (1993). *Multilingual multimedia*. Bridging the language barrier with intelligent systems. Oxford, intellect.

3376 Zähner, C. (1992). Foundations of ICALL. In: Thompson, J. & Zähner, C. (eds.), pp. 118-126.

SUBJECT INDEX

LIST OF CONTRIBUTORS

Robert C. Davis
Smith College
Center for Foreign
Languages and Cultures
Northampton, MA 01063
USA

Andreas Eck
Bergische Universität
Gesamthochschule
Fachbereich 4
Gaußstraße 20
D-42097 Wuppertal
Federal Republic of Germany

Hubert Eichheim
Goethe-Institut
Helene-Weber-Allee 1
D-80637 München
Federal Republic of Germany

Gabriele Fesl
Berlitz European Projects
Kaiserstraße 66
D-60329 Frankfurt a.M.
Federal Republic of Germany

Yoko Fujii
The University of the Air
2-11 Wakaba, Mihama-ku
Chiba City, 261
Japan

Gerlinde Hardt-Mautner
Wirtschaftsuniversität Wien
Institut für Englische Sprache
Augasse 9
A-1090 Wien
Austria

Masako K. Hiraga
The University of the Air
2-11 Wakaba, Mihama-ku
Chiba City, 261
Japan

Heidrun Jung
Wittelsbacherring 35
D-95444 Bayreuth
Federal Republic of Germany

Udo O.H. Jung
University of Bayreuth
Language Centre
D-95440 Bayreuth
Federal Republic of Germany

Paula Kalaja
University of Jyväskylä
Department of English
PO Box 35
SF-40351 Jyväskylä
Finland

Kurt Kohn
address for correspondence:
Rheingasse 10
D-78462 Konstanz
Federal Republic of Germany

Lienhard Legenhausen
Westfälische Wilhelms-Universität
Institut für Englische Sprache und
Literatur und ihre Didaktik i.G.
Johannisstraße 12-20
D-48143 Münster
Federal Republic of Germany

Sirpa Leppänen
University of Jyväskylä
Department of English
PO Box 35
SF-40351 Jyväskylä
Finland

William Savage
Asian Institute of Technology
Language Center
GPO Box 2754
Bangkok 10501
Thailand

Virginia Teichmann
Pädagogische Hochschule Karlsruhe
Bismarckstraße 10
D-76133 Karlsruhe
Federal Republic of Germany

Robert Vanderplank
Heriot-Watt University
Department of Languages
Riccarton
Edinburgh EH14 4AS
United Kingdom

Eileen Vick
University of Bayreuth
Language Centre
D-95440 Bayreuth
Federal Republic of Germany

Dieter Wolff
Bergische Universität
Gesamthochschule
Fachbereich 4
Gaußstraße 20
D-42097 Wuppertal
Federal Republic of Germany

BAYREUTHER BEITRÄGE ZUR GLOTTODIDAKTIK
BAYREUTH CONTRIBUTIONS TO GLOTTODIDACTICS

Herausgegeben von Udo O. H. Jung

Band 1 Heidrun & Udo O. H. Jung: The Dictionary of Acronyms and Abbreviations in Applied Linguistics and Language Learning. 1991.

Band 2 Udo O. H. Jung (Hrsg.): Praktische Handreichung für Fremdsprachenlehrer. Unter Mitarbeit von Heidrun Jung. 1992.

Band 3 Manfred Schewe / Peter Shaw (eds.): Towards Drama as a Method in the Foreign Language Classroom. 1993.

Band 4 Heidrun Jung / Robert Vanderplank (eds.): Barriers and Bridges: Media Technology in Language Learning. Proceedings of the 1993 CETaLL Symposium on the Occasion of the 10th AILA World Congress in Amsterdam. 1994.

Udo O. H. Jung / Gothild Lieber

An International Bibliography of Computer Assisted Language Learning with Annotations in German
Volume II

Frankfurt/M., Berlin, Bern, New York, Paris, Wien, 1993. VII, 197 pp.
ISBN 3-631-46376-6 pb. DM 59.--*

This bibliography is a sequel to volume I of the *International Bibliography of Computer Assisted Language Learning* compiled by the Senior Editor and published in 1988. The roughly 2000 entries mainly cover the period from 1987 to 1991. Together, the 3051 entries in volumes I and II constitute a fairly comprehensive picture of CALL around the world. This bibliography is not restricted to English as a first, second or foreign language. The articles indexed – some 600 of them have annotations in German – report on the teaching of Arabic, Bulgarian, Catalan, Chinese, Czech, Dutch, English, Esperanto, Finnish, French, German, Hungarian, Italian, Japanese, Korean, Latin, Polish, Russian, Spanish and Thai as target languages. A German and an English subject index help to locate entries.

Contents: Hardware · Courseware Development · Programming Languages · Authoring Systems · Word Processors · Hypertext · Interactive Video · Data Bases · Simulations · Text Reconstruction · Games · Translation · Testing · Software · Telecommunications · Concordances · Drill & Practice · Vocabulary Programmes · Evaluation · Artificial Intelligence